AF600714

UKRAINIAN WOMEN WRITERS AND THE NATIONAL IMAGINARY

From the Collapse of the USSR to the Euromaidan

Ukrainian Women Writers and the National Imaginary

From the Collapse of the USSR to the Euromaidan

OLEKSANDRA WALLO

UNIVERSITY OF TORONTO PRESS
Toronto Buffalo London

Toronto Buffalo London
utorontopress.com

ISBN 978-1-4875-0600-1 (cloth)
ISBN 978-1-4875-3310-6 (EPUB)
ISBN 978-1-4875-3309-0 (PDF)

Library and Archives Canada Cataloguing in Publication

Title: Ukrainian women writers and the national imaginary: From the collapse of the USSR to the Euromaidan / Oleksandra Wallo.
Names: Wallo, Oleksandra, 1980– author.
Description: Includes bibliographical references and index.
Identifiers: Canadiana 20190167904 | ISBN 9781487506001 (hardcover)
Subjects: LCSH: Ukrainian prose literature – Women authors – History and criticism. | LCSH: Ukrainian prose literature – 20th century – History and criticism. | LCSH: Ukrainian prose literature – 21st century – History and criticism. | LCSH: Women and literature – Ukraine – History. | LCSH: Nationalism and literature – Ukraine – History. | LCSH: Ukraine – In literature. | LCSH: Women in literature.
Classification: LCC PG3906.W64 W35 2019 | DDC 891.7/9808–dc23

Publication of this book was made possible, in part, by grants from the First Book Subvention Program of the Association for Slavic, East European, and Eurasian Studies and the Shevchenko Scientific Society, USA from the Olga Motsiuk Fund.

University of Toronto Press acknowledges the financial assistance to its publishing program of the Canada Council for the Arts and the Ontario Arts Council, an agency of the Government of Ontario.

Canada Council for the Arts

Conseil des Arts du Canada

Funded by the Government of Canada

Financé par le gouvernement du Canada

Contents

Acknowledgments

This book began more than ten years ago at the University of Illinois at Urbana-Champaign. I am deeply grateful to the faculty there, including Harriet Murav, Lilya Kaganovsky, Teresa Barnes, Dmytro Shtohryn, Michael Finke, David Cooper, and above all Valeria Sobol, who generously offered insights, sources, and words of encouragement. A fellowship from the Graduate College at the University of Illinois provided a full year of support that allowed me to complete much of the writing. The work continued at the University of Kansas, where comments and help from colleagues Svetlana Vassileva-Karagyozova, Stephen M. Dickey, Vitaly Chernetsky, and Ani Kokobobo, as well as a much-needed and timely course release, enabled me to reconceive this project as a book. Additional impetus came from one of the heroines of this study, Nina Bichuia, who agreed to sit down with me on several hot summer days in Lviv and share her fascinating memories of what it was like to be a Ukrainian woman writer in the Soviet era.

I owe a debt of gratitude to Stephen Shapiro at the University of Toronto Press, whose professionalism and kindness have made the publication process seem easy. The three anonymous readers of the initial manuscript have passed on sources and given invaluable suggestions that resulted in a better book. Of course, the responsibility for any errors and omissions that remain is fully mine. I gratefully acknowledge *East/West: Journal of Ukrainian Studies* for granting permission to reprint "'The Stone Master': On the Invisibility of Women's Writing from the Soviet Ukrainian Periphery" and Peter Lang for permission to use some material from "Ukrainian Women between Communism and Post-communism: Memory and the Everyday of Ideology in Oksana Zabuzhko's *The Museum of Abandoned Secrets*," which appeared in *The Everyday of Memory: Between Communism and Post-Communism*, edited by Marta Rabikowska. Publication of this book was made possible, in part, by a grant from the First Book Subvention Program of the Association for Slavic, East European, and Eurasian Studies.

Both my immediate and my extended families in the United States and in Ukraine have had to live with this project for many years; their unconditional love and unfailing support are deeply appreciated. My husband, Michael, and my daughter, Katria/Kaitlin, have shared a lot of my joys and burdens on this long journey from an idea to a published book. My warmest thank you – now and always – belongs to them.

Note on Transliteration

In transliterating from the Cyrillic alphabet, I have generally followed the modified Library of Congress system. Thus, proper names do not include the apostrophe to mark palatalization, Ukrainian names begin with "Ya" and "Ye" instead of "Ia" and "Ie," female first names end with "ia" instead of "iia," and male surnames end with "y" instead of "yi." In a few instances, authors' names appear in the form of transliteration that has already become customary through the publication of their works in English. However, the Library of Congress system has been preserved in the bibliography and the citations.

UKRAINIAN WOMEN WRITERS AND THE NATIONAL IMAGINARY

From the Collapse of the USSR to the Euromaidan

Introduction

Women, Literature, and the National Imaginary in (Post)colonial Ukraine

"To be a woman in Ukrainian literature of the 2000s, especially now, in the second decade, is not anything exotic anymore. What twenty years ago was marginal has become central," claimed Ukrainian writer Oksana Zabuzhko in 2013, during a week-long series of recorded conversations with a Polish journalist.[1] The fact that this epic, 400-page interview with a Ukrainian woman writer was done in the first place and then released in book form both in Poland and in Ukraine as a kind of "encyclopedia" of Ukrainian culture testifies to the truth of Zabuzhko's statement (Forostyna). So do the prestigious literary prizes awarded in the past two decades to Zabuzhko and contemporary women writers such as Yevhenia Kononenko, Maria Matios, Halyna Pahutiak, Tania Maliarchuk, and Sofia Andrukhovych, the introduction of the writings by several living women authors into secondary school and university curricula, and their works' adaptations for the stage and the screen. Since the collapse of the Soviet Union, the Ukrainian literary world has not only experienced a boom in women's prose writing,[2] but has also seen a number of Ukrainian women assume the roles of literary trendsetters and authoritative critics of their culture. As literary scholar Maria G. Rewakowicz notes in a recent monograph on contemporary Ukrainian writing, "the emergence and assertion of powerful women's voices comprises one of the most noticeable trends in literary discourses of post-independence Ukraine" (*Ukraine's Quest* 10–11). While several other studies have acknowledged this trend and have analysed examples of contemporary Ukrainian women's writing, including prose,[3] none have seriously considered the phenomenon and the process of this "emergence" and "assertion" itself. This book is the first in-depth study of *how* Ukrainian women's prose, after decades of being marginalized, was able to reemerge so powerfully in the post-Soviet era. Proceeding both chronologically and thematically, I tell the story of the gradual gains in public voice for contemporary Ukrainian women's prose writing since the collapse of the USSR.

The book examines the trajectory of this transformation of Ukrainian women's writing from "marginal" to "central," in Zabuzhko's parlance, by exploring the prose works and literary careers of several leading professional Ukrainian women authors of the same generation. Scholars of the Soviet period have dubbed it the "last Soviet generation," whereas in Ukrainian literature specifically, the term *visimdesiatnyky* (eighties writers) is the most common designation.[4] These authors first came onto the literary scene in the mid to late 1980s and are especially interesting because of the way in which their lives straddle the Soviet/post-Soviet divide. The only generation of women educated entirely under the Soviet regime, they had made their literary debuts under its disintegrating system, but built highly successful writing careers already after the collapse of the USSR. The female authors from this generation directly witnessed the Soviet-era marginality of Ukrainian women's prose writing in particular, yet were the first to renegotiate its status when doors opened for them to do so in the liberalized climate of *perestroika* and the first post-Soviet decades. Through talented literary work on timely topics and public intellectual engagement of post-Soviet Ukrainian culture and society, they were able to insert themselves into the centre of Ukraine's rapidly changing literary scene. In so doing, they paved the way to visibility and success for the subsequent generations of Ukrainian women writers.

This book focuses on three prominent and quite different women representatives of the eighties generation – Oksana Zabuzhko, Yevhenia Kononenko, and Maria Matios.[5] Zabuzhko and Matios have been jokingly referred to as "literary oligarchs" in today's Ukraine. Just like well-known contemporary male writers, such as Yuri Andrukhovych, Andrey Kurkov, and Serhiy Zhadan, these two women writers have been able to make a living through their literary careers, thanks to royalties for their books, literary prizes, fees for public lectures and readings, and writing fellowships.[6] Kononenko approaches this status, but she has combined her career as a writer with work as a literary translator and with professional responsibilities at the Ministry of Culture's Ukrainian Centre for Cultural Studies. These women have authored poetry and non-fiction, such as diaries, blogs, and essays as well as prose fiction. Zabuzhko and Kononenko have also written works of literary and cultural criticism. Through all of these activities, these women have proved to be authoritative commentators on some of the most pressing issues faced by Ukrainian culture and society today. Zabuzhko, especially, has been one of Ukraine's most active public intellectuals over the past two decades. Matios, in addition to exercising influence as a writer of popular literature, gained a political platform for sharing her views by becoming a member of the Ukrainian parliament in 2012.

Ukraine presents an interesting case study of how post-Soviet women authors have been renegotiating women's (and women writers') traditional roles and positions in and vis-à-vis their independent postcommunist nations.

Although scholars of the post-Soviet region have noted a general turn towards greater traditionalism in views on gender roles in the first decades since the collapse of the USSR, including public calls on women to "return to the home,"[7] the field of literature in the same period has seen a true blossoming and greater recognition of Slavic women's writing. The latter trend recently culminated in the first-ever award of the Nobel Prize for Literature to an East Slavic woman author, Svetlana Alexievich.[8] The Ukrainian case is especially curious because of the radical difference in the quantity and status of women's prose writing between the Soviet and the post-Soviet eras. While for Russia it has been argued that the Soviet system's promotion of women's education and employment facilitated a greater presence of female writers on the literary scene compared to the pre-Soviet period,[9] and therefore laid the groundwork for the post-Soviet boom in women's prose especially,[10] in Ukraine one observes a very different pattern. A vibrant pre-Soviet tradition of women's writing, with two outstanding women modernists, Lesia Ukrainka (1871–1913) and Olha Kobylianska (1863–1942), at its centre, gave way to a dearth of prominent Ukrainian female authors, especially in prose, between the 1930s and the 1970s[11] – so much so that some women writers of the eighties generation felt compelled in their early works to ask how a Ukrainian woman could write at all.[12] This fact makes the rapid rise of Ukrainian women's prose writing since the early 1990s all the more remarkable.

As I examine how Zabuzhko, Kononenko, and Matios managed to insert themselves, and women's writing more generally, into the contemporary Ukrainian literary canon, I argue that their success has largely hinged on their works' engagement with the "great" national issues, such as those of the traumatic Soviet past and Ukraine's post-Soviet challenges. This often implicit, yet enduring, cultural expectation of national themes in literary works can be traced back to Ukrainian literature's traditional role as the locus for the articulation and preservation of a sense of national identity in the absence of an independent Ukrainian state. In the late 1980s and the early 1990s, when women writers of the eighties generation were beginning to make their literary interventions, the Soviet state's disintegration made national identity and post-Soviet nation-building a topic of utmost importance. There was a pressing need to make sense of the historic changes and to forge "a new collective identity" for Ukraine as an independent nation (Hnatiuk, *Proshchannia* 17). Not surprisingly for "literature-centric" Ukraine,[13] much of this "national" discussion and construction happened in literary prose, with the newly emergent women writers actively participating in this process and contributing their visions of Ukraine's past and present. By engaging what this study calls "the national imaginary," Zabuzhko, Kononenko, and Matios created works that brought them wide popularity.

The degree to which such engagement has been intentional and bold can be illustrated by Zabuzhko's approach as a writer to the two key moments of national upheaval in Ukraine since the collapse of the USSR: the mass protests of the Orange Revolution in 2004 and the Euromaidan in 2013–14. Shortly after each revolution, Zabuzhko published or was involved in the publication of works that exhibited her great interest in the role of a chronicler of national history in literature. For example, Zabuzhko wrote in her brief preface to the multi-author non-fiction collection *Litopys samovydtsiv. Dev'iat' misiatsiv ukrains'koho sprotyvu* (*The Chronicle of Witnesses: Nine Months of Ukrainian Resistance*, 2014) that this volume appeared because she and her colleagues were convinced of the need for Ukrainians to learn how to depict their own "unfolding history" (7). Similarly, in her 2005 collection of fiction and non-fiction on the Orange Revolution, to which she gave a telling English title – *Let My People Go*, Zabuzhko wrote of her desire to find the right aesthetic forms that would permit her to capture "the people rising" and that "ascent of the spirit" that characterized the protests (181). Zabuzhko thought such depictions to be important for Ukraine because in her understanding, "a country speaks about itself in the voice of culture, not politics" (69). Furthermore, she specifically mentioned prose as the most natural medium for such an undertaking and expressed her keen interest in the process whereby through prose writing "history becomes culture" (8).[14]

Zabuzhko's ideas quoted above illustrate the connection between two of the key elements of my study – the active participation of prominent contemporary Ukrainian women authors in the shaping of Ukraine's national imaginary *through writing* and their search for suitable literary forms in which to represent their visions of the Ukrainian nation. For reasons explained below, prose genres were the ones in which this search primarily occurred, making prose highly significant for newly independent Ukraine. At the same time, for the Ukrainian women *visimdesiatnyky* themselves, a literary focus on the national was in no way fortuitous. I see it as part and parcel of their own search for a voice both as *women* writers and as *Ukrainian* ones.

This dual search helps explain why a lot of the "national" fiction and non-fiction by the women authors of the eighties generation has treated the topic of the nation through the lens of gender.[15] In the writing which I analyse in this book, Zabuzhko, Kononenko, and Matios discuss, reconstruct, and reimagine Ukraine's Soviet past and/or its impact on the national present from the perspective of a female subject. They place women in the centre of their narratives, as highly individualized characters and not mere symbols of the nation, and they give these protagonists critical voices in the texts. Doing so has permitted Zabuzhko, Kononenko, and Matios to illuminate a variety of women's viewpoints, experiences, and roles in twentieth-century Ukraine – something that until recently has hardly been done either by historians or by male prose writers.[16] In the case of works examined in chapters 4, 5, and 6, this emphasis on concrete women's lives in and vis-à-vis their communities – a kind of view from below – has also resulted in rich and nuanced national narratives, which serve to challenge black-and-white or monologic accounts about the Ukrainian national community.[17] In other words, it is often precisely the interjection of women's voices and perspectives that allow the narratives by Zabuzhko, Kononenko, and Matios to highlight the diversity of the national picture and the complexity of the national story – and thereby intervene in the national imaginary. At the same time, the dual focus on women and the nation has also permitted Zabuzhko, Kononenko, and Matios to work around the patriarchal stereotype that issues of gender relations and women's daily lives are the hallmark of "narrow-minded," "inferior" women's literature[18] – and thus to assert themselves on the Ukrainian literary scene.

The National Imaginary, History, and Literature

What is the national imaginary? I understand this term as a web of collectively shared, continually contested, and evolving imaginings of and about a national community. These imaginings are tied to popular national discourses, myths, and symbols (such as flags, anthems, and heroes) that are believed to hold the national community together and define the "uniqueness" of the nation – even if other nations share some of the same "unique" features. I concur with political scientist Walker Connor who saw as the chief property of a national community "a psychological bond that joins a people and differentiates it, in the subconscious conviction of its members, from all other people" (92). This bond may be forged and fostered on the basis of various elements and their combinations: ethnic, linguistic, cultural, political, and so on. The exact configuration of elements depends on the specifics of a nation's history and the ideological positions of elites who promote particular conceptions of the nation at different historical junctures. On the one hand, there are nations, like the United States, in whose imaginary the discourse of the state, with its notions of law and citizenship, predominates;[19] and on the other, there are nations, like Ukraine, whose long history of statelessness and legacy of exogenous policy make ethnocultural identity a strong element of its national imaginary.

Despite its singular form, the term "national imaginary" should not be understood as denoting something monolithic or common to all in the nation. As psychological anthropologist Claudia Strauss notes in her analysis of how the term "imaginary" has been used, "[b]ounded or self-identified groups may share some cultural understandings, or imaginaries, with each other, but be fractured with respect to other understandings" (323). Division over various aspects of the national imaginary has certainly taken hold in Ukraine, in part because of its colonial past. Since the early 1990s, scholars have written much about post-Soviet Ukraine's "unconsolidated" identity, especially with respect to language (Kuzio 248).[20] Yet regardless of the existing splits and contestation over various conceptions of Ukraine's collective national identity, I prefer the singular "imaginary" because this form aptly captures a nation's utopian striving for unity, or what Lauren Berlant has called "the common language of a common space" (21).[21] Additionally, the aspect of the Ukrainian national imaginary that is central to this study, that is, the role of women in and vis-à-vis the nation, has been relatively stable and uncontested, at least until recently.

My use of the term "imaginary" is not Lacanian. Instead, it builds upon Benedict Anderson's by now classic definition of nations as "imagined communities" and underscores the role of imaginative literature – narrative in general and fictional plots in particular – in shaping national imaginings. As Anderson has famously argued, the imagining of the modern nation has been facilitated by novels. The very structure of the novel connected the "simultaneous" pasts as well as the present lives of various characters, providing a textual figuration of their imagined national coexistence (*Imagined Communities* 26). The terms "imagined" and "imaginings" do not necessarily connote falseness or opposition to fact. Such a meaning has been occasionally (mis)attributed to Anderson, even though, as scholars have pointed out, he did not view nationalism as some form of delusion. Instead, he saw it as "a socially necessary creative act" that gives rise to new "forms of social organization" (M. Walsh 7). Yet in many specific historical cases, national imaginings have put forth hegemonic visions of national communities, which, for instance, included some members, such as women, only in certain circumscribed roles, and excluded others altogether.[22] In a similar fashion, while the term "national myth" does not necessarily imply that we are dealing with falsehoods, specific national myths have often obscured historical reality and/or promoted cultural values that have had devastating consequences for some members of a national community.[23] Nonetheless, myths prove to be indispensable for group identity, explaining the rationale for a community's existence in the first place.[24] The present study therefore pays attention to both the productive and the detrimental aspects of the national imaginary, following suit of the Ukrainian women writers examined here, whose works both affirm and critique the nation.

While literature has been historically important in the imagining of many nations around the world,[25] it has been crucial in the construction of Eastern European nations. As Andrew Wachtel points out, it is nineteenth-century poets, such as Adam Mickiewicz, Aleksandr Pushkin, and Taras Shevchenko, rather than revolutionaries or statesmen, who were recognized as the "founding fathers" of these national communities, because "these countries were seen as having been created on the basis of a shared national language and a literary corpus" (5). In the twentieth century, the Soviet state included poets like Pushkin and Shevchenko as important figures in its new literary canon – in part because with Stalin's ascent to power, the nation was reinstated as "a subject of history," albeit not as a discourse of political rights, but of cultural specificity

(Yekelchyk, *Stalin's Empire* 10). Writers in general and poets in particular also remained important in the Soviet era as opponents of the regime. In Ukraine, these were the oppositional voices of the *shistdesiatnyky* (sixties writers), as well as that of Shevchenko himself, much of whose poetry helped Ukrainians keep alive a non-Soviet sense of their "Ukrainianness."

Literary scholar Rory Finnin's insightful reading of Shevchenko's 1845 celebrated poem "My Friendly Epistle to My Dead, Living, and Unborn Compatriots in Ukraine and outside Ukraine" elucidates why poetry and not the novel was the dominant "national" genre in Ukraine prior to the collapse of the USSR. Finnin explains that while the novel, according to Anderson, helps imagine the nation as "a sociological organism moving calendrically through homogeneous, empty time" (Anderson, *Imagined Communities* 26), lyric poetry, through its vague, yet emotionally powerful, lyrical address and its "omnitemporality," "interpellates" national subjects across different historical periods and functions as "a message in a bottle," always "timely" because of its "timelessness" (Finnin 51–2). In other words, if a traditional realist novel gives readers a coherent "mental picture" of the nation, grounded in historical time, a lyric poem on the subject of the nation "hails" them in an Althusserian fashion, creating a feeling of belonging to a "national" community that is "outside of 'homogeneous, empty time'" (Finnin 45–6). This is how Shevchenko's "Epistle," addressed to his "Dead, Living, and Unborn Compatriots," has worked in Ukraine for many decades. Read, memorized, and recited by successive generations of Ukrainians who lived under foreign domination, it helped them feel part of an imagined timeless "national" community – identified not on the basis of an independent nation-state, but literally by a text. Shevchenko's "Epistle" is thus a specimen from that "literary corpus," in Wachtel's parlance, or a canon, on the basis of which an Eastern European nation like Ukraine was seen as "created," and which helped maintain a sense of a distinct Ukrainian national identity in the absence of political independence.

Because of its important political function, this "literary corpus" of Ukraine has had for many an aura of sacredness about it – so much so that in the early 1990s literary scholar Marko Pavlyshyn dubbed this model of the literary canon "the iconostasis."[26] Characterized by "hierarchy, immutability and ideological unanimity," this model was linked to a conservative vision of Ukrainian national identity – homogeneous, essentialized, and rigidly monolingual, with the language of the canon, standard literary Ukrainian, seen as the sole language of the nation ("Literary Canons" 5). Yet in the late Soviet and the early post-Soviet period, an alternative vision of the literary canon, and correspondingly of Ukrainian identity, emerged in Ukraine. Pavlyshyn called it "the new canon." Promoted mostly by the eighties generation of writers and critics, to which the Ukrainian women writers examined in this study belong, it included "re-established literary classics interpreted in ways not foreseen by the friends of the iconostasis, as well as new works that might broadly be described as modernist and postmodernist" (6). The proponents of the new canon likewise rejected the previously dominant model of national identity, and several of them, such as the members of the Bu-Ba-Bu literary group,[27] deliberately provoked the wrath of the iconostasis camp by displays of irreverence towards treasured national values.[28] And yet, despite their vociferous refusal to engage in literary nation-building, Pavlyshyn argued that these writers still did exactly that, since almost all of them wrote in Ukrainian.[29] Because language has been fundamental to Ukrainian national identity, and because literature, which is usually "segregated" by language, has been tied so closely to national identity in Ukraine, writing in Ukrainian in the early post-Soviet period was a "national" act – whether or not it was meant as such by the writer.

The conflict between the proponents of the iconostasis and the new canon was most pronounced in the 1990s and has lost its edge in the new millennium. The Euromaidan protests were most instrumental in bringing about a new level of acceptance of Ukraine's multicultural identity and prompting efforts to promote multilingual literature.[30] It also seems that the original conflict played out mostly among the *male* writers and critics representing the older and the younger generations – in the Ukrainian-inflected version of the classic struggle between literary precursors and followers as described in Harold Bloom's *The Anxiety of Influence*. While the Ukrainian women writers of the eighties generation seemed generally supportive of the "new canon" model, for them national identity was not the only factor that determined their position vis-à-vis the Ukrainian literary classics. The other crucial factor was gender.

Although Wachtel noted the general lack of "founding mothers" in Eastern European nations (5), Lesia Ukrainka did become enshrined in the Ukrainian canon as one of the three key figures in modern Ukrainian literature. As I show in this study, rereading the writings by Ukrainka and Kobylianska became a crucial way for the late Soviet and post-Soviet Ukrainian women authors to overcome what Sandra Gilbert and Susan Gubar have identified as female writers' "anxiety of authorship" (49). For the women writers in late Soviet and early post-Soviet Ukraine, this anxiety was acute because of a break in the Ukrainian women's writing tradition during the Soviet era. In the works of Ukrainka, Ukrainian women writers like Nina Bichuia, whose Soviet-era career I discuss in chapter 1, and Oksana Zabuzhko found a powerful example of aesthetically rich and complex women's writing. Indeed, their attitude towards this figure in the Ukrainian canon remains quite reverent.

Besides the appearance of alternatives to the literary iconostasis, post-Soviet Ukrainian literature has also witnessed growth in the cultural significance of prose, and especially the novel. As a widely recognized marker of a nation's distinctiveness and modernity,[31] the novel was deemed to be an essential literary form for independent Ukraine. Additionally, since the collapse of the USSR, the suitability of prose for "making sense of the nation" has become more important than poetry's above-mentioned capacity to function as a national "time capsule" (Finnin 52).[32] In independent Ukraine, as in Third World postcolonial nations, novels furnished "enabling" forms, "inscribing a national destiny into time" (Boehmer, "Stories of Women" 11). Such forms, of course, are especially needed in the postcolonial context: they impart a wholeness to the past of the colonized, which remains an untold or distorted story in the colonial period. The telling of this story from the perspective of the colonized is one of the most fundamental needs for a postcolonial nation.[33]

The case for applying the term "postcolonial" to the formerly so-called Second World countries, and to Ukraine in particular, has been made by a number of scholars, resulting in "a vibrant field growing from th[e] intersection" of postsocialism and postcolonial theory (Suchland 854).[34] Perhaps the best-known justification for viewing the post-Soviet space as postcolonial was given by David Chioni Moore in "Is the Post- in Postcolonial the Post- in Post-Soviet? Toward a Global Postcolonial Critique." In this 2001 essay, Moore successfully countered the most widespread objections to post-Soviet postcolonialism, including Russia's precarious identity between East and West, as well as the argument that unlike Britain or France, who were separated from their colonies by oceans, Russia (and the Soviet Union later on) took over adjacent territories.[35] He then compared the standard models of Western colonization, which include (1) "dynastic reach" to neighbours, (2) settler colonization, and (3) "colonial control over distant orientalized populations," to "Russo-Soviet" colonization. He argued that the latter included all of these types, albeit with some modifications, plus a new fourth type, which he proposed to call "reverse-cultural colonization" (118–21). According to Moore, Russo-Soviet colonizing efforts in Ukraine fit into the first and the fourth type. Russia's expansion into eastern and central Ukraine in the seventeenth and the eighteenth centuries could be characterized as "dynastic reach" into neighbouring territories, and the Soviet post-Second World War conquest of Western Ukrainian lands was an example of "reverse-cultural colonization" – because unlike the Western colonizers, who viewed their subject peoples as culturally inferior, the nations to the west of the Soviet Union, such as Poland or Hungary, considered themselves culturally superior to Soviet Russia and viewed the Soviet colonizers as "Asiatics" (119, 121). While Moore's examples of places with such a superior attitude were Budapest and Berlin, it is not difficult to find reports of similar views in Western Ukrainian towns. For instance, in his memoir, *L'viv ponad use* (*Lviv above All*), musician and writer Ilko Lemko remembers the 1960s of his childhood in this Western Ukrainian city as a time when "the wives of the Soviet officers – the so-called 'liberators' – who only twenty years ago had gone to the Lviv Opera wearing nightgowns, acquired some manners in the cultural environment of an ex-European city" (103).

However schematic, Moore's description of the two types of colonization of Ukrainian lands does explain why political and cultural divisiveness has been a central problem for contemporary Ukraine. For readers unfamiliar with the history of the region, the following very brief summary will provide some background for the subsequent discussion of Ukrainian national issues in this book. Split between the Russian and the Austro-Hungarian Empires until the fall of imperial rule during the First World War, most of the territory of present-day Ukraine was briefly united and proclaimed independent for the first time in modern history in 1918 – only to be divided again soon after, between the Soviet Union, Poland, Czechoslovakia, and Romania. Claimed by the reestablished Polish state, Western Ukrainian lands with the city of Lviv as their centre escaped the draconian Stalinist policies of the 1930s, which had devastating consequences in the newly formed Ukrainian Soviet Socialist Republic. Brutally enforced collectivization of agriculture in Soviet Ukraine led to the starvation of millions of Ukrainians in what became known as the Holodomor – the man-made famine of 1932–3. The short-lived revival of the Ukrainian language and culture, permitted by the Soviet authorities in the 1920s, ended in mass executions and deportations of hundreds of thousands of nationally conscious Soviet Ukrainian citizens during the Stalinist terror in the late 1930s.

In 1939, the Second World War began with the Nazi attack on Poland. In accordance with the secret pact between Hitler and Stalin, the Soviet Red Army "liberators" occupied Western Ukrainian lands, bringing Stalinist terror in the form of mass arrests and deportations, and setting in motion Moore's "reverse-cultural colonization." When Nazi Germany attacked the USSR in 1941, the Stepan Bandera–led wing of the Organization of Ukrainian Nationalists (OUN)[36] collaborated with the Nazis in an effort to establish an independent Ukrainian state. Right after the declaration of Ukraine's independence by the OUN, the Nazis arrested Bandera and many of his associates. Pogroms against the Jews and, ultimately, the Holocaust devastated Ukraine's very large pre-war Jewish population. The Ukrainian Insurgent Army (UPA), created by the OUN leadership in the early 1940s, fought primarily in Western Ukraine against the Soviet and the Nazi occupations, but also committed or instigated violence against civilians, most notoriously against the Poles in the region of Volyn in 1943. When the Soviets returned in 1944 to Western Ukraine – and stayed, claiming to have "reunited" the Western and Eastern Ukrainian brothers – the UPA continued to fight underground, in some areas well into the 1950s. The Second World War turned the territory of today's Ukraine into bloodlands, to use historian Timothy Snyder's well-known term, yet most of the lands of present-day Ukraine were "gathered" within the borders of one state as a result of the war.

The political and cultural climate in post-war Soviet Ukraine until the collapse of the USSR varied from decade to decade, fluctuating between waves of repression, especially against Ukrainian intelligentsia, and brief periods of liberalization. Under Soviet leader Nikita Khrushchev, Ukraine even acquired the dubious status of the second among allegedly equal Soviet republics (the first one, of course, was Russia). Yet this status had little impact on the detrimental cultural processes, such as increasing Russification and provincialization of Ukrainian culture. When the Soviet Union collapsed in 1991, independent Ukraine entered the rocky period of postcommunist transition with almost all Soviet structures and institutions intact. Political, economic, and cultural changes took place, yet in a rather haphazard fashion, with systemic reforms often impeded by the corrupt elites of the old Soviet and new post-Soviet regimes, as well as by the increasingly aggressive politics of Putin's Russia. Two waves of mass protests – the Orange Revolution in 2004 and the Euromaidan (or Revolution of Dignity, as it became known in Ukraine) in 2013–14 – were bold collective attempts to force meaningful change from below. The latter, however, so angered Ukraine's former colonizer that it responded with the annexation of Ukraine's Crimean peninsula and the initiation of the ongoing hybrid war in the Eastern Ukrainian region of Donbas.

This much-simplified account attempts to give some sense of Ukraine's claims to its (post)colonial status. In my own approach to Ukrainian literature and culture as "postcolonial," I build on the sizeable body of important scholarly work by Marko Pavlyshyn, Myroslav Shkandrij, Vitaly Chernetsky, Tamara Hundorova, and others who have proven the value of postcolonial theory for explaining fundamental aspects of contemporary Ukrainian cultural life.[37] Yet the works by Zabuzhko, Kononenko, and Matios themselves are informed by a sense of Ukraine's past being profoundly impacted by imperial or colonial domination.[38] Speaking of Ukrainians' lack of knowledge of their own history, Matios, for example, has stated that "the Ukrainian reality of the early twenty-first century is such that in our lives there are certain things from our recent past which one has to start retelling to people at a very basic level" (*Vyrvani storinky* 30). Like Zabuzhko, in her above-mentioned aspirations to be a chronicler of national history, Matios is convinced that this is one of the most urgent tasks in present-day Ukraine, and that it has to be taken on not only by historians but by writers in many genres.

Compared with narrative history, however, imaginative literature has an advantage in the enterprise of writing the past of the formerly colonized. Unlike history, fiction offers the creative licence to imagine what cannot be learned from documentary sources, and this means that fiction can proceed where historical inquiry stops for lack of "reliable" evidence.[39] In Ukraine, where there have been many recent efforts to write the past from the native's perspective, the difficulty of recovering local history has been acknowledged. For example, in attempting to write an account of what happened in the early Soviet period to the inhabitants of the multiethnic borderlands in what is today central Ukraine, historian Kate Brown was forced to look for a "path around documented evidence": "I turn to nontraditional sources: oral histories, memories, material culture, folklore" (13). For many historians sources such as memories and folklore are suspect, yet for a writer of fiction on national themes the same sources are precious keys to the past. Postcolonial women writers like Toni Morrison and Doris Lessing have relied on personal memories and folklore to write powerful fictional accounts of colonial times and have found that this approach allowed them to truthfully depict that historical experience.[40] As I demonstrate in this study, the Ukrainian women writers of the eighties generation have done something similar in their fictional explorations of Ukraine's Soviet past.

The kind of evidence used by Brown, Morrison, Lessing, and the women writers examined in this book points to the collective memory as an important source for and "location" of the national imaginary. According to psychologist and anthropologist James Wertsch, collective memory is "an inherently distributed phenomenon," "defined by an irreducible tension between active agents and the textual resources they employ, especially narrative texts" (*Voices* 174–5). These texts can produce "textual communities," and membership in such a community does not require personal reading of all the texts; sometimes mere participation "in the activities of a textual community" is sufficient for one's assimilation of "the textual material around which the group is organized" (Wertsch, "National Narratives" 28). The imagined community of the nation may be thought of as a kind of Wertschian "textual community": the "material" around which it is organized comprises cultural and historical myths and narratives, symbols, and values circulating in this community and continually defining its "identity" as well as producing its national imaginary through acts of collective remembering.

Because this is a continual and complex process, and because collective remembering is diffuse, the transmission of the national imaginary – from one generation to another, for instance – often seems quite nebulous. Members of a community are frequently unable to pinpoint exactly how they came to know a certain cultural narrative, why they believe this or that national myth, or why they share a particular value – they simply do. This lack of clarity only enhances the power of the national imaginary and makes it resistant to change. Wertsch's argument is that collective remembering occurs in part with the help of *narrative schematic templates*, which he contrasts with specific narratives that feature particular places, dates, and people. One such narrative schematic template, which Wersch finds operative in the Russian collective memory of the past, for example, is "the expulsion of foreign enemies" – based on "accounts of the Mongol invasion of the thirteenth century, the thirteenth-century invasion by the Teutonic knights depicted in Eisenstein's film, the Swedish invasion of Charles XII around the beginning of the eighteenth century, the Russo-Turkish wars involving Suvorov at the end of the eighteenth century, the Napoleonic invasion of the early nineteenth century, the German attack in World War II, and even the reign of communism in the twentieth century" ("National Narratives" 30). On the basis of post-Soviet Russian high school students' essays about the Second World War, Wertsch demonstrates that even if the students know little specific historical information about this war, their essays nevertheless show that students have somehow assimilated "the expulsion of foreign enemies" narrative template.

What Wertsch calls a "narrative schematic template" is nothing other than a plot structure, and his analysis of collective remembering demonstrates that plots play an important role in the organization and mediation of a national imaginary. In her study of the concept of "Rodina" (native land) in Russian culture, Irina Sandomirskaia goes so far as to suggest that "Rodina" is "first and foremost a 'plot,'" and while one cannot "referentially" point to it, one can "tell" it (24). Thus, if the genre of a novel enables one to imagine the nation in the most general terms – as a community of many people simultaneously existing in "homogeneous, empty time" – various plots capture the specific imagined characteristics of a national community and organize its history. Because plots are the bread and butter of imaginative literature and because, unlike a lot of narrative history,[41] literature often highlights its reliance on plots and various means of emplotment, it is an eminently suitable medium for generating and also deconstructing national plots, thereby intervening in the national imaginary.

In the works examined in this book, women writers do just that: they both generate and deconstruct various national plots, and occasionally, they explicitly analyse and critique Ukraine's master-narratives. Central among them are the narratives about women that have traditionally structured the Ukrainian national imaginary. In engaging these plots, Zabuzhko, Kononenko, and Matios bring to light how these stories have affected Ukrainian women's lives in the past and continue to exert influence on them in the present. And in many of their works, these authors endeavour to create new, less conventional plots for Ukrainian women.

Common Woman/Nation Plots

Scholars of the gender/nation nexus, such as Anne McClintock, have built upon the premise that nationalism is "a gendered discourse and cannot be understood without a theory of gender power" (McClintock, "No Longer in a Future Heaven" 261).[42] Why gender is so central to the nation has been explained in a number of ways – for instance, through the primordialist theory of the nation, which holds that a national community is just an extension of the family, or, as one British politician put it, "two males plus defending a territory with the women and children" (qtd in Yuval-Davis 15). Like a patriarchal family, then, the nation that is imagined in this way prescribes different roles for men and women, unequally distributing power and agency between them.

Sociologist Nira Yuval-Davis has argued that despite the differences between specific nations, their imaginaries usually share a common set of important, and therefore policed, roles which women are expected to perform vis-à-vis the nation. They are called upon to be (1) the nation's biological and cultural reproducers (through giving birth and raising its future loyal members); (2) its "symbolic border guards" (through marrying *inside* the nation); and (3) the symbolic "embodiments of the collectivity" (as figures for the nation's identity and "destiny") (23, 45). All of these roles have been ascribed to Ukrainian women in different historical periods, and they survived relatively intact through times of drastic political and ideological change. A 1970 essay, "Na sviato zhinky" ("On the Occasion of the Woman's Holiday"), by renowned Ukrainian dissident Yevhen Sverstiuk, illustrates these key imaginings about Ukrainian women's place in the nation and underscores the role of literature in generating and perpetuating particular Ukrainian woman/nation plots.

The essay's standpoint on Ukrainian women's status in society is clearly anticolonial, faulting both the Russian imperial regime and the Soviet system for making life extremely difficult for Ukrainian women. Sverstiuk points out that by forcing men to leave their families, either in search of jobs in other parts of the empire or as soldiers to fight in wars, the state has continually placed the burden of raising children and often taking on the role of breadwinner as well on women alone. He also calls out the Soviet regime for its hypocrisy in promising women equality with men in the public sphere, but in practice consigning many of them to the least prestigious, lowest-paying, and often manual, jobs "under the leadership and supervision of men." Yet throughout the essay, this sharp social critique is combined with mythologizing rhetoric that restricts women's roles to traditional ones, tying them to the nation's interests. For example, Sverstiuk spends most of the essay discussing the lot of the Ukrainian mother, whom he praises for safeguarding and passing on to the children "the language, the song, and the memory of their honest kinsfolk," despite the colonial circumstances ("Na sviato zhinky").

Sverstiuk refers to numerous female literary images, all created by Ukrainian male writers – as if to underscore how influential these have been in shaping the imaginings of Ukrainian womanhood. The central literary trope which he addresses is the composite image of Shevchenko's female characters, whose fate is captured by the paradigmatic literary plot of being seduced by a foreign man, impregnated, and abandoned to live out the life of shame: "… our greatest poetic genius tearfully sang the fate of the unwed mother (*pokrytka*), a mother who has been disgraced and humiliated, and on the barricades of our national distress he created out of her the image of Ukraine" (Sverstiuk). In addition to motherhood, two other typical national roles for women singled out by Yuval-Davis can be discerned in this passage. The tragic fate of a Ukrainian *pokrytka* is the result of a woman's failure to guard the symbolic ethnic/national borders by becoming sexually involved with a foreign man. And the poetic transformation of an individual woman's life into the paradigmatic national story turns the *pokrytka* into the embodiment of Ukraine's humiliating identity as a colonized nation.[43]

The imagining of the nation as feminine is certainly not unique to Ukraine, and Sverstiuk places his discussion of Shevchenko's *pokrytka* next to references to feminine images of free America and revolutionary France. Yet what is troubling in this politics of representation, especially if it consistently pervades discussions of women's lives, is the implicit refusal to see women "in anything other than a mythological light."[44] Instead of a focus on real-life issues that women face and often work actively to resolve, this discursive move takes them out of reality altogether, depriving them of agency, subjectivity, and intrinsic human value. Sverstiuk's essay demonstrates just how easy such slippage from a realistic portrayal of women's lives to the depiction of women as a national myth can be. Although it ostensibly sets out to praise women's achievements, as well as to critically discuss their status in Ukrainian Soviet society on the occasion of the women's holiday on 8 March, the essay ends up at one point unfavourably comparing Ukrainian women with the nation, mythically represented as a dishonoured yet saintly mother. This rhetorical opposition occurs when the nation's "daughters" are said to question their "natural calling" to become mothers to many children themselves and thus to reproduce the nation biologically. "One to two children per family is the formula for national extinction," comments the essayist.

Underlying all of these national roles and plots is the association of women with nature (primarily the body) and/or passivity. Both the individual *pokrytka* and the feminized Ukraine are victims of their circumstances – they are not independent actors but are rather acted upon. Even the seemingly active and "civilizational" rather than "natural" role of the cultural reproducer does not really allow women to *make* the cultural meanings they are supposed to transmit to future generations. They are often expected to be cultural *re*producers rather than cultural producers. Such an expectation makes the position of a woman writer – should she put forth new or iconoclastic cultural visions of the nation rather than reproduce the accepted old ones – quite problematic. This expectation is implied in Sverstiuk's essay "On the Occasion of the Woman's Holiday." It refers several times to Ukrainian women as talented creators/performers of folk songs and, by extension, literature. Yet the emphasis in these references is on "preserving" and "transmitting" the verbal art of the *people* rather than on writing one's own original work. Furthermore, the individual women authors who are mentioned – sophisticated modernist writers Lesia Ukrainka and Olha Kobylianska – figure only as the nation's progeny and the symbols of its noble character. Although each of these women writers created an entire series of active and unconventional female characters in their works, none are mentioned in the essay because they do not easily fit the presented national paradigm. Such treatment of these well-known Ukrainian women authors accords with the general patterns of their reception in both pre-Soviet and Soviet Ukraine: they were celebrated as talented literary figures and the nation's "achievement," but their works were read in a highly selective and sometimes manipulative fashion.[45]

Women writers of the eighties generation frequently faced the same problem. Although I argue in this study that writing about the nation has made these women writers popular in post-Soviet Ukraine, the reception of their works on national themes often revealed their culture's unease with, and sometimes even outrage at, the national visions put forth by these authors. As I show in the case of Matios, her acceptance into the Ukrainian literary canon on the basis of her two books on the subject of the nation was made possible by a partial misreading of these texts. While the critics and theatre directors who adapted her works for the stage welcomed her attention to historical themes that were forbidden under the Soviet regime, they largely ignored her gender critique of the national community. Another example is the hostile reception of Zabuzhko's first novel, *Poliovi doslidzhennia z ukrains'koho seksu* (*Fieldwork in Ukrainian Sex*), which I explore in chapter 3. By penning these works, Ukrainian women writers implicitly raised the question of who is authorized to speak about the postcolonial Ukrainian nation, and in what ways.

The parallels in the reception of Ukrainian women writers between the early and the late twentieth century are not the only similarities in the imaginings of women's place in the nation before and after the collapse of the USSR. Many of the ideas expressed in Sverstiuk's essay continue to enjoy popularity in present-day Ukrainian society. As historians Marian Rubchak and Oksana Kis, among others, explain, in the independence era the dominant model of Ukrainian womanhood was popularized under the name of *Berehynia*. Originally used to refer to ancient pagan female deities in the territory of present-day Ukraine, the term means "guardian" and came to stand for what is viewed as women's "natural" role as keepers of the home and tradition (Rubchak, "Collective Memory"). *Berehynia* has also been invoked in post-Soviet Ukraine as emblematic of the purported matriarchal roots of Ukrainian culture, which are often believed to translate into "exceptionally high social status and gender equality (if not all-out dominance)" for Ukrainian women (Kis, "(Re)Constructing Ukrainian Women's History" 156). Although Sverstiuk makes no mention of *Berehynia*, he does claim that women's equality with men has been one of Ukraine's ancient "national traditions," no doubt referring to the same set of beliefs. As Kis points out, however, these beliefs have little basis in reality ("(Re)Constructing Ukrainian Women's History" 156). Thus, the model of *Berehynia* is used to control women and keep them out of the public sphere (Hundorova, "Posttotalitarnyi kemp" 506). Paradoxically, even some Ukrainian women's organizations have embraced this model, and although they ascribed to it the broader function of "maternal care of the entire Ukrainian nation," this is a "public role, which can be performed at home" (Kis, "Choosing without Choice" 111).

Furthermore, *Berehynia* became the emblem of the entire nation in 2002 when a statue of a female figure symbolizing Ukraine's independence was unveiled on Kyiv's Maidan Nezalezhnosti – the location of independent Ukraine's mass protests, the Orange Revolution and the Euromaidan. The statue was immediately called by the then president of Ukraine, Leonid Kuchma, "the embodiment of the Berehynia of our Ukrainian family" (qtd in Kis, "(Re)Constructing Ukrainian Women's History" 158). As in the case with the *pokrytka* plot, the already severely circumscribed feminine model was now mythologically equated with the nation. In its monumental mission to both guard and embody the nation, *Berehynia* fixed the popular Ukrainian imaginings of "proper" womanhood and placed a formidable symbolic burden on real women currently living in Ukraine. It is both completely fitting and highly ironic that the Euromaidan protests, which sparked much debate about women's roles in the Ukrainian nation (discussed in chapter 6), unfolded under *Berehynia*'s watchful eye.

All of these common woman/nation myths were fashioned and actively promoted by male representatives of Ukraine's cultural and political elite. Serving the interests of either anticolonial resistance or post-Soviet nation-building, or both, these stories consistently used a female figure – whether victimized (*pokrytka*) or venerated (*Berehynia*) – as a means of generating emotional investment in the Ukrainian national project. Yet since the late 1980s, when the above-mentioned "new canon" literature made its first appearance in Ukraine, some male writers of the younger generation consciously worked to undermine various traditional national tropes, including "the mythical image of the Ukrainian Woman" (Pavlyshyn, "Ukrainian Literature" 118). Unfortunately, this did not automatically mean that their writings did more justice to women and their actual lives.

The works of the "new canon" by male writers almost invariably focused on the male hero, imagining him to be the sole central subject of Ukrainian history and culture. The acclaimed novels by Yuri Andrukhovych, for example, followed the adventures of Ukrainian male intellectuals burdened with a postcolonial inferiority complex. More often than not, Andrukhovych's heroes tried to compensate for their feelings of inadequacy with outrageous acts of machismo, as I discuss in chapter 3. The playful, ironic tone in which these escapades were related did little to justify their sexist character. Women did not fare better in the works by Valeri Shevchuk, the celebrated Ukrainian author from the sixties generation, who wrote in the Ukrainian variant of the postcolonial genre of magic realism, known in Ukraine as *khymerna proza* (whimsical prose). Women were either non-existent or marginal figures in Shevchuk's "whimsically" historical prose, or else they fit the archetype of the witch, exercising magical, evil powers over the helpless male characters.[46] In his prose from the early 1990s, women were also portrayed as sex objects with grotesquely depicted physical features.[47] While such writing no longer bound women to the ideals and demands of the nation through plots of mythologized motherhood, it turned them into the passive tools of male characters' (sexualized) postcolonial liberation, or else replaced women's stereotypical image of virtuous mothers with an equally stereotypical representation of demonized sexuality. Needless to say, when female writers of the eighties generation came onto the literary scene, they felt a pressing need to confront these stereotypes and to fashion different plots and other roles for Ukrainian women – including for themselves as women writers.

Rewriting Stories of Women and/in the Nation

As they began to write prose around the time of the Soviet state's collapse – and despite considerable differences of style and ideology between them – Zabuzhko, Kononenko, and Matios shared a deep interest in actual women's lives and a commitment to shed light on women's stories from the Soviet past and the post-Soviet present. In their early works as well as in the later "national" novels, these authors created complex, fully developed female protagonists who play a wide variety of roles in their communities, including that of critics of their culture. Zabuzhko and Matios, in very recent non-fiction books, have likewise promoted a focus on women's diverse roles during the Euromaidan. In so doing, these writers have affirmed time and again that women's lives are valuable and important in and of themselves, without being ascribed symbolic significance for the nation. Occasionally, they have also undermined popular woman/nation myths through irony or parody.[48]

Nonetheless, Ukraine's traumatic colonial past and tumultuous postcolonial present, which has included, among a plethora of social, political, and economic challenges, two revolutions and an ongoing hybrid war, are very much on these authors' minds and figure prominently in their writing. In effect, their lives, like many Ukrainian women's lives, have been profoundly shaped by the colonial experience under the Soviet system and by the many changes since the coming of Ukraine's independence. Thus, Zabuzhko's, Kononenko's, and Matios's works often pay special attention to how conditions of colonialism and postcolonialism have affected women and the relationships between the sexes, as well as show the multiple hierarchies and constraints that impact present-day lives of different Ukrainian women – from lower-class residents of rural areas or provincial towns to women intellectuals and politicians in the capital. In so doing, these women writers perform the opposite rhetorical move to the one present in the common woman/nation plots outlined earlier – instead of subsuming individual women's images and stories into one feminized symbol of the nation, they investigate the national story to shed light upon key issues in Ukrainian women's lives. Oftentimes such inquiry uncovers what scholars of postcolonial literature in the Third World have termed *double colonization* or *double marginalization* of women – that is, numerous and intersecting ways in which the latter have been targeted by colonial and/or native forces on account of both their gender and their ethnicity/nationality.[49] What also comes into focus is individual women's power and agency – sometimes used for positive change and sometimes used in a misguided fashion.

In a number of works examined in this study, these female agents do toil for the benefit of their nation, adopting a stance commonly found among Third World women activists who "allied themselves with modernizing, post-colonial national projects" (Vickers 90). In the Ukrainian context, this stance has been dubbed "national feminism."[50] While it is often criticized for allegedly prioritizing national interests over women's, this critique rests on an assumption that these interests never overlap, which, in turn, stems from Western feminism's wholesale rejection of the nation as a possible site for women's liberation.[51] As feminist political scientist Jill Vickers pointed out, the Western "tendency to theorize a single, common relationship between 'nation' and 'gender' has obscured the complexity of issues" (85). In fact, this relationship can vary in different historical and political circumstances, and it can be altered when circumstances change. This is so, Vickers explains, because "nation-states are not definitively formed when founded, but undergo 'rounds of restructuring' when opportunities can emerge for women to change the gender/nation relationships" (86). Despite a lengthy history of conservative imagining of women's roles in the nation, Ukraine has recently witnessed at least two key moments of national "restructuring," which have offered opportunities for rethinking women's roles. The first moment came with the collapse of the Soviet Union, and the second one emerged with the Euromaidan protests, followed by war in the Donbas. These two moments constitute the main chronological frame of my inquiry into Ukrainian female writers' literary engagement with the imaginings of women and/in the nation.

Zabuzhko, Kononenko, and Matios approach the relationship between women and the nation from rather different ideological standpoints. While Zabuzhko and Kononenko are familiar with Western feminist ideas and identify as feminists, Matios has on occasion stated that she does not know what feminism is. Her focus on women's stories stems in part from her predilection to pay attention to marginal figures who are often misunderstood by everyone around them and experience much suffering as a result. Matios's strong commitment to bring to light the tragic history of her native Bukovyna region during and after the Second World War through individual people's stories has often brought peasant women of various ages into the centre of her narratives. By truthfully portraying both their victimization and their agency in the most difficult of historical circumstances, and by giving them voice in her works, Matios has often shed light on the ugly aspects of nationalist thinking – while at the same time remaining firmly committed to the well-being of the Ukrainian nation. Since her entrance into top-level Ukrainian politics, Matios's allegiance to the nation has also prompted her to write critically about the inaptness of male-dominated Ukrainian government. Kononenko's and Zabuzhko's stances, by contrast, are more indebted to explicit critiques of patriarchy and a commitment to women's issues. Yet the two writers also differ from one another in their approach to the nation. While Zabuzhko's standpoint has been described as being very close to national feminism,[52] the same is not true of Kononenko, who remains more sceptical of nationalism. Because these writers hold a range of views on women and the nation, their works, when taken together, are representative of the variety of recent attempts in Ukraine to rethink the gender/nation intersections.

The true-to-life representations of women's experiences, which dominate in the works by these three authors, do not make this writing exclusively mimetic. Especially in their larger "national" works from the 2000s, which strive to maintain a double, simultaneous focus on women and the nation, Zabuzhko, Kononenko, and Matios resort to a variety of narrative techniques, intertextual play, and even fantastic elements to fashion and promote alternative imaginings of the nation's past and present, as well as of women's societal roles. One of this study's goals is to pay attention to such devices and to explore what these women writers' poetics reveals to us about their texts' politics. There is often more in these works than first meets the eye. In particular, this book analyses various modes of narration and emplotment that Zabuzhko, Kononenko, and Matios have used – and sometimes simultaneously deconstructed – in order to stage specific interventions in the Ukrainian national imaginary.

These aesthetic forms may be seen as performing the broad ideological function of "inventing imaginary or formal 'solutions' to unresolvable social contradictions" as described by Fredric Jameson (79). And in the cases when these forms are deconstructed by the women writers, it is done for the purpose of critiquing the "solutions" as unfit to resolve the given "social contradictions." After the Euromaidan protests, as I argue in chapter 6, Zabuzhko and Matios rejected fictional plots altogether as a mode for recording the experience of the protests and the ensuing war. Instead, they opted for non-fictional chronicles in which individual women's testimonies predominate.

Both the creative and the deconstructive moves, however, are important for these women writers, as their views on the nation are ultimately complex. Similarly to Third World postcolonial women authors, on the one hand women *visimdesiatnyky* affirm the nation as a "platform … from which to resist the multiple ways in which colonialism distorts and disfigures a people's history," and on the other, they critique it, partly in order "to reshape national cultur[e] in a way more hospitable to women" (Boehmer, *Stories of Women* 10, 12). As this study charts the development of women's prose writing in independent Ukraine, it examines how these two efforts intersect in the works of Ukrainian women writers of the eighties generation.

The chapters in this book trace the re-emergence, evolution, and reception of post-Soviet Ukrainian women's prose writing, using as examples representative works by Zabuzhko, Kononenko, and Matios, and analysing their interventions in the national imaginary. Chapter 1 sets the stage for the rise of women *visim-desiatnyky* by analysing the example of their female predecessor from the 1960s generation, Nina Bichuia. I describe her literary career and the publication history of some of her work to illuminate the Soviet Ukrainian historical, ideological, and institutional contexts that made it difficult for Ukrainian women writers to gain literary visibility before the collapse of the USSR. A close reading of Bichuia's last short story, "Kaminnyi hospodar" ("The Stone Master," 1990), explores her own perspective on writing literature within the Soviet context in the Ukrainian periphery. In chapter 2, I show through close readings of two early prose works by Kononenko and Zabuzhko that the Soviet-era break in the women's prose tradition in Ukraine was so dramatic that emerging female writers questioned the very possibility of writing in a patriarchal Ukrainian society marked by colonial legacy.

Chapter 3 focuses on Zabuzhko's bestselling novel *Fieldwork in Ukrainian Sex* (1996). My reading of this text is shaped by its reception in both the Slavic world and the West; I argue that many of the novel's vociferous critics, which faulted the author for being either "too" feminist or "too" nationalist, misread its politics because they elided the text's poetics. My analysis suggests that the voice of Zabuzhko's autobiographical heroine is a split, ambivalent one, shuttling between several powerful and conflicting discourses (Soviet, Ukrainian nationalist, and Western), and ultimately finding "home" in none of them.

Chapters 4 and 5 examine four larger works of prose fiction by Matios, Kononenko, and Zabuzhko published in the 2000s. These writings have garnered much attention from critics and readers, and have propelled their authors to the forefront of Ukrainian literary life. I read Matios's *Natsiia. Odkrovennia* (*The Nation. Revelation*, 2001) and *Solodka Darusia* (*Sweet Darusia*, 2004), Kononenko's *Imitatsiia* (*Imitation*, 2001), and Zabuzhko's *Muzei pokynutykh sekretiv* (*The Museum of Abandoned Secrets*, 2009) as foundational national narratives that at the same time are very women-centred. As these works engage the most fundamental questions of Ukraine's collective national identity, they also emplot women into the national story in ways that often contradict or complicate the traditional woman/nation plots.

Chapter 6 shifts the focus from fiction about women in the Soviet and early post-Soviet past to the chronicling of women's real experiences in the Euromaidan protests of 2013–14. It analyses how *Litopys samovydtsiv. Dev'iat' misiatsiv ukrains'koho sprotyvu* (*The Chronicle of Witnesses: Nine Months of Ukrainian Resistance*, 2014), conceived and contributed to by Zabuzhko, and Matios's *Pryvatnyi shchodennyk. Maidan. Viina . . .* (*Private Diary. Maidan. The War . . .*, 2015) represent women's, including writers' own, roles in Ukraine's most recent mass protests. I explore these representations in light of the significant debates on Ukrainian women's place in the nation ignited by the Euromaidan events. The chapter demonstrates how by means of the chronicle genre and an emphasis on women's own testimonies the two works created a rich and sometimes unconventional portrayal of how Ukrainian women "made revolution."

The conclusion sums up the role of women *visimdesiatnyky* in changing the status of Ukrainian women writers in contemporary Ukraine, as well as their narrative experiments in rewriting the traditional Ukrainian imaginings of gender/nation intersections.

1 On the Invisibility of Ukrainian Women's Writing in the Soviet Empire

"This phenomenon is difficult to explain, but in the Ukrainian Socialist Realist writing of the 1930s–1970s, there were very few women authors," acknowledges literary scholar Vira Aheieva in her monograph on the feminist discourse in Ukrainian modernism (*Zhinochyi prostir* 315). This fact is indeed puzzling, especially when one considers the flourishing critical recognition and subsequent canonization of women's writing from the turn and the first decades of the twentieth century, best seen in the cases of two celebrated Ukrainian women modernists, Olha Kobylianska and Lesia Ukrainka.[1]

Moreover, the situation in Ukraine appears to be quite different from what was happening in the literature of the Soviet metropole after the Second World War. According to literary scholar Beth Holmgren, the Soviet post-war era "is perhaps the first period in Russian literature when women signify as a major and distinctive group" (226). As proof, Holmgren cites the examples of Vera Panova (1907–1973), Antonina Koptiaeva (1909–1991), and Galina Nikolaeva (1911–1963), all of whom received the Stalin Prize for their works in the late 1940s and the early 1950s, with Panova being thus "honoured" three times. Holmgren goes on to mention Panova's and Olga Berggolts's later "key roles in precipitating the intermittent thaw in Soviet literature" and rounds off her evidence with a sizeable list of both dissident and more conformist women authors, which includes Evgenia Ginzburg, Lidia Chukovskaia, Lidia Ginzburg, Nadezhda Mandelshtam, I. Grekova, Inna Varlamova, and Natalia Baranskaia (226). Holmgren's explanation of this boom focuses on socio-economic reasons, such as Soviet-sponsored "equal-opportunity education and equal-opportunity employment" as well as the opened track for "upward mobility through Party membership" for "lower-class women" (226–7). This analysis leads the scholar to conclude that "surprising as it may seem, the Stalinist system proved to be an institutional and iconic enabler of women's writing" (228).

Even though the Soviet government promoted, at least on paper, equal rights for women's education and employment across all of the republics, Holmgren's conclusion has no bearing for women writers in Soviet Ukrainian literature. There is no "distinctive group" of prominent Ukrainian women writers – especially women writers of prose – to speak of until the 1980s,[2] and none of those Ukrainian women who did write during this period ever received the Stalin Prize or its later version, the State Prize of the USSR.[3] The only Ukrainian female prose writer who came close to being allowed into the Soviet literary canon was Iryna Vilde (1907–1982) – a prolific author from Western Ukraine who, at the time of this region's annexation by the Soviet Union, was already an established and popular writer and, thus, by no means a product of "the Stalinist system" that Holmgren writes about.[4] In fact, making Vilde's work fit the ideological and aesthetic strictures of the Soviet canon required her own renunciation or heavy reworking of her pre-war writings as well as a lot of conscious misreading of her later work on the part of some Ukrainian Soviet critics (Zakharchuk 49, 53).[5]

If not "an institutional and iconic enabler of women's writing," as Holmgren puts it, then what was the Stalinist and, more broadly, the Soviet regime to Ukrainian women authors? How did the Soviet state-controlled system of literary production influence women's writing in Ukraine – especially the writing of prose? These are important questions to address in order to understand the historical context for the re-emergence of Ukrainian women's prose writing in the *perestroika* and the early independence period.

Brutal Stalinist repression of Ukrainian authors of the generation preceding Vilde's, including such women writers as Zinaida Tulub (1890–1964) and Nadia Surovtsova (1896–1985),[6] further invalidates Holmgren's argument for Ukraine. Instead, it lends support to literary scholar Olia Hnatiuk's conclusion that the implementation of women's rights in Stalinist Ukraine often resulted in equal opportunity for intellectuals of both sexes to be persecuted for ideological, often nationalist "deviations." Hnatiuk mentions several strategies – one might call them "strategies of invisibility" – which Ukrainian women writers adopted in the early Soviet era to escape such an outcome. Some of them abandoned literature altogether, some chose translation or writing for children only, and some switched to Russian as a "safer" language ("Zhinoche oblychchia" 24). These circumstances suggest that in order to understand how the Soviet regime impacted women's writing in Ukraine, gender politics and attitudes in Soviet Ukraine have to be analysed together with the nature of the colonial relationship between the imperial metropole and its Ukrainian periphery, and the ways in which this relationship manifested itself in cultural production.

Taking both the Soviet colonial politics and the gender biases into account, this chapter attempts to illuminate the political, historical, and social contexts for women's writing in the Soviet Ukrainian periphery by examining the case of Nina Bichuia. She was one of very few Ukrainian women prose writers besides Vilde to achieve some prominence in pre-1980s Soviet Ukraine and was an important precursor of the generation of women prose writers who are the subject of this study.

Bichuia's publication history, the critical reception of her works, and her overall place in the Soviet literary world throw important light on both the differential literary politics between the Soviet metropole and its periphery, and on the specific ways in which such politics circumscribed women's literary careers in the Ukrainian context, often rendering them invisible by circumstance or by choice. I will first discuss the vicissitudes of Bichuia's literary career, and will then focus on her own perspective on her place as an author under the Soviet regime, expressed in her last short story, "The Stone Master."

Bichuia's Career

Born in 1937 in Kyiv, Nina Bichuia grew up in Lviv and lives there to this day. Being thirty years younger than Iryna Vilde, Bichuia published most of her works during the Soviet period of stagnation, between the late 1960s and the early 1980s. Like many women writers in the Soviet era, she made her literary debut with collections of stories for and about children: *Kanikuly u Svitlohors'ku* (*Vacation in Svitlohors'k*, 1967) and *Shpaha Slavka Berkuty* (*Slavko Berkuta's Rapier*, 1968). However, her finest work, according to most of her critics, was a series of masterful historical and psychological short stories published in the late 1960s and the early 1970s, including "Drohobyts'kyi zvizdar" (The Drohobych Astronomer), "Sotvorinnia tainy" (Creation of a Mystery), "Velyki korolivs'ki lovy" (The Great Royal Hunt), and "Buiest' Mytusyna" (Mytusa's Bravery) (Gabor, *Neznaioma* 62). All of these stories were written in Bichuia's idiosyncratic and intricate style, usually characterized as "modernist" by her contemporary critics. These fragmented and frequently plotless narratives are primarily devoted to exploring the characters' inner worlds and leave much unsaid and unexplained (Gabor, "Vyvorozhy" 28). Bichuia's first collection for adults, *Drohobyts'kyi zvizdar* (*The Drohobych Astronomer*, 1970), which included many of these stories, was well received: writer and essayist Vasyl Gabor mentions that it was reviewed positively in the literary press over twenty-five times ("Vyvorozhy" 28).

Yet the subsequent publication history of Bichuia's work is complicated. It illustrates the paradoxes and mechanisms of Soviet literary politics concerning the literature of the so-called Soviet peoples' cultures (*literatura narodov SSSR*) – in this case, Ukraine. In the beginning of the 1970s, the well-known Moscow-based translator Vladimir Rossels prepared a collection of Bichuia's stories translated into Russian for publication in the newly established series Biblioteka "Druzhby narodov" (Library of *The Friendship of Peoples* Journal) (Gabor, "Vyvorozhy" 30). Fittingly, the journal's name adopted Stalin's slogan from the 1930s that came to designate the official Soviet framework for organizing cultural production within the republics and cultural exchange between them. In Yuri Slezkine's sardonic assessment, this framework included both the official expectation that each Soviet nationality would produce its own set of "nationally defined 'Great Traditions'" and the official requirement "that all Soviet nationalities be deeply moved by the art of other Soviet nationalities" (Slezkine 226). In keeping with the latter objective, the journal started the new series to acquaint Soviet readers with the best non-Russian writing coming out of various Soviet republics. The publication in Moscow of Bichuia's collection as the first book by a Ukrainian author in the series would have signified a major breakthrough in the literary career of this young writer. However, because the Soviet metropole left it up to the republics to determine which of their cultural riches would represent them at the all-Union level (i.e., the "Great Traditions" were to be "nationally defined"), the publication of Bichuia's collection in Moscow had to receive official approval from Kyiv. According to Bichuia, the decision in this matter was made by the leadership of the Union of Soviet Writers of Ukraine. The literary authorities in Kyiv responded that Bichuia was too young to be the first writer to represent Ukraine in the new series and that her book, though of high quality, would have to wait (Bichuia, Personal interview). Despite Rossels's appeal to the older and better-known Vilde, who attempted to intercede for Bichuia with the Union in Kyiv, the book was shelved (Bichuia, Personal interview). Instead of Bichuia's volume, two books by Ukrainian writers appeared in this series in the early 1970s – a memoir about Ukrainian literary life by Yuriy Smolych (1971) and a novel, *Tsyklon* (*Cyclone*, 1972), by Oles Honchar. Both authors were heads of the Union of Soviet Writers of Ukraine around this time (Honchar until 1971 and Smolych briefly in 1971); both were men. It is hardly surprising that the collection by the young and relatively unknown woman writer from the Western Ukrainian periphery was initially denied its place in the series.

This incident is instructive in several respects. First, it illustrates the argument made by cultural historian Serhy Yekelchyk in *Stalin's Empire of Memory* about the significant degree to which local "Ukrainian cultural agents" were involved in the formulation and building of Soviet Ukrainian national culture (6). In this case, too, the Ukrainian literary authorities in Kyiv "acted as classic indigenous elites" in defending their right from the imperial centre to define what they saw as "their cultural domain" (6). Second, the incident underscores the constraints which the "Friendship of Peoples" discourse placed on the cultures of non-Russian republics. Because of its tokenist nature, it often automatically generated competition for prestige and resources among the local cultural elites. Last but not least, Bichuia's story has a gender dimension: the fact that in each of the republics the institutional framework for literary production was characterized by a rigid hierarchy with loyal men at the top guaranteed that, no matter how talented, a young woman writer like Bichuia could not be published in Moscow before the male leaders of the Ukrainian branch of the Union of Soviet Writers.

While Bichuia's collection in Russian finally did come out in Moscow in 1974, the same book in Ukrainian, which Bichuia submitted to the publishing house of the Union of Soviet Writers of Ukraine, "Radianskyi pysmennyk" (Soviet Writer), never saw the light of day. Gabor indicates that this manuscript received three extremely negative internal reviews.[7] The reviewers accused the author of painting an excessively dark picture of life as well as of being influenced by a repressed Ukrainian urban prose writer of the 1920s–30s, Valerian Pidmohylny, whose forbidden works Bichuia, by her own admission, had not in fact read at that time (Gabor, "Vyvorozhy" 30).

The seemingly odd scenario in which a Ukrainian writer had less difficulty publishing the same material in Moscow than in Soviet Ukraine occurred throughout the Soviet era, prompting some writers to seek out Russian-language publishers in the metropole before attempting to publish in Ukrainian.[8] Even in the relatively liberal early thaw period, Russian writer Vsevolod Ivanov encouraged the Ukrainian poet, and Bichuia's contemporary, Lina Kostenko, who was graduating from the Moscow Literary Institute, to stay on in Moscow and publish her first collection of poetry in the metropole: "It will be very difficult for you in Ukraine … Perhaps with a book published in Moscow, you will have an easier time in Kyiv" (Kostenko and Pakhliovs'ka 167).[9] The language of publication was part of the matter. As historian Joshua First explains, in the stagnation era especially, the use of the Ukrainian language "constituted a degree of cultural excess, something that lacked practical necessity and thus possessed potentially dangerous connotations" (12). He recounts an exchange in 1969 between Leonid Brezhnev and the First Secretary of the Communist Party of Ukraine, Petro Shelest, in which Brezhnev wondered "why publishers needed to print materials in Ukrainian when almost all Ukrainians also knew Russian" (12). More generally, however, "[t]he area of the 'legally allowed' was much narrower for a Ukrainian writer than for a Russian one" (Petrovsky-Shtern 277). After the brief period of liberalization during the thaw, Ukraine experienced a renewed, concerted effort on the part of the highest political authorities of the Ukrainian Soviet Republic to stamp out any manifestations of "bourgeois nationalism" – a label that in the post-war era came to be associated predominantly with Ukraine and that was used almost indiscriminately to condemn any type of activity or expression that appeared dangerous (First 10–11; Bazhan 45). Even Bichuia's innocuous vignettes from Ukrainian pre-Soviet history, an interest in psychology and urban themes, and an unconventional style were deemed subversive enough to merit a comparison with the "nationalist" Pidmohylny and to be refused publication in Kyiv. Translated into Russian, however, and placed within the "safe" context of Stalinist "Friendship of Peoples" discourse, which superficially celebrated Soviet cultural diversity, Bichuia's texts no longer evoked the ghosts of "bourgeois nationalism" or repressed Ukrainian writers of the 1930s.

Through much of her career, like many of her male Ukrainian colleagues, Bichuia suffered the brunt of differential colonial politics of censorship. In the more liberal late 1980s, she even chose to portray these differences in a work of literature. Her *Desiat' sliv poeta* (*Ten Words of a Poet*), published in 1987, scrutinizes a similar and historically true scenario of a Ukrainian writer finding a more hospitable reception for his work in the Soviet capital rather than at home. The novella details the fate of Mykola Kulish's drama, *Patetychna sonata* (*Sonata Pathéthique*, 1930), which was banned from the Berezil Theatre stage in Kharkiv, yet at the same time was performed with great success by the Tairov Theatre in Moscow. Bichuia's moving descriptions of how Kulish felt about the rejection of his play at home and its premiere in Moscow capture some of her pain about her own situation as a writer in Soviet Ukraine (Bichuia, Personal interview).

Yet Bichuia's situation was also impacted in significant ways by her specific location within the Soviet Ukrainian periphery. Vilde once described the drastic differences in permissible literary expression between Moscow, Kyiv, and Lviv in a pithy saying: "When they cut fingernails in Moscow, they cut fingers in Kyiv and chop off the entire hand in Lviv" (qtd in Il'nyts'kyi, *Drama* 86). The extent of literary policing in the peripheries depended both on the importance of the place within the imperial hierarchy and on the perceived degree of its potential rebelliousness. Kyiv was significant in its status as the capital of a key Soviet republic; moreover, it had an eventful past, full of struggles for national liberation. For these reasons, Kyiv was monitored very carefully. In contrast, the situation with Lviv seemed to be more ambiguous. On the one hand, it was the heart of the recently acquired Western Ukrainian lands and ranked high on the scale of suspected sedition because of its "nationalist" reputation (hence Vilde's aphorism). The appointed local and regional party officials were therefore perpetually on the lookout for the slightest manifestations of freethinking among the Lviv literati.[10] On the other hand, Lviv was twice removed from the metropole as the Western periphery of the larger Soviet Ukrainian periphery. This distance sometimes permitted one to deviate more from the official party line in literature – as long as one did not attempt to publish these literary "deviations" in Kyiv (Bichuia, Personal interview). Bichuia, who had firmly decided for herself that she "would not write about the Communist hero, the Komsomol hero, or the Pioneer hero," used the peripheral status of Lviv to her advantage throughout much of her career and published most of her stories in the Lviv-based literary journal *Zhovten* (*October*) where she had friends among the staff (Bichuia, Personal interview).[11] To be sure, this was another example of the consciously employed strategy of invisibility, though perhaps a less drastic one than those practised by some women writers of previous generations. By submitting her works for publication primarily in Lviv and by choosing to write largely on politically neutral topics, Bichuia, in critic Mykola Ilnytsky's characterization, "managed to find a 'hermetic zone' in which she was able to preserve the purity of her voice" even in those oppressive times (*Drama* 112).

Certainly, these strategies reduced Bichuia's chances of becoming a prominent author, as did her choice of themes and style. According to a memoir by prose writer and editor of the *October* prose section, Roman Ivanychuk, amid his circle of populist-minded colleagues in the 1970s, Bichuia "remained a solitary figure with her original, modernist style, which, alas, turned out to be unacceptable to our politicized and sentimental reading public" (*Blahoslovy* 79). What Ivanychuk meant by "politicized and sentimental" was partly a symptom of another aspect of state politics regarding the literature of the Soviet periphery: within "The Friendship of Peoples" discourse, the promotion of the national literatures of the non-Russian Soviet republics had in reality provincialized these literatures by limiting their function to expressions of their peoples' "essence" (Kas'ianov 180). As Joshua First put it, "[u]nder a Stalinist mode of 'national' representation, the landscapes and peoples of the Soviet periphery achieved recognition as unique within a folkloric ... vocabulary, replete with costumes, dancing peasants, and other evidence of 'national colour'" (27). Growing up on a steady literary diet of the simplified sentimental images of Ukrainian peasants in their colourful national garb, many Soviet Ukrainian readers and writers had come to believe that this is what Ukrainian literature really *is* and should be, if it is to be truly Ukrainian and capture "the spirit of the people." Bichuia's stylistically complex, psychologically nuanced, and fiercely unsentimental stories about individual intellectuals and urban life ran counter to such beliefs and readerly expectations.

The differences in literary politics between Moscow, Kyiv, and Lviv, and Bichuia's navigation of this institutional and ideological colonial matrix, impacted her literary visibility and shaped her reception by critics in curious ways. In part because of her ultimately successful, though belated, Russian-language publication in Moscow and the generally favourable critical reception of her stories in the metropole, she was once again noticed by the Ukrainian literary establishment. Toward the end of the 1970s, her name regularly appeared in the central Russian and Ukrainian literary press among the names of male Ukrainian prose writers active in that era. A survey of Ukrainian prose from the late 1970s published in Moscow's *Literaturnaia gazeta* (Literary Newspaper) in 1978 by Kyiv-based Ukrainian literary critic Vitaliy Donchyk is a case in point. Among scores of older and younger male Ukrainian prose writers who "became well-known to the all-Union reader," Bichuia was the only female author mentioned by Donchyk (Donchik 4). This is not to say that her works received very much thoughtful attention from Moscow or Kyiv literary critics.[12]

Rather, it seems that Bichuia became the token Ukrainian woman prose writer of her generation – frequently mentioned, yet less often critically appreciated.

In the attempts of her colleagues and literary critics to categorize her writing, Bichuia's gender often played an important role. To this day, many of those who write about Bichuia continue to mention that she was once characterized as "the queen of women's prose" of her generation by the Kyiv-based Ukrainian prose writer Valeri Shevchuk.[13] Bichuia herself, who dislikes this phrase, just as she generally disapproves of the division of literature into "men's" and "women's," was at a loss when I asked her what was meant by "women's prose" in the 1960s (Bichuia, Personal interview). She also found it difficult to name any other well-known Ukrainian women prose writers of whom she was supposedly "the queen" in the 1960s. She was right: as a 1984 review article of contemporary Ukrainian women's writing by female critic and prose writer Halyna Hordasevych noted, Ukrainian prose by women began to emerge only in the mid-1970s (116). Hordasevych, who meant by "women's prose" works by female writers that focused on a contemporary woman's inner world and life experiences, included in her review over half a dozen women authors' names, most of which are forgotten today.[14] She also discussed several pieces by Bichuia that featured female protagonists, paradoxically faulting the author for an excessive focus on their thoughts: "contemporary women do not have this much time to simply sit and think" (117). All of the above suggests that Bichuia's writing could not easily fit the label of "women's prose" as it was understood in the late Soviet era.[15] It seems that Shevchuk's "queen of women's prose" was a misnomer that, instead of inviting greater attention to Bichuia's work, made it easier to discount it.

Speaking more broadly, it appears that various stereotypes about creative women in general and women's prose writing in particular pervaded the literary circles of Bichuia's time. Ivanychuk, who later became Bichuia's closest friend, once described his initial scepticism about Bichuia's ability to write high-quality, serious prose when he first met her and saw "a slender green-eyed girl with long fair hair" ("Tema" 10). In a memoir about Soviet-era writers and artists in Lviv, poet Mykola Petrenko depicted their life as a valiant struggle against the Soviet functionaries and the system of cultural production they had imposed on Lviv. In this struggle, his almost exclusively male colleagues figured as knights and bohemians who fought valiantly against the system with their art, and drank their fear and worries away. Fittingly, the memoir is titled *Lytsari pera i charky* (The Knights of the Pen and the Shot Glass). Petrenko's vision of this period gives women mostly marginal, conservative roles: they are male writers' dutiful wives, caring mothers of small children, or, at most, the rare keepers of literary salons where "a tender woman's hand would serve you a cup of coffee and a sandwich" (82). Bichuia is mentioned once, and only as Ivanychuk's colleague. In general, the figure of a female writer or artist and her resistance to the Soviet system are virtually absent in the memoir.

As one can see from the example of Petrenko's work, such biased attitudes toward women writers were shaped in part by the stereotype of the arts as a male arena for fighting against the Soviet regime. This perception was a dominant one in Lviv, where Soviet rule was commonly viewed "as an alien force" (Risch 10).[16] Being a Western Ukrainian writer who felt the burden of colonial Soviet politics through much of her career, Bichuia certainly supported her male colleagues' efforts to resist the system (even though in her own writing she did not push the envelope as deliberately as some of them). Being a woman writer, Bichuia at the same time observed the male-dominated literary and cultural life around her – with all of its daring as well as its hypocrisy and blind spots – from a critical distance. She communicated this distanced perspective in her last short story, "The Stone Master," which first appeared in *October* in 1990.[17] Ivanychuk called this work by Bichuia "the quintessence of her intellectual expression" (*Blahoslovy* 106–7). Bichuia herself explained that her silence as a writer since "The Stone Master" was partly due to the fact that she had nothing further to say after finishing this story (Bichuia, Personal interview).

"The Stone Master"

"The Stone Master" is set in Lviv in the late 1970s and relates the thoughts, conversations, and experiences of a Ukrainian woman writer and her literary acquaintances. As Bichuia has acknowledged in interviews, the story is full of autobiographical details (Khudyts'kyi). Its female I-narrator expresses a lot of Bichuia's own ideas, fears, and regrets related to living and writing in post-Stalinist Western Ukraine. The historical, cultural, and social proximity of the subject-matter to the author makes "The Stone Master" into Bichuia's most overtly ideological text, yet it is still in keeping with her trademark style. In this story as in numerous others, Bichuia's disjointed, non-linear narration makes multiple attempts to tackle the main topic of the text by presenting disparate images, symbols, and scenes that illuminate this topic from various vantage points – usually in a self-consciously subjective and fragmentary way.

"The Stone Master" may be read as Bichuia's "last word" of sorts on the Soviet environment for writing literature, especially in the rebellious Soviet periphery of Western Ukraine. By analysing Bichuia's use of important literary intertexts and with the help of some recent theorizations about Soviet state discourse, I will demonstrate how "The Stone Master" imaginatively represents and criticizes the discursive regime established by the Soviet system and its effects in the Ukrainian periphery. Within this discursive regime, for multiple reasons, Bichuia's female writer-narrator finds it impossible to speak. The story is thus primarily about a female writer's painful and overdetermined silence, and it ends with a nightmarish image of her complete annihilation. As such,

"The Stone Master" offers additional insights into the conditions of invisibility impacting a female writer from the Soviet Ukrainian periphery.

The central event in "The Stone Master" takes place around a table where the I-narrator and a small circle of her male writer friends are sharing memories, almost twenty-five years later, about their reactions to the news of Stalin's death. The narrator remembers how upon hearing about it early in the morning, her father started jumping around the room in his underwear chanting "Zdokh! Zdokh!" ("He croaked! He croaked!"; 37).[18] Later at school, when the teacher locked up the narrator in the principal's office, asking her, because of her literary talents, to write a poem on the occasion of Stalin's death, all that kept coming to the girl's mind was her father's "Zdokh!" Caught between the impossibility of writing *that* and creating anything eulogistic, she finally got out of the sordid task by pretending she was so overcome with grief that she could not write at all. Although the narrator's companions laugh, finding the story amusing, the narrator's unease about their laughter generates a fragmented stream of other traumatic memories from the Stalinist past, both personal and national. The narrator pictures Stalin's ghost with a fake black moustache standing behind her friends' backs, joining in their laughter and drinking – making all of it possible, in fact, because it is their remembrance of him, however irreverent, that unites their little counter-community.

The portrayal of Stalin as an evil force and the master of the Soviet "house," complete with such stock features as his thick moustache and his pipe, mark this story as a fairly typical product of its time: in *Literary Exorcisms of Stalinism*, literary scholar Margaret Ziolkowski mentions a host of works by Russian authors from Aleksandr Solzhenitsyn to Aleksandr Bek that describe Stalin in similar terms. However, Bichuia's story is also different: it attempts to shift the focus from the pathologies of Stalin's person to the still totalitarian character of the Soviet system after Stalin. In this respect, Bichuia's most immediate intertext is the well-known sonnet "Koly umer kryvavyi Torkvemada" ("When the Bloody Torquemada Died") from a 1958 collection of poems by her then Lviv-based colleague Dmytro Pavlychko. Pavlychko's poem, which speaks of the sobbing populace after the death of Spain's tyrannical Grand Inquisitor and ends with the famous line "... zdokh tyran, ale stoit' tiurma" ("... the tyrant died, but the prison still stands"), was an early and daring allegory for the post-Stalinist Soviet society (qtd in Il'nyts'kyi, *Drama* 18; Risch 123). Bichuia referenced Pavlychko's sonnet by making both the verb "zdokh" and the theme of hypocritical sorrow over the dictator's death key in her own text. Yet if Pavlychko's work concludes with the simple assertion that "the prison still stands," Bichuia's story is an extended philosophical meditation on the nature of the Soviet system as a "prison." The analysis of the regime which Bichuia presents in "The Stone Master" leaves no stone unturned (pun intended): certainly, it blames the imperial centre and its rulers, but it also criticizes the local elites, including Bichuia's own circle of creative intelligentsia. It suggests important ethical questions about the very possibility and the cost of a writing career under this regime. In this sense especially, the choice of Pavlychko's work as this story's intertext is not accidental. Pavlychko's resounding "zdokh," written back in 1958 by a writer from the rebellious Western Ukrainian periphery, was meant as a gesture of resistance to the regime and became one reason why his collection was hastily banned upon its initial release. Yet as William Ray Risch pointed out, "[b]anning the book turned it into a bestseller" and ultimately propelled its author to literary fame (123). As a true "knight of the pen," to use Petrenko's metaphor, Pavlychko wrote in real life what Bichuia's female narrator did not dare put on paper in the fictional world of the story.

"The Stone Master" captures what I call, after the Slavic studies scholar Serguei Oushakine, "the discursive monopoly" of the Soviet regime – the fact that the regime reserved for itself and the subject positions authorized by it the exclusive right to produce authoritative discourse, which it refused to share with any other participants in the discursive field ("The Terrifying Mimicry" 214). Bichuia depicted the functioning of this discursive monopoly in stagnation-era Western Ukraine and its impact on her female writer-narrator through the narrator's recurrent nightmare, variations of which occur in the beginning, the middle, and the end of "The Stone Master." It is worth looking at the first variation of this dream in its entirety:

> A trampled green field extends between *me* and *the podium*, which was made of rough rust-colored planks hastily hammered together, and *the man behind the podium, holding a microphone in his hands*, exclaims something, shouting at the top of his voice, *but I don't hear a word, and this is all because someone has spread out such a boundless green expanse between us and also because of the fact that the microphone he's holding is not plugged into anything*; the cord droops, stretches out, and recoils like a long black snake, and maybe the man is even hissing like a snake, and although I understand that the man cannot hiss, I keep thinking that his voice is that absurd hissing, and there is not another soul in the vast green space – only I and that man who stands behind the podium holding the microphone, although it makes no sense to hold it because nothing can be heard anyway. (32; my emphasis)

The man at the podium in this nightmare is both an agent and a symbol of the Soviet regime's discursive monopoly. The man is fittingly not any specific, recognizable individual because it is his position at the podium rather than his person that endows him with the power to speak on behalf of the regime. Soviet visual propaganda (photos, monuments, posters, etc.) produced many stock images of the man at the podium (and very rarely – of a woman), their style depending little on whether the man was Lenin, Stalin, or some nameless Soviet hero exhorting the Soviet people to think or do one thing or another.

Although the man at the podium occupies a position authorized by the regime, his attempts to influence Bichuia's narrator with his discourse appear futile: she cannot hear a word of what he says because of the space between them and the fact that his microphone is not plugged in. I read the "boundless green expanse" between the narrator and the speaker as representing the distance between the Soviet centre and its periphery – in this case, one of the westernmost borderlands that historically proved to be particularly resistant to heeding the ideological messages of the Soviet metropole. The most interesting detail of this dream – the unplugged microphone – seemingly suggests that the regime has lost its discursive effectiveness. However, I think a more accurate interpretation of this image can be generated through Alexei Yurchak's theorization of the transformations that occurred in the Soviet authoritative discourse in the post-Stalinist era. While Stalin served as an external "master" of Soviet ideological discourse during his life, often personally directing and revising its content, after his death, this discursive regime underwent what Yurchak termed a "performative shift" (13, 24–6). As a result of this shift, "the performative dimension" of any public ideological act became more important than the constative one (24). In other words, the forms of various ideological acts and rituals remained intact while their actual content gradually lost its original significance.[19] Even though no constative meaning of the speaker's address in the dream can be deciphered, his speech act still works as a performance of discursive monopoly: he still occupies a position of power at the podium and still holds the microphone. This performance of power has a contradictory effect on the narrator: on the one hand, she finds it absurd and in a later variation of the dream she begins laughing uncontrollably; on the other hand, she reports being able only to laugh, but not to move, turn around, or say a word, as if she were petrified. This nightmare accurately represents the character of the late Soviet regime after the performative shift: while the content of its ideological discourse was perceived as ridiculous by many, the very shape of the discursive field persisted, continuing to hold the majority of the population in a subordinate position. The nightmare underscores the female narrator's position of powerlessness and silence within this discursive regime.

In contrast to the female narrator's arrested state in the nightmare, her fellow writer friends' ongoing irreverent reminiscing about Stalin's death and their lack of regime-prescribed mournfulness on the occasion looks like a display of counter-discursive power. Yet the ghost of the dictator is hovering behind them, and just like in the nightmare, the narrator feels unable to utter another word. She only listens quietly to her friends' stories and laughter. She hears the ghost laughing with them, giving them permission to mock him. Unlike her companions, the narrator realizes that even these oppositional tales are part and parcel of the same discursive field established under its master – Stalin. These stories do not escape the regime's discursive monopoly – first, because they do not come from a regime-authorized source (i.e., they are shared in private rather than in an official public setting); and, second, because they do not go beyond speech that revolves around the regime itself (i.e., they are still about Stalin).[20] Stalin's ghost enjoys how the narrator's friends "extend" his life by talking about him and relives his role of the master by putting on his fake black moustache. The moustache here does not represent Stalin as a historical person, but rather his function as the master of the Soviet regime with its discursive control – what Bichuia calls "The Stone Master" in the title of her story.

The title itself is an intertextual borrowing: it comes from Lesia Ukrainka's 1912 drama *Kaminnyi hospodar* (The Stone Master). Like her famous female predecessor's work, Bichuia's story portrays the contemporary social order's enduring power and immutability through the central symbol of "the stone master." Like the Commander in Lesia Ukrainka's drama, Stalin remains powerful even after death because the system he put into place does not cease to exist. Both Stalin and the Commander appear in the two texts as statues that come alive to ensure that the order over which they had presided remains intact. The image of a statue turned ghost is powerful in these contexts precisely because it communicates iconic, lasting status from the past (the statue) and the present dynamic influence (the ghost).

Recent critics of Lesia Ukrainka's drama have explicated its anticolonial meaning. One of this study's subjects, Oksana Zabuzhko, has read the drama's "key opposition" of austere, "stony" Madrid to freedom-loving, merry Seville as the contrast and conflict between Moscow and Ukraine (*Notre Dame d'Ukraine* 401). Literary scholar Myroslav Shkandrij has emphasized the play's dual critique of the imperial rule, symbolized by the Commander, and the shortcomings of the native opposition to it. In his analysis, Don Juan, who represents the Ukrainian oppositional forces, in the end "succumb[s] to the temptations of power and privilege" and thereby "exposes the superficiality of his … revolt" (*Russia and Ukraine* 202). Finally, both scholars have pointed out the drama's exposé of male drive for power: the Commander and Don Juan are alike in that they seek control both in the personal and in the public realm, and Donna Anna simply imitates this dominant masculine model of behaviour – to her own detriment.[21]

All of these ideas from Lesia Ukrainka's *The Stone Master* are echoed in Bichuia's story. The formidable totalitarian order established by Stalin is formally opposed by the female narrator's circle of male writer friends, who laugh and make merry. Yet the story shows that this childish laughter presents no real challenge to the system's discursive order. In fact, the narrator refuses to join in the merriment and instead remains silent precisely because she doubts that her friends' talk is effective or even ethical. While occupying the privileged position of a writer in their society – a position created and sanctioned by the regime itself – the narrator's friends continue to operate within its discursive monopoly even though they think they are rebelling against it. The direct critique of this position is not voiced by the female narrator herself, but by a young teenage daughter of one of the writers, who overhears their conversation and finally remarks: "Instead of talking about him [Stalin] all the time, you'd better hold a séance and summon his spirit … and ask him in person what he thinks about your present exceptional bravery" ("Stone Master" 51). The girl's taunt resembles the one by Don Juan's servant in Lesia Ukrainka's play: Sganarelle expresses his doubt that his master would be able to dine boldly with Donna Anna if the now dead Commander were in attendance (*Kaminnyi hospodar* 627). It is hardly an act of courage to celebrate a ruler's demise well after the fact, especially if at the same time you remain complicit in the oppressive system he had left behind (and if, like Don Juan and Donna Anna, you attempt to use this system to satisfy your own ambitions – something that numerous male Ukrainian writers have done throughout the Soviet era).

The story presents no easy exit from the system though. There is a sense that the fear instilled by the Stalinist regime will linger for many years to come. Yet in trying to grapple with the regime's legacy, Bichuia's female narrator intuitively seeks out the histories of the subaltern – those who were given no place and no voice whatsoever in the regime. That is why the female narrator repeatedly meditates on the victims of the Stalinist terror, first and foremost the Holodomor. Most of the terror images of the narrator derive from accounts of the older generation who personally witnessed it – especially her father. She assimilates her father's experiences as her own, and these terrifying visions continue to impact her even now: "While coming out of my apartment building in Lviv, I was often afraid to look to the side because I knew that back then, in Kyiv, Father saw, right under the gate, a woman in a beautiful embroidered shirt, with beads around her neck – dead from hunger" ("Stone Master" 44).[22] The story is filled with images of victims who have been silenced forever, and most of them are women. Whether consciously or not, Bichuia constructs a gendered hierarchy of subjection within the Stalinist system, with Stalin, the Stone Master, at its very top, and female terror victims as the regime's ultimate subaltern at its bottom. Her female narrator's silence throughout the story is at once an acknowledgment of the power of the regime's discursive monopoly, a sign of protest against her fellow writers' complicity in it, and a form of identification with the regime's subaltern, who cannot speak.[23] The latter point is vividly made by another of the narrator's nightmares. In it, she is sent on a mission to some nearby village to write down the songs of the women who wanted their art recorded before they died.[24] When she gets there, the narrator finds no village. Only a toothless, bald female child is sitting in the black snow, and she can tell nothing because she is mute. Horrified by this image of destroyed countryside and its suppressed cultural memory, the narrator is prompted to think about her own art, which, she feels, will also perish without a trace.

The story makes the linkage between the narrator's inability/refusal to speak and her silence as a writer most apparent in that central traumatic memory from the narrator's early youth, when, unwilling and unable to write either a eulogy for Stalin or a triumphant "Zdokh!" on the occasion of his death, she ends up writing nothing. In the story's present, the grown-up narrator periodically engages herself in an honest assessment of her writing career, lamenting an inability to write, as well as the lack of understanding for her writing: "You haven't written anything in a very long time, and it seems to you that the critics' bickering about the things you did write in the past resembles some senseless, wild dance on a still-fresh grave – your very own grave ("Stone Master" 40). This self-addressed passage exemplifies only one of the narrator's several moments of intense scrutiny directed at her "writerly" self. Throughout the story, these are always in the second person, unlike the rest of the narration. This mode of address affords the narrator an honest, critical look at herself while at the same time allowing her to avoid saying "I" and thereby owning up to her painful perceived failure as a writer. She ultimately traces this failure to the environment of discursive monopoly, in which only a very specific kind of writing, focused on the regime itself, would grant an author visibility.[25]

In this environment, the narrator sees no possibility to be understood or valued even in the future. Perhaps inspired by Marina Tsvetaeva's famous poetic address to her desk, Bichuia communicates this bleak prognosis in a striking coded image of her narrator's "writerly" self and its creations as a writing desk:

> Your big, old, solid, reliable table. Its two bulky sections support a heavy brown tabletop; the sections' drawers can be moved only with effort, as if they do not want to reveal their secrets to anyone … my table may turn out to be … useless later, sometime in the future, to someone who will realize its age, old-fashioned character, and bulkiness, and who will see nothing in its marks, stains, spots, its scratched-off polish, the charm, uniqueness, and mysteriousness of the pattern in its chestnut finish. ("Stone Master" 44–5)

The language of this description points to a similarity between the table's aesthetic details and Bichuia's own writing style, which has so many of its own unique "marks" and mysterious "patterns." As one contemporary commentator recently noted, Bichuia's stories, including "The Stone Master," are rarely straightforward but rather consist of cut-up and jumbled chunks, which the reader must attend to very closely in order to put them together (Riznyk 139).[26] Later the story sets up an opposition between the uselessness and probable future destruction of the narrator's writing table and the persistence of the stains from the red wine on the white tablecloth, left behind by Stalin's ghost. While her writing desk is a "mere used-up prop" that was simply a decoration in the "performance" of her life, the red circles from the wine glass on the tablecloth that symbolize Stalin's bloody heritage are permanent ("Stone Master" 51).

Significantly, the narrator mentions that her writing desk is not entirely her own: only one section of it belongs to her, whereas the rest is still her father's, full of his possessions. Just like her vision of the Stalinist past, her place and stance as a writer are shaped by the heritage of the previous generation. This heritage is full of trauma, but the narrator accepts its burden, even if it dooms her to a painful silence. She is persuaded that only the intimate knowledge and memory of this traumatic legacy can help disrupt and destroy the discursive monopoly, and prevent a future replay of the totalitarian past.

The ending of "The Stone Master" plays out a return of the terror-filled Stalinist era. In a grotesque scene at a Soviet second-hand shop, the narrator once again encounters a vision of Stalin – this time in the form of a stone bust that seems partly alive owing to the efforts of the shop assistant, who decided to resuscitate it and make him into her own, private devil. As the head of the bust turns and stares angrily at the narrator, the story ends with the last variation of the narrator's recurrent nightmare about the man at the podium. The green field between her and the man becomes filled with a multitude of people who can apparently hear him. The long cord of the microphone slithers like a snake at the narrator's feet, the crowd gets larger and larger, and it finally swallows up the narrator into its blackness. In this final nightmare, the constative dimension of the man's speech act is restored, and his discourse regains its full influence and authority, which is evidenced by his growing audience. The unavoidable, predatory character of this discursive monopoly is symbolized by the snakelike microphone, which now reaches the narrator. The horrific concluding image of the narrator vanishing into the crowd signifies that she has become both invisible and voiceless, part of the undifferentiated mass ruled by the regime.

Bichuia's story thus presents both a picture of the still-functioning Soviet discursive monopoly in the stagnation era – with its effects on her generation – and a warning about the possible return of its worst, totalitarian manifestations. The likelihood of its revival is shown to depend on forgetting or disregarding the terror-filled past and its numerous victims. In light of the present-day resurgence of Stalin's popularity and the state-sanctioned revisionism of the Soviet past in Russia, Bichuia's warning, issued in 1990, seems remarkably prescient.

While developing her strategies of resistance to the Soviet discursive regime, Bichuia's narrator employs silence as a radical way of evading the system's dictatorial power. The danger, of course, is that silence is easily misinterpreted – for example, as a sign of defeat. Perhaps, this is one reason why Bichuia felt compelled to write an entire story about a Soviet-era Ukrainian female writer's silence. In an afterword to a recent edition of her Soviet-era novellas, while thinking of her own silence as a writer, Bichuia spoke of it as a form of resistance: "It is possible to break the silence, although it does not mean that you have started speaking. Silence is sometimes more eloquent than any word" ("Taka sobi intryha" 334).

With its focus on the silencing of a female writer by the discursive monopoly established under Stalin, Bichuia's story powerfully refutes Holmgren's argument about "the Stalinist system" being "an institutional and iconic enabler of women's writing" (228). Instead, "The Stone Master" suggests that in the Ukrainian periphery, this system ended up greatly hindering women's writing – even if it did not intend to target women authors specifically. My examples from Bichuia's literary career show how various cultural policies and practices of the Soviet metropole combined and played out in the Ukrainian periphery in a way that often thwarted women writers' success and limited their visibility. Stalin's "Friendship of Peoples" discourse circumscribed literary production in the Soviet Ukrainian periphery in multiple ways. Not only did it provincialize Ukrainian literature, but it also created tight competition among Ukrainian writers for literary visibility at the all-Union level. The metropole invested top-placed Ukrainian establishment writers in Kyiv, all of whom happened to be male, with a decisive say in the competition, thus reducing women authors' chances to succeed. On a more peripheral level, and especially in the rebellious Western Ukraine, the regime's ideological pressure turned the process of cultural production into a "masculine" power struggle between Soviet literary ideologues and the creative intelligentsia. Prevailing traditional views of appropriate gender roles often deemed women writers unsuitable as potential participants in this struggle and instead segregated them in an ill-defined "women's prose" category. Bichuia's ultimate response to these traumatic circumstances was a pained silence – and "The Stone Master."

Despite its pessimistic ending, Bichuia's story does hint at the possibility of positive change in the future. While the narrator does not voice her objections to her circle of colleagues, who, it seems, simply cannot stop talking about Stalin, they are periodically interrupted by that teenage daughter of the narrator's writer friend. The girl keeps citing out loud from the book of aphorisms by the eighteenth-century French writer Marquis de Vauvenargues, which she is reading in Russian translation. Her seemingly random citations turn out to be an apt commentary on her father's and his friends' obsessive conversation and, more generally, on her parents' generation's uneasy relationship to the Stalinist regime. "The individual who cannot ingratiate himself with the monarch attempts to gain the favor of the minister or, at least, his lackey," quotes the girl at one point ("Stone Master" 33). With this quotation, the girl interrupts the narrator's memories of private reflections, during the commemoration ceremony on the day of Stalin's death, about how many of her peers pretended to cry for Stalin and how many were watching her, ready to inform the authorities of her lack of mournfulness. Unlike the narrator, and despite her young age, the girl is not afraid to express her opinions out loud, although her father keeps snapping at her, trying to get her to go to bed and leave them alone. The narrator, however, recognizes in the girl's comments something her own generation needs to hear, and she asks the girl to keep reading out loud from Vauvenargues.

In an oblique way, then, "The Stone Master" suggests that it will be up to the younger generation to make sense of the Soviet era and its many traumas. In the image of the nameless young girl created by Bichuia, I see a representation of the new generation of women writers in Ukraine – the ones who, unlike Bichuia's narrator, did not live through the Stalinist period themselves and are therefore not haunted by the personal memories and fears of the past. Nevertheless, these younger women grew up in the Soviet Union, observed the fear- and trauma-ridden lives of their parents and older compatriots, and were moved to make sense of it all – in prose genres, which seemed to them most suitable for the purpose. With the coming of the more liberal *perestroika* period and the eventual crumbling of the Soviet regime, a new generation of women writers did emerge in Ukraine – after decades of marginalization of Ukrainian women authors and their virtual silence within the Soviet Ukrainian literary scene. Scholars of contemporary Ukrainian literature have referred to the emergence of an entire wave of new women prose writers as "a conspicuous blossoming" and have called the writing they produced since Ukraine's independence "remarkably vibrant."[27] It is to them and their writing that I turn next.

2

How Can a Ukrainian Woman Write?

The women writers of the eighties generation, who emerged on Ukraine's literary scene just as the Soviet regime was beginning to crumble, were born at approximately the same time as Bichuia's young girl in "The Stone Master." Born in the late 1950s or the early 1960s, this generation of female authors had still experienced firsthand – both as women and as women writers – what Michael Naydan termed as "the repressive and congenitally patriarchal nature of the Soviet system."[1] Because of this environment and the disrupted tradition of Ukrainian women's prose, which some of these women authors acutely felt, finding a path to literary success was no easy task for these writers. They needed to articulate anew for themselves as well as for their culture what it means to be a *Ukrainian woman writer* – with all three of these terms demanding rethinking, and the concept as a whole prompting renegotiation of women's and women writers' traditional roles in the Ukrainian national imaginary. One can begin to understand how Zabuzhko, Kononenko, and Matios – three key women authors of the eighties generation – navigated this social and cultural terrain by exploring and comparing the trajectories of their literary careers.

Born in 1960 in the city of Lutsk in northwestern Ukraine, Oksana Zabuzhko received an undergraduate degree in philosophy (1982) and a graduate degree in aesthetics (1985), both from the Taras Shevchenko University in Kyiv. She made a very early literary debut as a poet at the age of ten, but her first collection of poetry, prepared for publication in the mid-1970s, did not come out until 1985. This delay was the result of a new wave of repressions against the Ukrainian intelligentsia in Kyiv, a series of events which also touched Zabuzhko's parents (Gabor, *Neznaioma* 116–18). Her first prose works appeared in 1988–92 in literary journals, but her major breakthrough was the 1996 autobiographical novel, *Poliovi doslidzhennia z ukrains'koho seksu* (*Fieldwork in Ukrainian Sex*), which is currently in its thirteenth edition in Ukraine. Since then, in addition to shorter works of prose, Zabuzhko has published several collections of essays and correspondence, as well as three major works of literary/cultural criticism on the foundational figures of Ukrainian literature: Taras Shevchenko, Ivan Franko, and Lesia Ukrainka. For a number of years, she also maintained her own columns in several Ukrainian periodicals. Her magnum opus is the controversial 820-page novel *Muzei pokynutykh sekretiv* (*The Museum of Abandoned Secrets*, 2009) – a family saga that attempts to reconstruct and rethink Ukrainian history from the 1940s to the 2000s. Most recently, two volumes of non-fiction written and/or contributed to by Zabuzhko have appeared in the wake of the Euromaidan protests. Zabuzhko's public visibility, participation in countless national and international forums, involvement in the publishing of contemporary Ukrainian literature, and numerous prizes, as well as film and theatre adaptations of her works, have all contributed to her current image as Ukraine's premier woman writer and cultural figure.

Born in Kyiv in 1959, Yevhenia Kononenko obtained degrees in mathematics (1981) and French (1994) from prestigious Kyiv universities. Her initial forays into literature were translations of French poetry, while her own poems and stories appeared in print after 1991 (Gabor, *Neznaioma* 232). Her first published collection, like Zabuzhko's, was a volume of poetry (1997), to be followed by many works of prose. She made a name for herself with short stories about contemporary urban women's lives (the collection *Kolosal'nyi siuzhet* [*A Phenomenal Plot*], 1998, followed by many others). In the early 2000s, she switched to novels, publishing works such as *Imitatsiia* (*Imitation*, 2001), *Zrada. ZRADA made in Ukraine* (*Betrayal*, 2002), and *Nostal'hiia* (*Nostalgia*, 2005). Kononenko is credited with successfully transplanting the detective novel genre onto the Ukrainian cultural landscape (*Imitatsiia*). She is also the author of the autobiographical feminist essay *Bez muzhyka* (*Without a Guy*, 2005), numerous translations from French, and many cultural studies articles and essays, some of which examine the public images of Ukrainian women writers, including Zabuzhko (the collection *Heroini ta heroi* [*Heroines and Heroes*, 2010]). Most recently, Kononenko has published some short novels (*Rosiis'kyi siuzhet* [*The Russian Plot*, 2012] and *Ostannie bazhannia* [*The Last Wish*, 2015]) and several more collections of short stories. Her writing has been translated into many languages and recognized with a number of Ukrainian and international literary prizes.

Born in 1959 in the village of Rostoky in the Bukovyna region, Maria Matios graduated in 1982 from the Chernivtsi State University with a degree in Ukrainian language and literature. Her early works included poetry, with six collections published between 1983 and 2002 (Gabor, *Neznaioma* 374–5). Critical acclaim and widespread public recognition, however, came to her with the publication of two prose volumes in the early 2000s – a collection of short stories, *Natsiia* (*The Nation*, 2001), and the novel *Solodka Darusia* (*Sweet Darusia*, 2004), about the Soviet occupation and eventual annexation of Bukovyna during the Second World War and the lives of the Ukrainian peasants traumatized in its wake. In 2005, Matios was awarded the Taras Shevchenko National Prize for *Sweet Darusia*. Numerous translations and stage adaptations followed, and a film adaptation, co-produced by Ukraine, Poland, and the United States, is in progress. Since then, Matios has been highly productive, writing in a variety of prose genres, including non-fiction. Her recent books include the autobiographical volume *Vyrvani storinky z avtobiohrafii* (*Pages Torn Out of My Autobiography*, 2010); novels, *Armahedon uzhe vidbuvsia* (*Armageddon Has Already Taken Place*, 2011) and *Cherevychky Bozhoi materi* (*Shoes of the Mother of God*, 2013); and her memoir of the Euromaidan events and the beginning of the war in the Donbas, *Pryvatnyi shchodennyk. Maidan. Viina . . .* (*Private Diary. Maidan. The War ...*, 2015).

While these three women writers could not be more different in their personalities, worldviews, and writing styles, the brief sketches of their literary careers suggest a number of commonalities in their paths to literary recognition. It is interesting that all three started out writing or translating poetry, only later switching to prose fiction, in which all of them gained cultural visibility, fame, and speedy canonization. The connection between genre and popularity seems far from accidental. During the Soviet era, poetry, especially lyric or love poetry, was the most popular and culturally acceptable niche for Ukrainian women writers. Thus, while there was a dearth of women writing prose fiction until the late Soviet era, there were a number of women poets, Lina Kostenko being the premier example. And although Kostenko's poetry clearly broke out of the "women's ghetto," as Zabuzhko has once characterized the status of women's lyric poetry in Soviet Ukraine,[2] the work by her fellow female poets, such as Iryna Zhylenko (1941–2013), Hanna Svitlychna (1939–1995) or Svitlana Yovenko (b. 1945), did not, at least not during the Soviet era.[3]

Another safe and socially sanctioned niche for Ukrainian women authors was writing for and/or about children, something which Bichuia pursued early on. Such Ukrainian women writers as Natalia Zabila (1903–1985), as well as mother and daughter Oksana Ivanenko (1906–1997) and Valeria Ivanenko (1926–1968), spent most of their literary careers working within this niche. As Ukrainian historian Olena Stiazhkina reports for the year of 1965, among the authors who specialized in writing for children in Ukraine's Union of Soviet Writers, women constituted the majority, even though women writers accounted for only 10 per cent of the Union's overall membership (63–4). Women authors were so closely associated with writing works for children that, in the early 1970s, the leadership of Soviet Ukraine established the annual Lesia Ukrainka Literary Prize, awarded for excellence in children's literature. As Stiazhkina pointedly comments, "[w]hen making such a decision, the state officials spent little time reflecting on what Lesia Ukrainka had to do with children's literature; consciously or, most likely, unconsciously, they relied on the stereotype 'woman-child,' and this was sufficient to fit Lesia Ukrainka's oeuvre within the established, conservative view on the place of women in the literary process" (64).

Although commonly stereotyped as "feminine" forms of literature, lyric poetry and works for children were a means for women to get their foot in the door of Ukraine's Union of Soviet Writers, but accomplishing that rarely gained them enough recognition and material benefits to enable them to become full-time professional writers.[4] At the same time, classical Soviet literature's "privileged genre" was the novel, which could best accommodate socialist realism's ideological didacticism.[5] Consequently novels were carefully policed and real or perceived infractions often got their authors into deep trouble with the Soviet censors. For instance, Ukrainian historian and prose writer Raisa Ivanchenko (b. 1934) quickly experienced the wrath of the communist ideologues of Soviet Ukraine after she made her literary debut in the early 1970s with a controversial novella and a historical novel about the prominent nineteenth-century Ukrainian thinker Mykhailo Drahomanov.[6] And while many of her male Ukrainian colleagues who wrote historical fiction suffered the same fate,[7] it is telling that her subsequent works – collections of shorter prose mostly about love, *Liubyty ne prosto* (*It Is Not Easy to Love*, 1976) and *Ne rozmynys' iz soboiu* (*Do Not Lose Your Way*, 1980) – read like a conscious attempt to retreat into safe thematic territory and thereby rehabilitate oneself in the eyes of the Soviet authorities.[8]

For reasons explained in the introduction, the novel did not lose its privileged status in the post-Soviet years, but even gained in cultural importance in Ukraine. The history of the Taras Shevchenko Prize, established in Soviet Ukraine in 1961 and still awarded annually in Ukraine today as the most important *national* prize, suggests such a continued privileging of the novel, and especially for female awardees.[9] Having started out in one of the two traditional women's niches, Zabuzhko, Kononenko, and Matios "wrote" themselves into literature and even the literary canon by writing outside of them, and especially by authoring novels that addressed the "great" national issues of Ukraine's Soviet past and post-Soviet present. However, when these women authors were penning their first prose works, they seemed to be acutely aware of working against the cultural grain specifically as *women* writers – so much so that they made the problem of being a woman author in late Soviet/early post-Soviet Ukraine a central focus in some of their early prose fiction.

Two works that engage this theme most explicitly are Zabuzhko's novella, *Inoplanetianka* (*The Alien Woman*, 1989), and Kononenko's short story, "U nediliu rano" ("On Sunday Morning," 1992). These two texts are remarkable not only for their frank discussion of the social obstacles to women's writing in Ukraine, but also for the complex intertextual strategies they employ to position their authors in a very particular way vis-à-vis Ukraine's literary tradition and even to attempt a rewriting of this tradition. Like Bichuia's "The Stone Master," Zabuzhko's and Kononenko's fiction establishes an intertextual connection to well-known works by the canonized Ukrainian women writers from the beginning of the twentieth century. While Bichuia's story borrows its title from Lesia Ukrainka's 1902 drama, Kononenko's story invokes by its title the 1908 novella *V nediliu rano zillia kopala* (*On Sunday Morning She Gathered Herbs*), by Kobylianska, and Zabuzhko's *The Alien Woman* explicitly engages in its text the 1908 drama *Kassandra* (*Cassandra*), by Ukrainka. In so doing, all three late Soviet/post-Soviet texts seek to claim literary authority for the women who wrote them: "[a]n intertextually constructed text consciously positions itself on the axis of the cultural tradition; it forces its way into the tradition, intending, among other things, to benefit from proximity to the works already accepted, and often sanctified, by cultural memory" (Parts 16). By intertextually engaging the works of the two celebrated Ukrainian women modernists, Kononenko and Zabuzhko attempt to draw their own lineage to the pre-Soviet tradition of Ukrainian women's writing, bypassing the Soviet era. In addition, they strive to bring out and re-emphasize the gender aspects in Ukrainka's and Kobylianska's work that were previously marginalized and de-emphasized in the process of their cultural canonization, thereby making a bold attempt to rewrite Ukrainian literary history.

In a provocative essay from the late 1990s, "Kanon klasykiv iak pole gendernoi borot'by" ("The Canon of Classics as a Gender Battlefield"), feminist literary scholar Solomia Pavlychko has poignantly summarized the curious history of Ukrainka's and Kobylianska's literary canonization:

> Ukrainian criticism, represented almost exclusively by men, preferred to look past the plays by Lesia Ukrainka, past her feminist statements, past her disregard for social conventions, praising and canonizing her early "revolutionary" poetry. The latter, in its aggressive, masculine imagery, the motifs of struggle, strength, and the word as the weapon, appealed to the populists and corresponded to their ideas about the role and mission of literature. Yet her dramas as well as articles, prose fiction, some poetry, and letters are filled with scepticism, a critique of populism and a search for an alternative to it and to herself in her early "manifestation" … In the literary histories and in the enormous literature on Lesia Ukrainka, there is not a trace of this inner split; her feminism and her disappointment in what she thought was a completely unjust reception of her work have been completely forgotten … A similar falsification, a misrepresentation of truth characterized the canonization of Olha Kobylianska. (215–16)

While the 1990s in independent Ukraine have ushered in a major rereading of the works by the Ukrainian women modernists, especially from the point of view of gender, I think it is remarkable that this rereading was first started by the new generation of women writers in their prose fiction rather than by critics who have finally acquired access to Western feminist methodologies after the collapse of the Iron Curtain.[10] That Kononenko and Zabuzhko were clearly promoting such a re-reading through their stories is also evident in the specific texts from Ukrainka's and Kobylianska's oeuvres selected as their intertextual referents. Both *Cassandra* and *On Sunday Morning She Gathered Herbs* are works in which the two women modernists responded to important myths in European and Ukrainian culture that have generated classical literary works by (mostly) male writers. Kobylianska's novella is her version of the Ukrainian folk ballad, allegedly composed by the legendary seventeenth-century female folk-poet Marusia Churai, about her poisoning of her unfaithful fiancé. Ukrainka's *Cassandra* reworks the Greek myth about the fall of Troy around the tragic figure of the eponymous prophetess. Both texts rewrote the cultural myths in question from a woman's perspective. In choosing to engage these myths in their prose fiction, Kononenko and Zabuzhko affirmed and furthered this modernist project of cultural rewriting. And the fact that the two myths have to do with the issue of the recognition of women's expression within traditional societies made these texts especially attractive to these young women writers emerging on the Ukrainian literary scene of the late 1980s and the early 1990s.

Poems Like Potions: Women's Writing as Taboo in Kononenko's "On Sunday Morning"

The legend of Marusia Churai, perhaps the first Ukrainian woman poet in history, has generated an enormous number of literary works from Ukrainian, Polish, and Russian writers in the nineteenth and the twentieth centuries.[11] The figure of Marusia herself had long been an important cultural heroine in the Ukrainian national imaginary. Kononenko, who had written about the Ukrainian cult of Marusia Churai in a 1999 cultural studies essay, "Spivocha dusha Ukrainy" ("The Singing Soul of Ukraine"), first took up this national myth in her 1992 short story, "On Sunday Morning." Via an intertextual engagement of Kobylianska's novella on this legendary theme, "On Sunday Morning" reworks Marusia's story for Ukraine's early post-Soviet period and thereby tests the limits of this myth.

Marusia Churai, who allegedly lived in seventeenth-century Ukraine around the time of Bohdan Khmelnytsky's uprising against the Polish Commonwealth,[12] entered the Ukrainian imaginary as a talented writer of folk songs and ballads, among which "Oi ne khody, Hrytsiu ... " ("Do not go, Hryts ... ") is considered to be autobiographical. According to the text of the song, Marusia poisoned her beloved, Hryts, with a potion made of magical herbs after she discovered that he had proposed marriage to another woman. The song, especially its final stanza, which contains Marusia's direct speech, suggests that this was a premeditated act of revenge, intended to punish Hryts for loving two women at once. However, as Kononenko points, Marusia's current status as a cultural heroine rests not so much on her dramatic love story, but rather on her reputation as a gifted writer of folk songs:

> In the Ukrainian culture, it is not only literature (and especially poetry) that is considered sacred, but also its "mother ancestor" – the folk song. Ukraine is a singing nation. The song is the soul of the Ukrainian people. The Ukrainian language sounds like "the song sung by nightingales." … The singing voices of Ukraine are the pride of our motherland. The list of similar clichés on the "song" theme can go on and on. "The singing Ukraine" is a stable metaphor which has transformed into a fixed stereotype. It is only natural that one of the first national heroines of Ukraine, in the chronological sense, is the legendary author of folk songs, Marusia Churai. ("Spivocha dusha Ukrainy" 235)

In the nineteenth-century Ukrainian cultural imagination and to this day, Marusia Churai has been associated with this highly valorized myth of Ukraine's "singing soul," but in order to preserve her positive image, the other part of the story – her poisoning of Hryts – had to be somehow redeemed or reworked. The two "products" of Marusia's legendary life, her songs that helped sustain Ukrainian culture and her potion that poisoned Hryts, had to be reconciled in some way. In her essay, Kononenko describes some of the literary attempts to create a thoroughly heroic image of Marusia in various time periods: her nineteenth-century transformation from "a betrayed lover who has poured out her sorrow in lyrical ballads" to "the author of heroic songs that inspired the Ukrainian people to fight against their oppressors" in the work of the now forgotten Russian writers; the Soviet-era reworkings of the image of Hryts into a disloyal coward ("apparently, 'the enemy of the people,'" as Kononenko quips); and the undoubtedly masterful nationalist rewriting of the Marusia myth in Lina Kostenko's celebrated novel in verse, according to which Marusia's poisoning of Hryts was an accident ("Spivocha dusha Ukrainy" 237–8). In all of these works, despite their disparate ideological underpinnings and a wildly varying level of literary merit, Marusia's song-writing persona overshadows and/or redeems her personal drama with Hryts, and her crime is reinterpreted as an excusable act of passion, a deserved punishment of fate, and/or a tragic mistake.

Against the background of these myth-making efforts, Kobylianska's 1908 novella and Kononenko's 1992 short story look very different. Completely uninterested in contributing to the heroic national Marusia Churai myth, Kobylianska even gives her female protagonist a different name (Tetiana) and focuses instead on the story of the poisoning, close to how it is told in the folk ballad. By her own admission, Kobylianska wrote her novella partly in response to the 1892 play *Oi ne khody, Hrytsiu, ta i na vechornytsi* (*Don't Go to Parties, Hryts*), by the well-known Ukrainian playwright Mykhailo Starytsky, who used the first line of the ballad for the title of his folk drama.[13] Kobylianska's polemic with Starytsky, who turned the story of Marusia and Hryts into a buoyant theatrical melodrama with much folk singing and dancing, surfaces already in her choice of the title for the novella. While Starytsky's title points to the central chronotope of his play – the Ukrainian village *vechornytsi*,[14] Kobylianska's title, *On Sunday Morning She Gathered Herbs*, is a line from the third stanza of the ballad, which details Marusia's preparation of the potion and the actual poisoning:

> On Sunday morning she gathered [dug] herbs,
> On Monday she washed them out,
> On Tuesday she cooked them,
> And on Wednesday morning she poisoned Hryts. (Qtd in Kobylians'ka 1)

Such a title shifts the emphasis from Hryts and the social milieu of the village, which are central in Starytsky's drama, to Kobylianska's female character Tetiana, the psychological motivations of her actions, and the forest outside the village where Tetiana prepares for her desperate act. Starytsky's play is a melodramatic rendering of a series of misunderstandings in a complicated tangle of love triangles actively promoted by the male villain of the play, who is a much more important character than Marusia. In contrast, Kobylianska's novella is an in-depth study of a young woman's psychological response to what she perceives to be the "evil" around her, which the text suggests is the systemic "evil" of the patriarchal society's double standards for men and women.

Such an interpretation of *On Sunday Morning She Gathered Herbs* becomes evident in part from its structure, for the betrayal of Tetiana by Hryts is not the only one in the text. It is preceded by the story of a Gypsy woman, Mavra – a completely new and unexpected plotline inserted by Kobylianska into the Marusia legend and frequently attributed by critics to the novella's Neo-Romantic roots. Upon giving birth to a blue-eyed, white-skinned boy, Mavra is almost killed by her Gypsy husband, rejected by her community, and abandoned by her father in the forest next to the village where Tetiana's mother lives. Mavra's father leaves her baby son at the door of a rich household in the same village, and its inhabitants later adopt the boy and name him Hryts. Mavra is rescued by Tetiana's mother and helps her bring up the little Tetiana, becoming her "second mother." Eventually though, she moves out of the village into a hut in the forest where she makes a living telling fortunes and selling various medicinal and magic herbs. She is the one who passes on to Tetiana the knowledge of herbs and of life in general. When Hryts first courts Tetiana and later abandons her for another girl, Mavra, who at one point discovers that he is her son, interprets his "dual" nature, his love for two women, as a consequence of her own betrayal of her husband. After Tetiana, who has lost her sanity, poisons Hryts, Mavra says that her own sin is discharged.

This basic plotline has led many scholars to argue that the novella is built around the concept of sin, which is partly true.[15] However, to argue that it is only Mavra's transgression that leads to Hryts and Tetiana's tragedy means to take grief-stricken Mavra's final point of view rather than that of the novella's implied author, whose position is subtly suggested through a variety of means. Mavra's own earlier comments on her illicit love story, its parallels to Tetiana's story, and the similar treatment they received from men show that Mavra is very aware of the society's double standards. "You think he was punished? … Punishment has not reached him, only me," says Mavra to Tetiana about the outcome of her love affair with a rich white nobleman (Kobylians'ka 17). And when Hryts is chastised by Mavra for how he treated Tetiana, he only laughs in response and says: "It is okay for a man to love two [women]" (Kobylians'ka 41). It is precisely this "evil" [*lykho*] in Hryts rather than him as a person that Tetiana, already delirious at this point, decides to kill: "Is Hryts to blame? No, Hryts is not to blame, her heart tells her that Hryts is not to blame. It is something else. This evil that is hidden in him is to blame, it is stopping him … Evil!!! It is to blame, and it must be killed. She will kill it" (41). Tetiana's madness in the novella is therefore not simply a reaction of a fragile psyche to a lover's betrayal; it is artistically necessary as a reaction that is diametrically opposed to Mavra's "rational" response to her own treatment by men – accepting it as the norm of society, which no one single-handedly can change. The permanence and the immutability of this societal order are symbolized in the novella through the monotonous rustling in the wind of the spruce trees that surround the village nestled in the mountains: "Wherever you look, everything is the same. The same sea of green, an unchanging lullaby … Whether it's summer, whether it's winter, whether it's sunny, whether it's raining – everything remains the same. It's the same song with the same monotonous rhythm. The same lullaby, the same rustling" (1). This image is ubiquitous in the text: the novella begins with it, its action takes place to the accompaniment of the rustling, and the same rustling is heard once again after the death of Hryts, suggesting that even Tetiana's desperate rebellion against this order cannot alter the ways in which it functions.

Thus, in *On Sunday Morning She Gathered Herbs*, Kobylianska rewrites the Marusia myth by focusing on the second of its two seemingly incompatible components: the nation-rejuvenating song and the poisonous potion. Her interpretation of Marusia's potion-making as an act of a woman's rebellion against the patriarchal order is completely unique among the many other literary versions of this legend. It is, however, precisely this rewriting that Kononenko chooses to engage in her contemporary story, relying on Kobylianska's key symbols and motifs to advance a critique of another crucial aspect of the national Marusia myth – its implicit claim of Ukrainian culture's absolute valorization of women's poetic expression.

Kononenko's "On Sunday Morning" relocates the female poet – a contemporary "Marusia Churai" – from her rural patriarchal setting into a seemingly progressive, urban environment of early post-Soviet Kyiv and imagines what her life would have been like had she actually married her "Hryts." The change of setting and circumstance is so drastic that, were it not for the story's intertextual title, the reader could easily miss the connection of this text to Kobylianska and the Marusia myth. The story, told in free indirect discourse, gives us the perspective of Kononenko's nameless heroine on her mundane, uneventful life in a loveless marriage and her difficult coexistence with her husband and her mother-in-law in a cramped city apartment. This barely tolerable life situation affords the female poet freedom to think and write only on Sunday morning. The story takes place entirely on one Sunday morning, while the heroine's husband and son are still asleep and her mother-in-law has gone on her ritual round of local food markets. The heroine slips into the kitchen where she stealthily recovers a handwritten notebook of her poems from behind the jars of jam in the cupboard. As she rereads them, she begins to reflect on her life. She remembers how one time, during her pregnancy, she came home and sat down immediately to write down a few poetic lines, inspired by the freshness of the rain outside. Her husband's response was to stuff the piece of paper on which she had jotted down the lines into her mouth. "[A]fter that incident, whenever images whirled in her mind like tropical butterflies, and the faint rustle of a cosmic wind echoed in her ears, the taste of ball-point ink would appear on her tongue."[16] This traumatic episode of Kononenko's post-Soviet "Marusia Churai" story brings together the already familiar elements of Marusia's song and Marusia's potion. Only now, in a grotesque twist, the song becomes the potion: the heroine's poetic lines are fed to her by her own husband – the contemporary Hryts figure – gagging her and leaving a poisonous aftertaste in her mouth.

After this and other instances in which her husband mocked her poetic aspirations, the heroine resigned herself to hiding her poetry, limiting her writing to Sunday mornings. Thus marginalized and forced into concealment, the heroine's poetry-writing becomes an illicit activity, akin to Marusia's (or Tetiana's) gathering of the magic herbs on Sunday morning instead of going to church like the rest of the peasants – or, in post-Soviet Kyiv, instead of sleeping or going shopping. The culminating moment of the story comes in the heroine's remembrance of a past event, which briefly illuminated her gloomy existence. Once at a party, she met a man who enjoyed talking to her and happened to tell her that he had found a three-stanza poem, written on a yellow index card, in a library book. As she began to recite her very own poem to him, which she had once left in that book, the man started kissing her, the poem producing an effect of something like a love potion. In an ironic reversal, it turns out that the fondest memory of Kononenko's "Marusia" character is a sexual liaison with somebody other than her "Hryts."

At this point in the story, the Marusia Churai myth collapses entirely. By placing her "Marusia" heroine in a drab post-Soviet marriage, Kononenko tests the most optimistic and vital beliefs on which the Marusia myth is built: Marusia's passionate and faithful love for her Hryts as well as a culturally universal valorization of her poetic expression. According to Ukrainian historian and ethnographer Oksana Kis, creative activities such as song writing were traditionally the province of young, unmarried women, who learned and honed this art form in the circle of their female peers. By contrast, a married woman was expected to devote herself mostly to practical household tasks.[17] The unmarried songwriter Marusia Churai fit this cultural norm, which is partly what gave credence to her cult. Although Kis writes about the culture of the second half of the nineteenth and the early twentieth century, Kononenko's story shows that little has changed in the cultural expectations for women since that time – despite the Soviet proclamations of "women's equality." Kononenko's heroine is contrasted in the story with her mother-in-law, who had moved to Kyiv from a nearby village, and unlike her, is concerned with doing the "right" things for a woman with a family: procuring food, getting good bargains, and so on. It is in this contrast that Kononenko's intertextual play with Kobylianska's text is most subtle and ingenious. Early on in the story, the heroine recalls how her mother-in-law criticized her potato-peeling skills: "How can you peel off so much of the potatoes? Did you plant them? Did you *dig them up* [*ty ii* kopala]?" ("On Sunday Morning" 151; my emphasis). The Ukrainian phrase for "dig them up" uses the same word in the same grammatical form as the last part of Kobylianska's Ukrainian title of her novella, *V nediliu rano zillia kopala* – the word that is omitted in the title of Kononenko's story but supplied here. The point of contrast is clear: instead of digging potatoes, as "befits" a married woman, the heroine spends her Sunday mornings in the taboo activity of "digging magic herbs," which is Kononenko's intertextual metaphor for writing poetry. Furthermore, playing on Kobylianska's image of wind, the sound of which foreshadowed different dramatic events in the novella, Kononenko calls her heroine's poetic inspiration "the cosmic wind" while the heroine's mother-in-law only uses the word in a crude, folksy expression, "*khodyty do vitru*" (to go to the wind), a euphemism for "to go to the bathroom" ("U nediliu rano" 5). Finally, like the monotonous rustling of the spruce trees, which in Kobylianska symbolized the immutability of the social order against which Tetiana rebelled, Kononenko's heroine reminisces in the kitchen to the non-stop rumbling of the streetcars outside her window. This image denotes the unchanging tedium of the heroine's life, which was untouched even by the kind of experience that set off the entire dramatic chain of events in Kobylianska's novella – a woman's extramarital affair.

In the dysfunctional post-Soviet family, which Kononenko portrays in "On Sunday Morning" as well as in her other stories from the early 1990s, there is neither genuine love nor adequate space or time for a woman's creative self-expression. The chief irony of this story, however, is that the writing of poetry for a married woman turns out to be a greater taboo than her adultery. The heroine's writing is perceived by her family to be an unseemly occupation, and it is so marginalized that it is implicitly equated with witchcraft and ultimately leads the heroine into an illicit love affair, however brief and inconsequential. Kononenko's critique of a woman writer's position in her own, post-Soviet Ukrainian society emerges most strongly in the intertextual juxtaposition with Kobylianska's novella and through her play with the basic elements of the heroic Marusia Churai myth. As Kononenko enters into dialogue with these popular "texts" of the Ukrainian literary and cultural tradition, she attempts to rewrite this tradition through her critique, but also to write herself into the company of its best female commentators, such as Kobylianska. Kononenko's critique and project of cultural rewriting, as well as her strategies for claiming literary authority for herself, were not a singular phenomenon in late Soviet/early post-Soviet Ukrainian literature. In *The Alien Woman*, Zabuzhko tackled the same theme and relied on a similar repertoire of strategies in a project of rewriting and self-authorship similar to Kononenko's.

Mythologizing Women's Writing: Freedom, Truth, and Liminality in Zabuzhko's *The Alien Woman*

In the second half of the 1990s, as part of the new intellectual project to reinterpret the Ukrainian modernist works from a gender perspective, Zabuzhko put forth a major feminist critique of the dramas of Ukrainka. She suggested that collectively they amount to "a grandiose 'rereading' of European cultural history" from a woman's perspective ("Zhinka-avtor" 175). However, a decade before its publication – and eighteen years before the appearance of her 600-page monograph on Ukrainka's dramas, *Notre Dame d'Ukraine* – Zabuzhko emphasized Ukrainka's radical rewriting of cultural myths in her own early novella, *Inoplanetianka* (*The Alien Woman*). In this text, Zabuzhko directly engages, explicates, and applies to her own time the philosophical questions raised by Ukrainka in her 1908 poetic drama, *Cassandra*. In Zabuzhko's words, this drama turns the mythic history of the fall of Troy into "a tragedy of a female voice that went unheard" ("Zhinka-avtor" 175).

In her study of female mythic figures in women's literature, Anja Grothe has argued that in a larger sense "Cassandra can be read as a paradigm of the silenced woman author."[18] This is exactly how Zabuzhko sees Ukrainka's Cassandra: Zabuzhko constructs the prophetess as an ancestor and a spiritual sister to the future generations of women writers, including to the heroine of her novella, Rada. If we consider Cassandra and Rada as their respective authors' alter egos (a reading invited by Zabuzhko's critical comments on Ukrainka's work and by my analysis of the structure and narrative strategy in *The Alien Woman*), these two texts acquire a metafictional dimension. They become commentaries on the nature of creative writing in general and of the potential of women's writing in particular.

In *The Alien Woman*, a very self-aware and articulate young writer, Rada D., has a mysterious encounter with a "Messenger" – a creature from "beyond" who comes to offer Rada absolute freedom in transcending the limitations of human existence. The text makes it clear that Rada receives this visit because she herself is "an alien woman" in her society, in possession of a powerful literary talent that is metaphysical in nature: the only reason Rada is able to see and hear the Messenger is because she is connected with "the other" worlds, and her works are true art because they "come" to her from "beyond." Rada's speculation as to who the Messenger is reveals not only her erudition ("… who are you? … Ivan Karamazov's devil? Or the one who bought the soul of Adrian Leverkühn?"; 172), but also the fact that she does not hesitate to place herself among the celebrated *male* literati: "So this is what was happening with all of them shortly before their death – with Gogol and with Franko, who was rumoured to have gone mad. And Swift's silence … Also the poets with their mysterious deaths – from Shelley to Svidzinsky" (225). However, while the well-known male writers and literary characters are only mentioned in the text, Rada's alignment of herself with Ukrainka's Cassandra runs throughout the novella and is important for all of its major themes. One of them is what writer and literary scholar Liudmyla Taran identifies as the novella's portrayal of the process whereby a creative woman asserts her identity in "the male world" (*Zhinocha rol'* 21). For Zabuzhko, this was a crucial autobiographical theme at the time. *The Alien Woman* was one of her very first prose works, and as such, it is astounding in its boldness. Not only does it make big statements about the true nature of art and portrays a woman writer who, in a very nonchalant manner, likens herself to the most established male authors; it also re-establishes a tradition of women's writing in Ukraine by evoking Ukrainka's legacy and making Zabuzhko's alter ego, Rada, Cassandra's literary heiress.

In discussing the process of how a woman writer deals with the literary tradition before her, Sandra Gilbert and Susan Gubar have famously revised Harold Bloom's concept of "the anxiety of influence" and argued that a female poet experiences instead "an even more primary 'anxiety of authorship' – a radical fear that she cannot create" (17).[19] Confronting this anxiety, a woman writer does not perceive her literary predecessors as a threat, as male authors tend to do, but rather actively seeks out a female precursor in her literary tradition who "proves by example that a revolt against patriarchal literary authority is possible" (49). She thus finds reassurance and support in such a literary ancestor. Gilbert and Gubar's theory elucidates Zabuzhko's purposes in making Cassandra and her creator so central in *The Alien Woman*. By aligning Rada with Cassandra, and herself with Ukrainka, Zabuzhko is claiming a place for herself in the tradition of Ukrainian women's writing. Moreover, Zabuzhko enlists Ukrainka and her Cassandra to help her advance a curious gendered theory of art, one which is implied in *The Alien Woman*. She does this by drawing parallels between Rada's literary talent and Cassandra's gift of prophesying, thereby presenting Rada's writing as prophetic in some sense and therefore superior to other ways of writing.

Zabuzhko highlights several similarities between Cassandra's prophesying and Rada's writing. Cassandra's visions and Rada's artistic works have an "otherworldly" source; they are presented as dictated "truth" rather than invention. Neither woman has any real control of her gift, a gift which serves only as a conduit for the prophecies/literary texts. Moreover, both Ukrainka and Zabuzhko emphasize the role of vision in their heroines' ability to grasp "the truth." Cassandra firmly states the primacy of vision in her prophetic gift: "I don't know anything except what I see" (Ukrainka, *Kassandra* 93). In *The Alien Woman*, Rada's former husband accuses her of observing people only from a distance rather than letting them get close to her, and she herself reports that her gift of writing is grounded in her ability to see people and herself differently. Zabuzhko's insistence on the all-important role of vision for Rada's writing is what allows her to claim an affinity between prophesying and writing, and thus between Cassandra and Rada.[20] The final important similarity between the two heroines is that both have to use language as the primary tool for transmitting their visions. This requirement turns out to be problematic for both: Cassandra's main struggle throughout the drama is to make her compatriots understand and believe her prophecies; and Rada's first complaint to the Messenger is about her inability to write because she has lost faith in language and her own ability to communicate. The inadequacy of language for expressing Cassandra's and Rada's visions is an important key to understanding Zabuzhko's theory of art as a gendered theory.

A number of scholars of women's writing have relied on Lacan's theory of the symbolic to explain the difficulties that exist for women in adopting language as a tool. As literary scholar Martha J. Cutter summarizes, "symbolic language suppresses multiple meanings – which recall the libidinal multiplicity of the pre-symbolic realm – installing unambiguous and discrete meanings in their place" (91). Furthermore, symbolic language in Lacanian theory "reserves the 'I' position for men," consigning women, who lack the phallus, Lacan's symbol of authority, to "a negative position in language" (92).[21] Yet the suppression of multiple meanings by the symbolic language is precisely what enables understanding: only by knowing exactly what somebody means by this or that word or phrase can you make sense of her utterance. Cassandra's problem lies in the fact that she cannot make her prophecies understood by people because they are presymbolic and atemporal. She sees images of tragic future events, but they are difficult to comprehend because they can be interpreted in multiple ways. To make them understood, she would have to force meaning onto them, but she refuses to do so because of her commitment to the truth – however incomprehensible this truth may be to others. Cassandra's dilemma becomes painfully obvious in a conversation with her sisters:

> ANDROMACHE: How can we believe you if your prophecies / are always so untimely and unclear?
> POLYXENA: You prophesy disaster without telling / wherefrom and why disaster will appear.
> CASSANDRA: Because I do not know it, Polyxena.
> ANDROMACHE: Then how can we believe the mere words?
> CASSANDRA: It's not mere words, I see it all, my sisters. I see Troy perishing.
> ANDROMACHE: But why? Who will destroy it? / The Atridae? Achilles?
> CASSANDRA: Sisters, I don't know. (Ukrainka, *Kassandra* 99–100)

Zabuzhko appropriates the prophetess's vacillation between vision and language, and between truth and understanding, for her theory of art. By making Rada's literary gift highly dependent on personal visions and by claiming that these visions have an "otherworldly" source, Zabuzhko creates a dilemma for her character similar to Cassandra's. Rada is positioned between the reality of this world and the "other," between language that has been, in her opinion, used up by others and her unique visions. Consequently, Rada must choose between remaining true to her visions, thereby risking not being understood and appreciated, and describing what people want to hear and can understand, using unambiguous language.

What Zabuzhko implicitly suggests in *The Alien Woman* is that this liminal position is the station of a woman writer. It is a lonely place, yet it allows one to create truly visionary art, of which those living completely within the bounds of the symbolic order are incapable. Although Zabuzhko does not say so directly, it becomes clear from the radical opposition she sets up between Rada and her male mentor, the writer Valentyn Stepanovych, as well as several other male characters, that this liminal position can be understood as *feminine*. Men, by virtue of their gender, are less likely or willing to occupy it and, by extension, to create what Zabuzhko believes is true art.[22]

Like Helenus and Cassandra in Ukrainka's drama, Valentyn Stepanovych and Rada are perfect antagonists. The descriptions of Valentyn Stepanovych, his way of writing and even his study leave little doubt about his complete entrapment in the symbolic order: "For him, the world was fixed clearly and firmly, like the orderly structure of a crystal"; "... this phrase was already redundant, but this is precisely how Valentyn Stepanovych wrote – taking every glimmer of an idea to its unambiguous and conclusive end"; "Everything in this study was heavy … among this weightiness of established things, one would probably feel quite unable to work" (*Inoplanetianka* 211, 190). While Rada is generally critical of Valentyn Stepanovych, there are two things about him which she truly envies: his outstanding command of language and his all-Ukrainian literary fame. Not incidentally, these achievements represent the two important privileges of the masculine position within the symbolic order – the ability to master the symbolic language and the authority that this mastery grants. Unlike Rada, who is after some elusive sense and transcendental truths, Valentyn Stepanovych is content to simply *describe* in his work, the element of creativity in his writing being limited to his skilful use of language. Further, his fame is a direct result of his authoritative and, above all, unambiguous, pragmatic use of language: his works are easy to understand because they describe what is known and appealing to other people. In this sense, Valentyn Stepanovych is very much like Helenus in *Cassandra*: he gives people what they want and he privileges language over truth ("Helenus: You think that truth gives birth to language? / I think that language births the truth" [*Kassandra* 139]).

At one point in the novella, Zabuzhko makes explicit, on the one hand, the alignment of Rada and Cassandra, and on the other, that of Valentyn Stepanovych and Helenus. She cites Cassandra's dialogue with Helenus about the relationship of truth and language in prophesying, yet radically re-evaluates Cassandra's status in the world vis-à-vis that of Helenus. Rada claims that Cassandra's gift of prophesying, which she cannot control, is in fact a sign of a peculiar kind of freedom, and this freedom characterizes her, Rada, as well:

> … that force which tore people out of the established, inhabited flow of circumstances-that-cannot-be-ignored and threw them into the dark abyss of the unknown had, I just know it, the same nature as Cassandra's "voice" and as my "writing dictated from above" … to recognize it and to walk towards it … – that is freedom, the second degree of freedom. (*Inoplanetianka* 201)

This is certainly an unusual way to read Cassandra's situation. Cassandra's prophetic gift made her very unhappy: it alienated her from her family and everyone else in Troy and prevented her from being with a man she loved. More than once in the drama, Cassandra herself laments being unable to free herself from her visions. Most critics have interpreted Cassandra's gift as a curse, yet Zabuzhko rereads Cassandra from a different perspective.

In ascribing to Cassandra and Rada "the second degree of freedom," Zabuzhko is referencing a long-standing philosophical tradition of dividing freedom into two types: negative and positive. This distinction was considered in detail by the philosopher and political theorist Isaiah Berlin in his well-known lecture "Two Concepts of Liberty" (1958). As philosopher Ian Carter summarizes, "[n]egative liberty is the absence of obstacles, barriers or constraints. One has negative liberty to the extent that actions are available to one in this negative sense. Positive liberty is the possibility of acting – or the fact of acting – in such a way as to take control of one's life and realize one's fundamental purposes." Using this definition, one might say that Cassandra does not have negative freedom because her prophetic gift is a constant obstacle on her path to happiness. At the same time, one can see her as having positive freedom because she acts on her gift: she chooses to lend voice to her visions and thereby realizes a higher purpose of serving the truth. For Zabuzhko's Rada, the second degree of freedom is of greater value: it enables one to realize a higher ideal by transcending the firmly established symbolic order, which allows one only a very primitive kind of liberty – "the liberty of a graphomaniac to replace any of the words he wrote with a different one, or to stop writing altogether" (*Inoplanetianka* 194).

The Alien Woman shows the insufficiency of negative liberty by stressing how enchanted Valentyn Stepanovych is by Rada's freedom, confessing that freedom is the most essential thing for a writer. That he has no positive freedom himself becomes clear towards the end of the novella, when Rada discovers that Valentyn Stepanovych had plagiarized her ideas in his new book. She explains his action to herself by his choice of fame over liberty: "For his myth, for a registration [*propyska*] in people's consciousness, Valentyn Stepanovych has paid with his freedom, without even noticing it. Poor Valentyn Stepanovych, what else is he supposed to do now if not to steal it from others?" (222).

Thus, Zabuzhko's theory of what constitutes true art makes the second degree of freedom, or positive liberty, an indispensable condition for a writer. To attain this freedom – more often than not – the artist has to go beyond the laws of the symbolic order, beyond everyday human existence, and pursue her visions, however extraordinary and incomprehensible they may be to the rest of the world. This is why the Messenger tells Rada that an artist is not entirely human. The contrast between Rada and Valentyn Stepanovych demonstrates that Rada is capable of going against the symbolic order towards positive freedom in part because her feminine position of liminality enables her to be less trapped in the symbolic order and less seduced by its promise of power than Valentyn Stepanovych.

How gender pertains to prophesying and writing in the two works can be further traced through the symbols of masculinity and femininity repeatedly used in these texts. Aheieva analyses the opposition of two such symbols – the sword (*mech*) and the distaff (*priadka*) in *Cassandra*. While the sword is clearly a symbol of aggressive masculinity, distaff is the tool used in traditionally feminine work. Aheieva concludes that, in the drama, Cassandra rejects both the stereotypical masculine and feminine roles – both the sword and the distaff (*Poetesa zlamu stolit'* 162). Because she is a prophetess, Cassandra cannot be easily placed in the feminine world symbolized by the distaff, despite such attempts by her brothers: "Deiphobus: You picked up your distaff and that is good, / in truth, it so much more befits a woman / than that prophetic speech, so start your spinning / and do not prophesy" (*Kassandra* 119). At the same time, Cassandra refuses to kill an enemy with a sword, giving up a unique chance to prove her loyalty to her compatriots. Even though Cassandra prefers the peaceful distaff to the sword, neither of the stereotypical gender roles represented by the two tools suit her. There is, however, a third gender symbol in *Cassandra* for which Aheieva's analysis does not account. It is the prophet's staff (*paterytsia*), which is the symbol of the prophet's spiritual authority. It is interesting that in Ukrainian the word for "staff" is derived from the Latin *pater*, suggesting that the role of the prophet has been traditionally reserved for men. A symbol of masculine authority, the staff in the hands of Cassandra puts her in an uncertain position. One can say that the staff is a visual equivalent of Lacanian symbolic language instituted by the Law of the Father. The staff represents the power of this law and as such, it marks a profound irony of Cassandra's situation: it is precisely the power and the authority in her society that she lacks. At the end of the drama, Cassandra breaks the staff and renounces her status of a prophetess. Aheieva argues that Cassandra does it because she has already seen a vision of her approaching death, and there is no longer any use for prophesying (*Poetesa zlamu stolit'* 147). While I agree with this claim in general terms, there is an interesting detail in the text that can make the reading of the drama's ending more nuanced. Right after breaking her staff, Cassandra asks Clitemnestra to give her some work (presumably feminine work such as spinning yarn). That Cassandra did not simply give up her prophet's staff, but replaced it with feminine work, signifies her acceptance, for however brief a moment before her death, of a woman's negative and *silent* position in the symbolic language. The ending of Ukrainka's drama is thus quite pessimistic, showing Cassandra's defeat by the symbolic order.

In addition to the concept of positive freedom, the use of feminine and masculine symbols in *The Alien Woman* constitutes a rewriting of *Cassandra* by Zabuzhko. There is no sword and no staff in the novella; however, a gendered symbol close to Cassandra's distaff – knitting – is employed throughout the text. It first appears during Rada's recollection of her attempts to fit in and find meaning in the mundane activities of her society. As a child, following the example of the older girls, she desperately wished to learn how to knit, thinking that this activity holds a meaningful secret to the "essence" of existence. Once she masters knitting, Rada is very disappointed:

> Moving needles, an endless yarn thread unwinding out of the little plastic bag, knit one, yarn over, knit two together – there was no mystery behind all of this, no secret society existed, nothing but the soft growing body of the knitted garment, its knotty texture, and the all-consuming calculations, which I took *for an exquisite fantastic language* that had transported our girly circle into adulthood. (*Inoplanetianka* 187; my emphasis)

Rada's association of knitting with language is made even more explicit when she later uses the metaphor of knitting to describe Valentyn Stepanovych's manner of speaking: "Lord, how infuriatingly masterful and indefatigable was his speech, as if he were knitting: knit one, yarn over, knit two together" (219). Knitting in this case represents the writer's mechanical mastery of the symbolic language. While in *Cassandra* the symbolic language was represented by the staff, which underscored masculine authority, *The Alien Woman* deliberately emphasizes this language's inferiority by equating it with the mechanical act of knitting and thereby undermining the supreme value that is usually ascribed to it. In other words, if Ukrainka emphasized the symbolic order's overwhelming power, Zabuzhko stresses its mechanical, uncreative nature.

This reversal of usual value hierarchies in *The Alien Woman* – the devaluation of the masculine symbolic order as lacking in freedom and true creativity, and the ascription of higher value to the feminine position of liminality, which allows a woman writer to create real art – constitutes the radical rewriting of *Cassandra* by Zabuzhko. The latter uses Ukrainka's pessimistic reinterpretation of the Cassandra myth to create a new, positive myth of women's writing. While the drama ends with Cassandra's silence, the ending of the novella is literally the first sentence of Rada's new work – *The Alien Woman* itself:

> After some time, Rada D. was sitting at her writing desk, having put a new sheet of paper into the typewriter. Hesitating for a moment – the paper seemed threatening in its whiteness, like an unfilled space on an old map – she finally typed her first lonely sentence:
>
> There was something about the Messenger she didn't like right away. (*Inoplanetianka* 226)

Filling blank sheets of paper with the story of her encounter with (or vision of?) the Messenger, which in itself is a rewriting of the male authors' popular literary myth, Rada takes the readers into the heretofore uncharted territory of a Ukrainian woman writer's creative laboratory – the process whereby a vision is transformed into a work of verbal art.

Zabuzhko goes to great lengths to encourage readers to accept her version of *Cassandra* and to assure them that Rada's writing from the liminal feminine position is both possible and admirable. Her choice of a novelistic genre rather than a dramatic one allows her to tell Rada's story from this character's perspective and from that of a narrator who is sympathetic to Rada. Zabuzhko's use of free indirect discourse in the novella supports and strengthens Rada's authority. Free indirect discourse has been used by many women writers "to authorize intelligent and morally superior women as critics and interpreters of their society" (Lanser 74). Unless this narrative mode is used in an ironic way, it allows the writer to create "a completely authoritative heroine" (77). This was undoubtedly Zabuzhko's goal in *The Alien Woman*. Another interesting feature of Zabuzhko's narrative technique, which she employs in this novella as well as in later works, is the frequent, almost kaleidoscopic switching between the first-, the second-, and the third-person narration. Rada's second-person address is directed not at another character or the reader, but at herself, which draws the readers into Rada's most intimate conversations with herself and encourages their identification with her. At the same time, the fact that all three narrative positions – the "I," the "you," and the "she" – refer to Rada creates a solipsistic textual universe in which she is simultaneously the narrator, the character, and the audience. No opportunities are left for the reader to identify with Valentyn Stepanovych, Rada's husband, or even the Messenger; they are presented through Rada's point of view and this presentation forcefully dismisses them all.

Much has been written in literary scholarship about the prevalence of the autobiographical in Zabuzhko's fiction.[23] This observation also applies to *The Alien Woman*. Yet the novella features a special structural trick in its ending, quoted above, that makes Zabuzhko and Rada appear to be the same person. The circular structure of *The Alien Woman* – the ending which is also its beginning – raises the question of who the real author of the work is. The text makes it clear that the author is Rada because it is she who writes its first sentence, included again at the end of the novella. However, the work itself was obviously published with Zabuzhko's name on the title page, which formally equates the author with the character. This feature highlights the metafictional dimension of *The Alien Woman* – Zabuzhko's early prose work about the difficulty, but *not* the impossibility, of women's writing, including her own. By making Ukrainka's *Cassandra* central to her work, Zabuzhko reminds us of the tradition of women's writing in Ukraine that existed prior to the Soviet era and inserts herself into it. And by re-evaluating the gender implications of the drama, especially those suggested by its pessimistic ending, Zabuzhko creates a positive myth about the ultimate value of women's writing.

If Kononenko's story dramatized post-Soviet Ukrainian women's obstacles to creative self-expression, Zabuzhko used her novella to find a way for herself, and the woman author more generally, out of the difficulties and thereby foster and affirm women's writing. At the same time, by engaging in an intertextual dialogue such famous literary predecessors as Kobylianska and Ukrainka, Kononenko and Zabuzhko attempted to revive the tradition of feminist women's writing in Ukraine and to write themselves into it. After several decades of Ukrainian women prose writers' relative silence, these two women authors entered the literary scene with works that addressed the possible reasons behind this silence – continuing, in their different ways, Bichuia's attempts to account for it in "The Stone Master."

Taken together, the three texts by Bichuia, Kononenko, and Zabuzhko create a multifaceted portrayal of a Ukrainian woman writer's position in late Soviet and post-Soviet Ukraine. Bichuia reveals how circumscribed this position was by the institutional and ideological strictures and practices of the official Soviet culture, as well as by the local Ukrainian accommodations and forms of resistance to it. Kononenko's story describes the challenges that often awaited a Ukrainian woman writer in the private sphere. While the Soviet regime had claimed to have liberated women, "On Sunday Morning," like many other works by Ukrainian female authors from the late 1980s and the early 1990s, shows that not much had really changed in the Soviet and early post-Soviet Ukrainian society's dominant views on "appropriate" gender roles. Kononenko emphasizes this lack of change by cleverly reworking and deconstructing a popular Ukrainian myth that supposedly illustrates traditional Ukrainian culture's valorization of women's poetic voices. Finally, Zabuzhko's novella responded to what seemed like an immutable societal gender order, including in the world of literary production, by reversing its value hierarchies and mythologizing women's writing as inherently different – and better – than men's.

3
Voicing the Self: The First Ukrainian Bestseller by a Woman Writer

In addressing questions about the place and the worth of a woman author in the late Soviet and early post-Soviet Ukrainian society, the short prose works by Bichuia, Kononenko and Zabuzhko bring up a number of themes that come to the forefront in later women's writing. These include the issue of the repressive Soviet past and the lingering national traumas resulting from it (Bichuia's "The Stone Master"); maltreatment of women and the profound disconnect between the sexes (Kononenko's "On Sunday Morning"); and the loneliness and marginality of a creative, intellectual woman in a society that does not hear or value her voice (Zabuzhko's *The Alien Woman* as well as Bichuia's and Kononenko's texts). In the first post-Soviet decade, no other Ukrainian work managed to bring together and articulate these themes with greater force and intensity than Zabuzhko's 1996 bestselling novel with the provocative title *Poliovi doslidzhennia z ukrains'koho seksu* (*Fieldwork in Ukrainian Sex*; hereafter *Fieldwork*). This work has been since recognized by many as one of the key texts in post-Soviet Ukrainian literature, and its successive editions and translations continue to be printed, read, and debated in Ukraine and beyond.[1]

Yet the novel's reception has been quite ambivalent. In Ukraine, its initial publication caused a scandal (albeit not without Zabuzhko's conscious efforts to elicit precisely such a reaction). A significant number of hostile reviews lambasted the author for the novel's subject-matter, especially its treatment of the Ukrainian male character's colonial inferiority complex, manifested in the sexual abuse of the woman narrator. Quite a few reviews also criticized its stylistic features, be it its veiled autobiographical narration or its angry, sarcastic tone.[2] More serious commentators acknowledged that the novelty of this text, which at first glance seemed to be just another failed love story, lay in its examination of the nexus of gender and Ukrainian national identity. Yet different critics, depending on their own ideological affiliations, found the work to be – paradoxically – either too feminist and subversively anti-nationalist, or too nationalist and hence "deficient" in its feminism. For example, an early review in the newspaper *Ukrainske slovo* (*Ukrainian Word*) criticized Zabuzhko's novel for deconstructing the traditional image of a woman in Ukrainian culture and acting "against population needs" of the nation because the protagonist displayed ambivalent attitudes towards motherhood.[3] On the opposite side of the ideological spectrum, Serguei Oushakine, in his introduction to a special volume of *Studies in East European Thought* dedicated to the changing roles of intelligentsia in Eastern Europe, described Zabuzhko's stance as "somatic nationalism ... in the Ukrainian version of postcolonialism" and suggested that the feminist identities emerging in post-Soviet Ukraine were "a product of elaborate (and at times twisted) cultural translation" ("Introduction" 247–8). As a result, *Fieldwork* earned Zabuzhko a perplexing reputation as a nationalist who is not good enough for many nationalists and as a feminist who is not good enough for many (especially Western) feminists. A compromise solution that emerged a good decade after the publication of *Fieldwork* was to call Zabuzhko a "national feminist."[4]

At the same time, as Zabuzhko pointed out in her interviews, numerous women readers of different ages found that the novel gave eloquent expression to their own gendered experiences of life in the Soviet Union and post-Soviet Ukraine. As Zabuzhko herself reported, female readers communicated their admiration to the author with phrases such as "This is my story!," "It reads as though you were sitting in my kitchen, and I was pouring my heart out to you!," and "I feel as though I wrote it!" (Hryn and Zabuzhko 18). "Never before did I realize to what extent half of the nation had been deprived of a direct voice of their own when it came to the most intimate, everyday life experiences," commented the author on this feedback (Hryn and Zabuzhko 18–19). By having her autobiographical female narrator express and analyse her own position – the experience of being caught in a web of personal, historical, and ideological pressures and discourses, characteristic of the early post-Soviet Ukrainian context – Zabuzhko did not simply write a story that resonated with her female readers. Rather, it seemed that she opened up a heretofore unavailable discursive space for Ukrainian women.

A few perceptive commentators, such as Vitaly Chernetsky and Natalia Monakhova, have noted the relevance of Gayatri Chakravorty Spivak's theorization of the female subaltern for Zabuzhko's text.[5] As both scholars pointed out, Spivak's analysis of the female subaltern subject's double silencing and abuse by the imperial colonizing and the local colonized masculinities is highly applicable to *Fieldwork*, a work in which a Ukrainian female intellectual takes on the difficult task of breaking this silence and shedding light on this abuse. While I agree with this general line of reasoning, I would like to further flesh out this argument. Taking another, closer look at Spivak's insights about the subaltern woman subject will elucidate both the politics and poetics of Zabuzhko's novel, as well as its contradictory critical reception. In the course of this rereading of

Fieldwork through Spivak's arguments and through other concepts from postcolonial and cultural theory, Zabuzhko's engagement with and critique of the Ukrainian national imaginary and its gendered aspects will become clear.

In Search of a Space from Which to Speak

The central claim of Spivak's renowned essay "Can the Subaltern Speak?" answers the title question in the negative, demonstrating through a meticulous historical discursive analysis of *sati* (the Indian ritual of widow self-immolation on the deceased husband's pyre) and its abolition by the British colonizers that, in fact, "[t]here is no space from which the sexed subaltern subject can speak" (307). It is so because the male is the default figure "both as object of colonialist historiography and as subject of insurgency," which usually leaves women outside of official narratives altogether (287). When women do appear in these narratives, they figure in them as objects of discursive manipulation, spoken for rather than speaking themselves. Spivak illustrates this idea with two statements that summarize the legal and cultural battle over *sati* between the British colonial rulers and the Indian nativists: while the actions of the former can be "understood as a case of 'White men saving brown women from brown men,'" the latter's defence of *sati* boils down to a statement that speaks for the subaltern women: "The women actually wanted to die" (297). Not only do both statements leave no room for the female subaltern herself to speak about *sati*, but they also, as Spivak shows, make the figure of the self-immolated Indian widow into a battleground of powerful discourses: "Between patriarchy and imperialism, subject-constitution and object-formation, the figure of the woman disappears, not into a pristine nothingness, but into a violent shuttling which is the displaced figuration of the 'third-world woman' caught between tradition and modernization" (306).

To unearth the subaltern women's voices from the long history of this "violent [discursive] shuttling," Spivak argues, is a challenging task. It is itself fraught with the risk of, in the end, speaking for them, which would leave the female subaltern "as mute as ever" (295). Yet this task must be faced, according to Spivak, by postcolonial female intellectuals, who can chart this history and, in so doing, at least begin a search for a subaltern woman's consciousness. The essay's final example of such a search is the story, unearthed by Spivak, of a young Indian woman's desperate attempt to rewrite the hegemonic "social text of *sati*" by committing a ritually unsanctioned suicide (308). This story emphasizes the urgency of the postcolonial female intellectual's task, as the young woman's subversive rewriting was ignored and misinterpreted even by her own family and acquaintances.[6] The female subaltern's efforts to carve out a space from which to speak a different message about herself from within the available hegemonic discourses failed, and her message went unheard.

The double dilemma outlined by Spivak – the female subaltern's inability to speak herself and be heard, and the danger that, in telling the subaltern's story, even a well-meaning postcolonial intellectual will end up speaking *for* her – is given a unique solution in Zabuzhko's novel, for *Fieldwork*, to use Zabuzhko's own characterization, is a "confessional" work (Hryn and Zabuzhko 20). It takes its autobiographical female narrator, named, like Zabuzhko herself, Oksana, as its object of investigation – announced in the title as "fieldwork in Ukrainian sex." It thus positions her as both a Ukrainian subaltern woman and a postcolonial female intellectual who analyses the subaltern's history (or, rather, *her*story). Such a positioning is accomplished in part by the text's split narration. The latter alternates between an authoritative first-person voice that reports and explains the heroine's story in the form of an imaginary lecture to an international academic audience (marked as "ladies and gentlemen" in the text, with the English address transliterated in Ukrainian) and as an intimate narrative – combining first-person and third-person narration, free indirect discourse, and a second-person address to oneself, with fragments of poetry interspersed. This narrative relives the painful feelings and personal details from the narrator's past.

The authoritative voice of the female intellectual addressing a Western audience

> ... so, ladies and gentlemen, please do not be in a hurry to qualify the presented case of love here as pathological, because the speaker has not yet stated what is most important – the main point, ladies and gentlemen, lies in the fact that in the research subject's life this was her first *Ukrainian* man. Honestly – the first. (*Fieldwork* 30; emphasis in original)[7]

The intimate voice that mixes narration in all three persons and includes poetic fragments

> ... I can't take this anymore! – and so her prophetic dream came true – an old dream from a year ago, visited upon her long before they met: a sapling at the crossroads, trembling and rustling, someone invisible is setting a bonfire below, the strike of a match, and oh – in a flash! – the sapling is consumed by fire ... and so in a place where a moment earlier the sapling glittered with shades of light green against the blue sky there now protrudes a bitter, blackened skeleton. On the occasion of which, girlfriend, allow me to congratulate you.
>
> A budding tree in a naked row – Why in such hurry, you foolish thing? (*Fieldwork* 82)

The changes in the narrative voice are frequently quite seamless. As in Zabuzhko's *The Alien Woman*, this text's narration also switches rapidly from the first to the second to the third person, but the added function of this device in *Fieldwork* is to preserve the unity of the split narrating heroine. Simultaneously, the construction of all the voices and personas of the narrator is further complicated by anger, sarcasm, ironic performance, and the narrator's bitter self-awareness, which underscore the narrator's ambivalence about her embattled position. By means of this complex narrative structure, Zabuzhko attempted to create a space from which a Ukrainian subaltern woman could speak. Her narrator avoids the danger of speaking for another, as that "another" in *Fieldwork* is herself; and at the same time, through putting on an authoritative first-person voice of a woman intellectual, she strives to increase the chances of her subaltern "self" to be heard and understood, especially by Western audiences that are largely ignorant about Ukraine and the problems faced by Ukrainian women.

Furthermore, *Fieldwork* confirms Spivak's insight into the insidious power of hegemonic discourses, be they imperialist or nativist, to manipulate, co-opt, and obliterate a female subaltern and her history. Since these are the discourses that have heretofore constructed "the woman," they furnish and circumscribe the space from which a female subaltern subject must speak. *Fieldwork* dramatizes what Spivak dubbed as the "violent shuttling" of the figure of a subaltern woman between the powerful discourses of "tradition and modernization" (306), which in the early post-Soviet Ukrainian context are the ones of Soviet colonialism and Western cultural dominance (both presented as "modernization") as well as Ukrainian populism and anticolonial nationalism (both wedded to Ukrainian traditions).[8] The novel's autobiographical heroine is at once a victim and a product of these discourses – at least of the Soviet and the Ukrainian ones. While her female postcolonial intellectual persona, in her first-person authoritative voice, attempts to explain the hold of these discourses on the female subaltern and to diminish their power through sarcasm and scathing critique, her female subaltern persona performs her own imprisonment in and loyalty to them (especially the discourse of Ukrainian nationalism), even as she also occasionally laments their continued force. In *Fieldwork* such ambivalence emerges and is illuminated in the most obvious point of intersection between gender and national identity: it is the narrating heroine's choice of a Ukrainian lover and her willingness to put up with his abusive sexual behaviour, at least for a time, just because he is Ukrainian. Even as the narrator's subaltern persona expresses her attachment to this man through remembering numerous intimate details of their relationship and, for instance, the seeming fulfilment in it of her dream for a *Ukrainian* family that would bring forth the next generation of Ukrainians, her postcolonial intellectual persona recognizes this kind of behaviour as "national masochism" and ironically refers to herself as "poor sexual victim of the national idea" (*Fieldwork* 53, 103).

It is precisely critics' general lack of attention to the complex narrative structure, as well as other *literary* aspects of *Fieldwork*, that has brought about such a broad range of ideological (mis)readings of this novel. Those commentators who accused Zabuzhko of a subversive anti-nationalist stance have focused mostly on the criticisms of the Ukrainian imaginary made by the intellectual voice of the novel's narrator, while ignoring her other persona's allegiance to her Ukrainian identity. And critics like Oushakine or Uilleam Blacker, who found Zabuzhko's feminism lacking precisely because of her nationalism, have taken the performance by the narrator's female subaltern persona of her dependence on nationalist and essentialist gender discourses to be Zabuzhko's only and final word on the matter.[9] However, Zabuzhko's project can be fully understood only if we take seriously the productive tension created by the voices of the novel's split narration and pay close attention to other technical aspects of *Fieldwork* – especially its use of language(s).[10]

Finally, Spivak's analysis is applicable not only to *Fieldwork*'s form, but also to its theme, as demonstrated through the suicidal thoughts of the novel's severely depressed heroine. From the novel's first sentence, in which the narrator tells herself that she wouldn't do it "today," to its last word, which signals that the heroine has decided to go on living, the entire text may be read as the narrator's tortured, extended debate with herself (often in front of the mirror in which she examines herself) on why she should or should not take her life (*Fieldwork* 1). The text seems to suggest that the immediate reason for the narrator's desire to end it all is her failed romantic relationship, and it is this relationship and especially its sexual aspects that have been the focus of most literary scholarship on *Fieldwork* up to the present time.[11] While certainly important, so much so that it gives the novel its title, such a focus has the inherent danger of trivializing Zabuzhko's intricately woven, convoluted text. To take the narrating heroine's failed affair with her Ukrainian lover, Mykola, as the centre of the narrative and the principal reason for her depression and thoughts of suicide is to perform a rhetorical gesture similar to that of the Indian hegemonic discourse on *sati*, which validates the loss of a man as the only understandable reason for a woman's desperate decision to take her life. Instead, I argue that, like Spivak's young female rebel, Bhuvaneswari Bhaduri, who went to great lengths to send a different message to others in her suicide, Zabuzhko's narrator charts a complex personal and cultural history of oppression, silencing, and invisibility that throws a different light on her contemplated act of self-annihilation. In this light, the heroine's disastrous love affair emerges as only the most obvious, surface theme of the story that she tells.

In Search of a Home … in Language

Like the protagonists of the works by Bichuia, Kononenko, and Zabuzhko examined in previous chapters, the narrating heroine in *Fieldwork* is a writer (a poet, to be exact). Unlike their soul-searching, however, hers takes place not in Ukraine but outside it – during her stay in the United States as a Fulbright scholar in the mid-1990s. Thus, the third major preoccupation of the novel, in addition to gender and nation, is "dissemination" – defined by Homi Bhabha, in one sense, as "that moment of scattering of the people," the experience of "mass migration" that has so profoundly changed the modern world and its nations ("Dissemi-Nation" 291). For the heroine of *Fieldwork* – a former Soviet subject from behind the Iron Curtain – travelling to and teaching in the West is at once a dream come true (a literal fulfilment of her reiterated wish "to break out" [*vyrvatys'*]) and a painful experience of displacement.[12] Although Oksana knows English well enough to lecture in it, the text continually underscores the foreignness of her surroundings and of various objects and concepts of American culture by leaving their names in English (with footnoted definitions and explanations in Ukrainian). She also feels profoundly alone, especially because, as she discovers, few in America know much about Ukrainians or Ukraine:

> … you had simply grown tired, after all these years of homeless wandering, of loving the world *all alone* – of passing, anonymous and unrecognized, through all the dusky airport terminals, the restaurants and bars with their warm lights, the seashores with their shuffle of incoming waves against the rough sand, the early-morning hotels with coffee in the lobby – "Where are you from?" – "Ukraine." – "Where's that?"[13] – you had grown tired of *not being* in this world. (*Fieldwork* 33; emphasis in original)

The physical condition of dislocation to the West, with its accompanying feelings of loneliness and even non-existence, further destabilizes Oksana's sense of self, already undermined by her recent romantic failure and the lingering traumas from her Soviet past. As a result, *Fieldwork* becomes a record of the narrator's painful identity crisis, which is expressed in the novel as a search for "home," or, more precisely, for a feeling of being at home (*vdoma*). Yet the novel never expressly defines what this feeling is in positive terms; rather, the narrator intimates what it could be by cataloguing all those circumstances that make it impossible for her to feel at home anywhere in the world, as well as by recalling a few remarkable instances in which she did experience "being at home."

In part, Oksana's crisis can be understood as a specifically postcolonial one: postcolonial studies scholars Bill Ashcroft, Gareth Griffiths, and Helen Tiffin define this crisis as "the concern with the development or recovery of an effective identifying relationship between self and place" (*The Empire Writes Back* 8). This identification, and with it a "valid and active sense of self," is often lost, they argue, as part of the colonial experience of "dislocation" or "displacement," which "is always a feature of post-colonial societies whether these have been created by a process of settlement, intervention, or a mixture of the two" (9). Elsewhere Ashcroft, Griffiths, and Tiffin explain exactly how this dislocation occurs in societies that are colonized through conquest, and this explanation is very fitting for Ukraine:

> … dislocation in a different sense is also a feature of all invaded colonies where indigenous or original cultures are, if not annihilated, often literally dislocated, i.e. moved off what was their territory. At best, they are *metaphorically dislocated*, placed into a hierarchy that sets their culture aside and ignores its institutions and values in favour of the values and practices of the colonizing culture. Many post-colonial texts acknowledge *the psychological and personal dislocations that result from this cultural denigration.* (*Post-Colonial Studies* 75; my emphasis)

While many citizens actually experienced physical displacement under the Soviet regime (imprisonment in the Gulag or exile, for example), what Zabuzhko focuses on most of all in *Fieldwork* is the *metaphorical* dislocation of Ukrainians, the erosion of their "valid and active sense of self" because of "the cultural denigration" of the Ukrainian language and of the local traditions and institutions. Writer and translator Maksym Strikha, in a contribution to a multi-author project on Ukrainian popular culture, identifies the Ukrainian language as the most important, fundamental element of the Ukrainian national imaginary and charts the history of this language's "denigration" – from the bans on the use of Ukrainian in the Russian Empire to its reflection in the popular attitudes towards Ukrainian in the late Soviet era. He writes that as recently as in the 1980s, the "typical reaction" of many in the streets of Kyiv to conversations in Ukrainian between a father and his child, for example, would be comments such as "he looks like a cultured man, yet doesn't know Russian" or "Why are you ruining your child's life?" ("Mova" 424). Similarly, Zabuzhko herself, in an essay on language and state power, acknowledges the crucial function of the Ukrainian language for her culture and writes about belonging to the generation of Ukrainian intelligentsia who grew up deprived of a native language environment, because outside their home in Kyiv there were few opportunities to hear Ukrainian ("Mova i vlada" 101). *Fieldwork*'s autobiographical narrator likewise experiences this metaphorical dislocation, as well as the real threat of physical displacement, and they are primary reasons for her inability to feel "at home."

Growing up with a dissident father, with terrifying memories of repeated home searches and a constant fear of his possible arrest, as well as the burden of her father's over-protectiveness and control bordering on abuse, the narrating heroine remembers her childhood home as a dangerous and oppressive space from which she yearned to escape (*vyrvatys'*) (*Fieldwork* 129). As she bitterly remarks, there was nowhere to escape in Soviet Ukraine:

> There *was* no breaking out – all around nothing but Communist Youth League meetings, political education classes, and the Russian language [*chuzha mova*]. One

> only ventured out there (like a four-year-old to a stool in the middle of the room to recite a poem for aunties and uncles) in order to reproduce, in ringing tones and tape-recorder accuracy, all that had been learned from them and them alone, and only this guaranteed *safety* – a Gold Medal on leaving high school, a Diploma of Red Distinction at university, and then ever so carefully along the tightrope [*prosuvannia "po veriovochke"*] … (*Fieldwork* 145–6; emphasis in original)

Outside of her childhood home, Zabuzhko's heroine could obtain the longed-for feelings of safety only in exchange for ideological compliance with the Soviet regime, its institutions, and its practices, including the displacement of Ukrainian through Russification ("all around … the Russian language" – identified in the original as *chuzha mova* – a foreign language). Significantly, the passage above expresses the Soviet discourse's pervasiveness and power to silence the subaltern through an image of rote poetry memorization and its recitation – an act in which a discourse is shown to literally *speak through and for* its subject and one that has special meaning for Zabuzhko's heroine, who is a poet herself. This passage suggests that for the narrator in *Fieldwork*, "being at home" is closely associated with being able to speak her own text, rather than somebody else's, and in her own language. Early on, the novel describes how the narrator experiences feelings of "at-home-ness" precisely on an occasion when she is given a chance to publicly read her own poetry:

> … at a writers' forum in one Far Eastern country where out of politeness they asked you to read in your native language ("you mean, it's not Russian?"[14]) – and you began reading then, in insult and desperation listening only to your own text (you were sick to death of their "Russian" even then), concealing yourself within it the way one slips into a lit house at night and locks the door behind, and midway you suddenly realized that in the frozen silence you were being heard [*shcho zvuchysh v dzvinkii … tyshi*]: *mova* – your language, even though nobody understood it, in full view of the public it had concentrated around you into a clear, sparkling sphere of the most refined, crafted glass inside which magic was happening, this could be seen by all … you finished your piece – enveloped, crystal-clear, protected, now that would have been the time to realize that your home is your language, a language only about a few hundred other people in the whole world can still speak properly – it would always be with you, like a snail's shell, and there would not be another, non-portable home for you, girl, ever, no matter what you do. (*Fieldwork* 10–11; emphasis in original)

This telling passage sheds light on what the narrator means by "feeling at home." It is not tied to possessing an actual house of her own ("non-portable home"), or to the physical territory of Ukraine (the poetry reading is taking place in a foreign country), or even to the condition of her language – Ukrainian – being recognized or understood, since in this case, as before, Oksana is mistaken for a Russian speaker, and no one in the audience can comprehend what she is saying. In this case, the translation inaccurately states that Oksana was being "heard," whereas in the original, she only "sounded." The feeling of home for the narrator is created by the act of speaking for herself, reciting her own text in Ukrainian. To the sound of her language, she ascribes some magical protective quality and essentially finds her identity in it.

Oksana's location of her "home" in her language confirms the principle which Ashcroft, Griffiths, and Tiffin see as ubiquitous in postcolonial writing – in this literature, they find "a repetition of the general idea of the interdependence of language and identity – you are the way you speak" (*The Empire Writes Back* 53). *Fieldwork*, however, extends the application of this statement from the language or a mixture of languages an individual speaks to *the manner* of speaking as well. The passage cited above, for example, describes the narrating heroine feeling completely at home in an odd, hermetic, non-communicative situation, where her speech, instead of establishing some sort of communicative interaction between her and the audience, actually serves as a barrier between them. This type of speaking, I would argue, is paradigmatic for the embattled identity of the Ukrainian intellectual (of either gender), which Zabuzhko dramatizes and analyses in her novel.

The Insular Ukrainian Identity

Many conceptions of identity have underscored the importance of the interplay between the self and the Other for identity formation. Mikhail Bakhtin has famously described this process in terms of dialogic exchange (287), and Stuart Hall saw "the relationship between you and the Other" as one of identity's crucial constitutive elements (345). Zabuzhko's novel scrutinizes a historical situation in which the self is significantly shaped by the ubiquitous presence of a powerful and hostile Other – the Soviet regime – represented by its secret police, informers, and other agents whose goal it is to make sure that the ideology of this Other is a vital part of each self. *Fieldwork*'s narrator describes what it is like to grow up engaged in the constant *forced* "dialogue" with this "evil" Other: "you grow up in a flat that is constantly bugged and surveilled and you know about it, so you learn to speak directly to an invisible audience: at times out loud, at times with gestures, and at times by saying nothing, or when the object of your first girlish infatuation turns out to be a fellow assigned to spy on you" (*Fieldwork* 111). The constant presence of this Other is shown to have a profound effect on the speech of the self. To protect herself, the heroine learned early on to hide her real thoughts and even at times her speaking in Ukrainian from anybody who could be linked to the Other, which was almost everyone but her immediate circle of family and friends. Thus, when a boy whom the narrator met in a high school academic competition asked her if she was familiar with the works of the banned Ukrainian writer, Volodymyr Vynnychenko,[15] she gave him a politically correct answer, "tapping out each syllable in precise Pioneer Girl fashion" and speaking in Russian (*Fieldwork* 144). In light of such a history of identity formation, the novel seems to suggest, a (non)communicative situation in which an individual can speak her own "text" publicly and in her own language, yet be protected from another's potentially threatening entrance into a dialogue, can truly seem like a safe haven – a utopian "home."

Nevertheless, *Fieldwork*'s narrator recognizes the pathological character of such a closed off, insular identity – when she gets a chance to observe it up close and in the extreme form in her lover, the Ukrainian artist Mykola. Upon their initial encounter, Oksana experiences that rare feeling of "at-home-ness" she had at the poetry reading abroad. That is because Mykola is her first Ukrainian partner, with the same language and the same traumatic baggage of displacement and denigration, which both of them experience especially acutely as Ukrainian cultural producers. Initially, Oksana sees in this relationship a chance for a real partnership. They could explore the world together and make names for themselves in the West through their creative expression as *Ukrainian* artists. Yet the heroine quickly becomes disillusioned, for she discovers a dark side to the insular structure of identity that characterizes her lover and (to a lesser extent) herself.

In describing the reasons behind the failure of Oksana and Mykola's relationship, many commentators have focused on the sexual abusiveness of Mykola, stemming from his traumatic colonial past. While the novel does foreground this reason, it also highlights other aspects of Mykola's character that made this relationship unviable. All of these aspects are symptoms of his insular identity formation. For instance, the narrator deplores Mykola's lack of interest in the outside world: upon joining Oksana in the United States, he remains completely closed to experiencing the foreign Other and makes no effort to learn English.[16] By contrast, the narrator herself, who has already travelled abroad repeatedly, seems more open and welcoming to the fascinating foreign world around her: "you liked that bar, the dull bottle-green of the décor … the night outside the distant windows, its thick, brown murkiness melting the candy-yellow street lamps – everything at once, because only thus can you enter an *alien* world: accepting everything at once, with all your senses, and you know how to do that (*Fieldwork* 32–3; emphasis in original).

Oksana also sees Mykola's "hermetic" identity, which is what he himself calls it (*Fieldwork* 58), manifest itself in his use of language as a protective mask from the Other:

> … he opened up to share something inside him only very gradually, creakily … for outsiders he smeared himself with a thick coat of an impenetrable, though, one

> must admit, very masterful sort of chitchat, all kinds of gags and games generously flavored with spicy irony, but she was not one to be fooled by that, she also had her (hah!) elaborate and ever-so-tightly fitted … linguistic mask, and when he tried to hide behind his – hey, there, if you're gonna play, no cheating! – she preferred to slice that papier-mâché apart with a knife. (*Fieldwork* 59–60)

Oksana recognizes Mykola's *manner* of speaking – the "impenetrable" chatter that hides the real self from the Other – as disguising one's real meaning through irony. She has learned, through her identity formation under the Soviet regime, to use similar defensive strategies herself. Yet unlike Mykola, she realizes that what these strategies do is preclude real communication, making a dialogue and therefore a genuine partnership impossible. This communicative disconnect turns out to be just as damaging to Oksana and Mykola's relationship as the sexual abuse, and the narrator sees the roots of both in Mykola's insular identity.

While *Fieldwork* recognizes this type of identity as characteristic of both genders, the novel also suggests that it is an especially acute problem for Ukrainian men in Soviet/post-Soviet culture. In a theoretical essay, "Zhinka-avtor u kolonial'nii kul'turi" ("A Woman Writer in a Colonial Culture"), written in an effort to better understand the hostile reception of *Fieldwork* in Ukraine, Zabuzhko argues that cultural denigration under the Soviet regime affected Ukrainian men more than women by virtue of the fact that the Soviet society, in its structure and culture, remained a patriarchal one and the public sphere continued to be dominated by men. Therefore, if women, unable to realize their creative potential in the public sphere, could psychologically "retreat" into the private sphere of home and family, men were likely to find such a retreat much more challenging and psychologically traumatic. They thus turned out to be "more dependent on the social environment 'outside [the home]'" and much more susceptible to cultural denigration ("Zhinka-avtor" 163). *Fieldwork* illustrates this idea not only through Mykola, but also through other male characters. The image of the father of Oksana's female friend, Darka, vividly shows how the denigration of Ukrainian culture and the ubiquitous presence of the Soviet state Other, especially in the public sphere, affected the manner of speaking and the identity of Ukrainian men:

> … a year earlier Darka's father had died – he was an award-winning musician, a deputy, and in his day practically a member of the Communist Party Central Committee, although, it's true, even he got into a little trouble for "nationalism," so he started playing at state concerts, while his wife, who had gotten used to a comfortable life, would nag him to death *if ever he tried to give a toast at official banquets in Ukrainian – even if uttered thickly and stupidly, playing the jester with his "howdy-doody" wordplays*, the Central Committee official representative – a

> concrete slab in a gray suit – sat disapprovingly silent: not a single muscle moved on his impenetrable, seemingly waterlogged, face, ai-ai-yai, we're in trouble now, "and you were gonna go on that trip to Canada," the wife yelped, taking off her coat in the hall while a pregnant Darka … was grinding up some coffee in the kitchen for her father … and her old man, after walking into the kitchen and lighting up a cigarette (first breaking a few matches), *told his daughter roughly (also, like his wife, in Russian): "I know, I'm merely a sociopolitical buffoon,"* and this phrase stayed with her always, a hammered-in nail. (*Fieldwork* 101–2; my emphasis)

This passage shows, once again, the self being forced to hide behind a language mask, this time of a fool and a buffoon, in the presence of the threatening Other. This strategy, however, is used here to avoid potential accusations of nationalism because of the man's use of Ukrainian in the official Soviet public sphere. Darka's father consciously adopts a comical and self-demeaning tone – in the already low speech genre of a toast – as if to reassure everyone present that his Ukrainian is not dangerous and does not carry with it any hidden challenge to the official *status quo*. Nevertheless, even this self-inflicted denigration of one's language is perceived with displeasure by the authorities (the Communist Party's Central Committee representative) and instils fear into Darka's mother for her husband's future career advancement. Significantly, the final assessment of himself as a "buffoon" (*shut*) is given by Darka's father in Russian – suggesting perhaps that his Ukrainian has become so inextricably tied to the mask of buffoonery that it is not suitable for expressing such a serious and bitter truth about one's identity.[17]

The "Gender War" in Early Post-Soviet Ukrainian Literature

While *Fieldwork* does much to portray the psychological roots of Ukrainian men's insular identity and their colonial inferiority complex, it also powerfully critiques this identity and exposes the tendency of some Ukrainian men, like Mykola, to seek compensation for their denigration in how they relate to women. When the narrator informs Mykola that their relationship is over, the latter tellingly asks Oksana if she feels like a female "victor," using the Russian word "побєдітєльніца" and thereby revealing that on some level, he viewed their relationship as a sparring match rather than an equal partnership (Zabuzhko, *Poliovi doslidzhennia* 21). By employing the Russian feminine noun for "victor," pronounced with great irony (which the text reflects through the Ukrainian transcription of the word), Mykola simultaneously distances himself from Oksana, aligning her with the Russian-speaking colonizing Other, and mocks the very idea of a woman being victorious in anything. His compensation for his past experiences of colonial humiliation becomes especially evident in this scene.

Although inspired by the real prototype from Zabuzhko's love life, the image of Mykola emerged also as the author's response to a cultural and literary type of a Ukrainian man that became popular in Ukraine in the early post-Soviet years. Zabuzhko has acknowledged this fact in her interviews,[18] and in her aforementioned essay, "Zhinka-avtor u kolonial'nii kul'turi," she explained in more detail what she perceived to be a glaring absence of fully drawn, complex women characters in contemporary Ukrainian fiction by men. On the one hand, Zabuzhko argued, there was the "'sexually liberated' men's prose," populated by immature male characters (created by equally immature male authors) and only the specific women's body parts in which they were interested ("Zhinka-avtor" 189). On the other hand, she stated, there were works by seemingly less "juvenile" male writers, who nevertheless displayed complete "lack of interest" in the fate of those identical female caricatures whom they created for the benefit and diversion of their male protagonists (189). From the sum of these statements, it is not difficult to recognize which male author in particular Zabuzhko had in mind as the chief target of her criticisms. Yuri Andrukhovych – the most successful Ukrainian male writer of Zabuzhko's generation and the leader of the male literary group, Bu-Ba-Bu – is a well-known creator of a whole series of juvenile and misogynist "macho" characters, modelled to a large extent on his own persona and contributing to what Tamara Hundorova called "the image of the Ukrainian [male] bohemian of the 1990s" ("'Bu-Ba-Bu,' karnaval i kich" 16). In a way, the main debates on the Soviet past, the nation, and gender of the first half-decade of post-Soviet Ukrainian literature crystallized on the pages written by Andrukhovych and Zabuzhko – and in dialogue, both overt and covert, between them. Solomia Pavlychko once referred to these debates as a "gender confrontation or war" ("Vyklyk stereotypam" 186).

Andrukhovych's second novel, *Moskoviada* (*The Moscoviad*, 1993), published three years prior to *Fieldwork*, came to be widely considered a key Ukrainian text in the project of "postcolonial de-centering of Russian/Soviet imperial discourses" and a symbolic "farewell to the empire" (Polishchuk 296; Hnatiuk, *Proshchannia* 481). A Ukrainian parody of *The Odyssey* and a nod to Venedikt Erofeev's drunken travel narrative, *Moskva-Petushki* (*Moscow to the End of the Line*, 1970),[19] *The Moscoviad* features as its narrating hero a perpetually inebriated Ukrainian poet who, like Andrukhovych did himself, studies at the Maxim Gorky Literary Institute in Moscow in 1989–90. There he witnesses what is described as the death throes of the Soviet empire. Physically displaced to the imperial centre, the protagonist engages in what Chernetsky sees as a "paradigmatic instance of 'writing back to the centre of the empire,'" deconstructing through mockery and linguistic play Soviet ideological myths, institutions, and discourses ("The Trope of Displacement" 222). As in Andrukhovych's other novels, *The Moscoviad*'s protagonist is a carnivalesque adventure hero – a buffoon – as is evidenced by his escapades, "linguistic behaviour" (Hundorova's term), as well as his clownish (and distinctly un-Ukrainian) name, Otto von F.[20] At the end of the novel, the author actually dresses Otto von F. in a buffoon's mask, thereby laying bare his carnivalesque device. Otto attends the macabre apocalyptic ball/conference of all political leaders of the Russian and Soviet empires and shoots them all, as well as himself. These killings turn out to be symbolic rather than real (Catherine II, Lenin, and other leaders shed rags, not blood, and Otto reappears alive on a train back to Ukraine), suggesting that underlying the novel is a desire to exorcise the "evil" Other of the Soviet empire from one's identity and thereby articulate a new self.

In this journey to a new identity, Otto's primary "weapon" is not a gun, but rather language, as some scholars have pointed out (Bodin 65). His manner of speaking may be understood as a Ukrainian colonial subject's appropriation of language as a mask, a protective barrier, as well as of Ukrainian speech as a form of self-denigrating buffoonery – both captured by Zabuzhko in *Fieldwork*'s characters of Mykola and Darka's father, as analysed above. Just as mimicry in a colonial culture has the potential to be a "menace" to colonial authority because it may become mockery, as Homi Bhabha has argued, the buffoon's self-denigrating and masked linguistic performance may, through irony and ambiguity, be turned against the colonizing Other ("Of Mimicry and Man"). This ploy is illustrated by a toast that the inebriated Otto gives at a shady Moscow pub, in front of a few friends, who accuse him of nationalism, and a general half-drunk Russian-speaking audience. Otto begins by assuring everyone in a friendly tone that he has benevolent feelings for all people, that he supports the idea of unity and brotherhood of nations, and then proceeds to give as proof – in the same sincere tone – his numerous sexual liaisons, including with members of other nations and races, suggesting that he has thus enhanced unity in the world with his body. His "proof," of course, ironically undercuts his earnest proclamation of loyalty to the familiar Soviet slogan about the brotherhood of nations, but the mask of sincerity hides the mockery, making Otto's position and person seem ambiguous: is he simply a fool to make such a statement, a drunk whose thinking is temporarily clouded, or is he consciously engaging in parody and subversion? The toast is also filled with folksy Ukrainian sayings, appropriate for a simpleton's speech delivered in his "provincial" language: "I cannot just sit … silently, as if I just swallowed a horseradish" (Andrukhovych, *Moscoviad* 50).[21] Finally, it contains ambiguous puns that poke fun at the Soviet state but masquerade as the slips of a drunk's tongue: "now, when I drink acrid beer in the midst of a wasteland … when around me is one great Asian, sorry, Eurasian plain [*rivnyna*], sorry, country [*kraina*]" (50). In form, Otto's toast does not differ from the toast given by Darka's father in Zabuzhko's *Fieldwork*: like the latter, Otto fools around, engages in punning buffoonery, and uses folksy expressions ("uttered thickly and stupidly, playing the jester with his 'howdy-doody' wordplays" [*Fieldwork* 101]). Yet in an appropriation and redirection of these devices, initially used by Darka's father to make himself and his Ukrainian seem unthreatening to the Soviet Other, Andrukhovych's Otto transforms the figure of the buffoon and his language into the very opposite – a "menace" and a challenge directed at the colonizing Other.

Andrukhovych's re-appropriation and re-evaluation of the Ukrainian buffoon from a position like that of Darka's father ("I'm merely a sociopolitical buffoon") to a figure with freedom and power to undermine his society's oppressive conventions appeared to be quite revolutionary in early post-Soviet Ukrainian culture. Many renowned literary critics and scholars of Ukrainian literature were genuinely intrigued by Andrukhovych and Bu-Ba-Bu, praising their use of Bakhtinian carnival and its liberating reversals, the playful performance of postcolonial hybridity, and the ironic attitude of Andrukhovych's buffoons, not only towards the Soviet myths but also towards the Ukrainian nationalist discourse.[22] Zabuzhko, however, found the figure of the buffoon problematic in several ways, which she alluded to in *Fieldwork*, thus implicitly engaging in a polemic with Andrukhovych.

Zabuzhko's first and main criticism of the Ukrainian buffoon character had to do with his extreme misogyny. Incidentally, this characteristic is true of the buffoon as a literary type in general and not only of its Ukrainian incarnation. In "Living by His Wits: The Buffoon and Male Survival," literary scholar Peter F. Murphy writes that the buffoon lives his life predominantly in male company and perpetually "acts out a contempt for women grounded in the traditional belief that they are available for sexual pleasure but never to be trusted or taken seriously" (1125). At the same time, the buffoon depends on sex with women as well as on alcohol consumption in order "to confirm his always shaky masculinity" (Murphy 1132). He also constantly brags competitively about his drinking and sleeping around, although frequently his exaggerated stories meet with nothing but laughter. Andrukhovych's Otto clearly fits this description. He spends much of the novel drinking and engaging in the most outrageous sexual escapades, although since he is the novel's narrator and an incorrigible braggart, many of these episodes are to be taken with a grain of salt.[23]

However, Otto's contempt for women and his treatment of them as sexual objects also has specifically Ukrainian historical roots. This fact emerges only vaguely in *The Moscoviad*, but is picked up and given a detailed treatment in Zabuzhko's *Fieldwork*. Among Otto's letters to an imaginary exiled king of Ukraine, two are noticeably parallel: one describes Otto's relationships with women and the other tells the king about the protagonist's relationship with the KGB. The letter about the women is a typical buffoon's tall tale that exaggerates Otto's manly attributes and describes women of all ages and several nationalities chasing after Otto, who, as a result, is frequently forced to maintain liaisons with two women at once. Sexual contact, however, is not the only basis of these relationships. In most cases, Otto's facility with language leads to what he calls "sex in words," where women engage him in endless conversations on a variety of subjects or where he exhausts them with reading long poems, such as *The Odyssey*, out loud – pretending that he is the poems' author (Andrukhovych, *Moscoviad* 61). Each of these women aims to "catch" Otto and never let him go, but he always manages to get out of the relationship – until he meets a Russian woman who is a professional snake catcher and later turns out to be a KGB agent. This stereotypical braggart's tale receives another, more sinister layer of meaning because of its parallelism with Otto's letter about his dealings with the KGB. Like the women, this Soviet institution is out to "catch" Otto and involve him in a "relationship." It takes him out on "dates" (*pobachennia*), frequently with two agents at once. Most of the time during these "dates" is spent in endless, exhausting conversation, often on the subject of poetry and Otto's poetic talent, which the agents promise to help Otto develop if he agrees to cooperate with them. Otto stalls for time, using as much of his buffoon's wit as he can; he also tries to refuse, saying that when a guy wants to seduce a girl, he will promise her anything – only to dump her when the "deed" is done (95). Yet, threatened with persecution of his family members, he is forced to agree to become an informer. He is spared the guilt and shame of betraying his compatriots only because the Soviet regime soon begins to crumble.

Meant to be humorous and playful, Otto's equation of women with the KGB, and through it with the colonizing Other, actually reveals how much his identity has been shaped by his repressive colonial history – so much, in fact, that he views a relationship with *any* Other, including women, exclusively as a power struggle. Zabuzhko, who was well aware of this dynamic, gave an explicit critique of it in *Fieldwork*. This critique is evident in the above-mentioned scene when Mykola sarcastically asks Oksana if she feels like a female victor and in Zabuzhko's underlying argument that many Ukrainian men tend to compensate for their colonial humiliation through contempt and violence – both physical and verbal – directed at women.

Zabuzhko's second, related, criticism of the Ukrainian buffoon as a literary type and a cultural model of behaviour has to do with the fact that the buffoon's re-appropriation of the colonially imposed mask does not essentially change the "hermetic" structure of his identity, or what I have described above as the insular Ukrainian identity. As with Darka's father, the colonizing Other still remains Otto's main "interlocutor" in the ongoing identity-defining dialogue. The power dynamics might have shifted, and now it is Otto who directs (mostly verbal) violence at the colonizing Other rather than vice versa. Yet this reversal does not open up the dialogue to any other possible interlocutors and therefore has limited potential to transform identity. This imparts to the character of Otto and to *The Moscoviad* in general a sense of confinement, of being stuck, which does not diminish even by the end of the novel.

As mentioned before, Zabuzhko portrays the insular identity as a general problem of the Ukrainian self – one that has affected both genders, albeit differently. In addition, it has shaped the nation's collective self-perception. In *Fieldwork*, the heroine's authoritative intellectual persona explicitly reflects on this problem. The heroine expresses her frustration with this pathology of the Ukrainian identity, even if her postcolonial subaltern's voice laments her inability to free herself of such unfortunate thinking:

> In psychiatry, I believe it's called victim behavior, but there's nothing I can do about it, it's the way I was taught; and in general all that Ukrainians can say about themselves is how, and how much, and by which manner they *were beaten*: information, I must say, not very enticing for strangers, nonetheless, if there's nothing else in either your family or your national history that can be scraped together, you slowly but surely begin to take pride in this – hey, come see how they beat us, but we're not yet dead – my Cambridge friends rolled on the ground with laughter when you translated the beginning of your national anthem as "Ukraine has not died yet" – "What kind of anthem is that?"[24] –and truly, a pretty screwed up little opening line. (*Fieldwork* 115; emphasis in original)

Fieldwork's narrating heroine recognizes that Ukrainians' fixation on the colonizing Other and the violence they experienced from it only exacerbates their inferiority complex and perpetuates the insular structure of their identity. As Hall once put it, "[i]dentity is a narrative of the self; it's the story we tell about the self in order to know who we are" (346). Zabuzhko observes that the victimization narrative has become so prevalent among Ukrainians that it has turned into the meta-narrative of the Ukrainian national imaginary, which is evidenced by the fact that this basic plot has become enshrined in the nation's anthem. The anthem, as one of any nation's chief symbols, encapsulates the main elements of the nation's historical and cultural specificity; it is the story (song) of the national self which is told (sung) not only to the self, but also to the world. Oksana aptly points out that the problem with the story that Ukrainians tell the rest of the world about themselves lies not only in the fact that it is self-denigrating, but also in the act of telling itself. Such a story, if artfully told, also normalizes the self-denigrating pose, suggesting to others that perhaps such a history and identity are not that bad after all.

> I'm making the point, ladies and gentlemen, that it's not such a great thrill to belong to a beaten nation, as the fox in the folktale said, the unbeaten rides on the back of the beaten – and that's what the beaten one deserves, the problem is that in the meantime that beaten one manages to sing, let's say, the ballad of the misfortunate captives,[25] and in this way – legitimates his own humiliated position, because art, don't you know, always legitimizes, in the eyes of the outsider, the life that gave it birth; and in that fact lies its, that is, art's, gre-eat [*sic*] deception. (*Fieldwork* 116)

With bitter self-awareness, Zabuzhko directs her critique not only at *The Moscoviad*, but also at her own self and the story she tells in *Fieldwork* – the artful narrative of her autobiographical heroine's direct victimization by the Soviet regime as well as its indirect manifestation in the disrespectful and abusive behaviour of her lover, who has been victimized himself. Zabuzhko realizes only too well the dangers and the pathological effects of such a narrative, yet she still finds that the story must be told – as an act of personal and national self-therapy ("[l]iterature as a form of national therapy" [*Fieldwork* 158]); as an address and self-explication to foreign audiences, who know so little about Ukrainians (which in itself is another effect of Ukraine's colonial past); and also as an attempt to open up the insular Ukrainian identity to the world.

Towards the "New Ethnicity"

In *How Our Lives Become Stories: Making Selves*, Paul John Eakin suggests that "acts of self-narration play a major part" in "a lifelong process of identity formation" (101). Both *Fieldwork* and *The Moscoviad* are autobiographical narratives about the journey of the Ukrainian self through the labyrinths of the traumatic past to a (hopefully) new identity. To see if something like a new identity emerges in these texts, it is instructive to compare how the two novels end. In many ways, their endings are very similar. Both Otto and Oksana in the novels' final scenes are in transit: Otto is taking a train to Kyiv to get out of Moscow, which is perishing in what seems like an apocalyptic flood, and Oksana has just boarded a plane, presumably also for Kyiv, having completed her fellowship year in the United States and her "fieldwork in Ukrainian sex." Both protagonists express feelings of anger and disappointment about their lives up to this point, filled as they were with experiences of violence, repression, and crushed hopes and dreams. Both voice a belief that a new chapter of their lives is beginning. Nevertheless, the two endings are also different in a subtle but important way.

As he lies on the train's topmost berth, which is normally used only for luggage, Andrukhovych's Otto composes in his mind his final letter to the imaginary king of Ukraine, in which he once again articulates his resentment of his people's colonial past and a desire to know what will happen to Ukrainians in the future. He also emphatically states that his escape from Moscow is really a *return* home.

> Since tonight I am not running away but coming back. Angry, empty, and with a bullet in my skull to top it all off. Why the hell would anyone need me? I don't know that either. I only know that now almost all of us are like this. And what remains for us is the most persuasive of all hopes, passed on to us from our glorious ancestors – that it will work out somehow. The main thing is to survive until tomorrow. To make it to the station called Kyiv. (Andrukhovych, *Moscoviad* 185)

In his final sentences, which, paradoxically, look *forward* to coming *back*, Otto rhetorically reintegrates himself into his nation. His "I" gets swallowed up by the uniform "we" of the Ukrainian people ("now almost all of us are like this"), and on behalf of this imagined community, he voices a vague hope in the nation's future survival ("it will work out somehow"). Otto's urgent desire to return home and the collective, uniform voice of the nation reiterating one of its fundamental beliefs – the belief in its survival despite the circumstances ("Ukraine has not died yet") – suggest that no new identity has really emerged as a result of Otto's "self-narration."

In a cogently argued lecture, "Ethnicity: Identity and Difference," Hall puts forth the concept of "the new ethnicity" (347–9). He argues that we cannot do away with identity and ethnicity completely because "[t]here is no way … in which people of the world can act, can speak, can create, can come in from the margins and talk … unless they come from some place, they come from some history, they inherit certain cultural traditions" (347). Ethnicity is what gives people a place, a positioning from which to speak. Yet Hall also argues against "essentialist ethnicity," which is backward-looking, unchanging, and stuck in the past. Instead, he proposes that a new conception of ethnicity is emerging in our fast-paced, mobile, and diverse world: "The notion of an identity that knows where it came from, where home is, but also … knows you can't really go home again" (349). As Hall explains further, "[i]t is a new conception of our identities because it has not lost hold of the place and the ground from which we can speak, yet it is no longer contained within that place as an essence. It wants to address a much wider variety of experience … Those are the new ethnicities, the new voices. They are neither locked into the past nor able to forget the past" (349).

While Otto in *The Moscoviad* does not manage to break out of the insular and essentialist Ukrainian identity, the ending of Zabuzhko's *Fieldwork* suggests that Oksana is beginning to move in the direction of "the new (Ukrainian) ethnicity." This is evident first and foremost in the change of temporality in *Fieldwork*'s final scene. If most of the previous narration was turned to the colonial past or the heroine's present in the United States, the novel's final fragment begins with a sentence in the future tense, which, significantly, looks forward to the trip itself rather than the homecoming. (Kyiv or Ukraine is not even explicitly mentioned as a destination, although it is safe to assume that Oksana is going there.) Further, despite the bitter sense of disappointment which the heroine articulates in this scene, she explicitly states that she no longer wishes her life to end, and the reason she gives for this change of mood is very interesting:

> When I was young, I dreamed of such a death: plane crash over the Atlantic, an aircraft dissolving in the air and the ocean – no grave, no trace. Now I wish with all my heart that the plane land safely: I like to watch the tall, sinewy old man with the hooked nose and deeply furrowed lines running down from his eyes … and

> the Spanish-looking brunette with the unbuttoned leather coat – she's on board with two children … a girl of about five, narrow tanned face in a baroque frame of promisingly capricious curls, flashes her eyes and her smile up and down the aisle in all directions, glowing with excitement – her first trip! and her eyes stop on me:
>
> "Hi!" she shouts happily.
> "Hello there!" say I. (*Fieldwork* 161)
>
> [— Хай! — щасливо випалює вона.
> — Хай! — кажу я.] (*Poliovi doslidzhennia* 142)

Having completed her "fieldwork," or "research," as Oksana herself calls it in English at one point in the text, Oksana has managed to come to terms with her painful past. The passage above suggests that she has resolved to stop dwelling on it and has put it aside, together with the thoughts of suicide. This decision makes her free to finally turn away from the mirror and an examination of her own self, and to begin to look at others. In this act of opening up her previously insular identity to the world, she encounters ethnically different others, like the Hispanic mother and daughter. With the latter, she engages in as minimal a conversation as can be, yet it is a very important one for Oksana and for the novel.

"Хай" in this conversation, as some commentators have pointed out,[26] functions as an interlingual pun, which is, unfortunately, lost in the English translation: it is a Ukrainian transcription of the English greeting "Hi!," but spelled in this way, it also means something like "Let it be!" in Ukrainian. In reply to the little girl's greeting, Oksana says "Хай" and means it both as a "hello" and a "let it be," the latter referring to her life, her colonial past, and all other disappointments which she had voiced throughout the novel. This is the first instance in *Fieldwork* when the heroine uses an English word or words without underscoring their difference from Ukrainian by leaving them in the Latin script and/or using them as a means of "othering," putting the English language and American culture at a distance from her own. Here, instead, "Хай" becomes the heroine's way to establish genuine contact with the Other – both the girl and the English language. This is a significant step for the Ukrainian poet Oksana, who identifies so much with the Ukrainian language that she locates her home in it and who has earlier in the novel complained that living in a foreign-language environment (be it Russian-speaking Soviet Ukraine or the English-speaking United States) pollutes her native speech. Earlier, she had also described a strategy widely used by her and others to keep the foreign words from "making their home" in the Ukrainian speech: "to role-play, like we all do, using your voice to take the foreign words into quotation marks, place a kind of clownish-ironic stress on them like they were a citation" (*Fieldwork* 29). This is basically a strategy out of the repertoire of the Ukrainian buffoon, so the characterization "clownish-ironic" is very appropriate here. Although the reader cannot hear the intonation with which Oksana says her final "Хай," the context around it leaves no doubt that she says it sincerely and without irony.

All of these clues suggest that in its final scene, *Fieldwork* moves in the direction of "the new ethnicity" for Ukrainians, as Hall defined it. This beginning of a transformation partly becomes possible because Zabuzhko has seen the drawbacks of the kind of Ukrainian identity Andrukhovych had constructed in his work. More importantly though, *Fieldwork* takes place in a foreign country, where both Zabuzhko and her autobiographical heroine are exposed to a different other and have a chance to observe the self from this other's point of view.[27] The experience of physical displacement to the United States thus plays a crucial role in enabling a move beyond the insular and backward-looking structure of identity to a new "I," which is the last word of the novel.

This new self is not essentialist or static: in fact, its hallmark lies in its movement between different discourses, expressed in the novel's poetics as the tension between the narrator's different voices, and in its ultimate opening up to others in dialogue. At the same time, however, the position of this self is informed by the histories of personal and national oppression which *Fieldwork* recounts – it "knows where it came from," as Hall put it. And yet, this position is also based on a refusal to be contained by this legacy and a rejection of the Ukrainian national imaginary's victimization meta-narrative, encapsulated in the national anthem's first line. By the very act of pinpointing this master plot that underlies the Ukrainian national imaginary and by dramatizing and analysing its self-denigrating effects throughout the novel, Zabuzhko undermines its grip on the structure of her own identity and, perhaps, the collective Ukrainian identity as well.

Fieldwork as a Bestseller: The Subaltern's Voice That Has Been Heard?

Fieldwork's iconic status as the first bestselling novel by a Ukrainian woman writer perhaps testifies to the fact that Zabuzhko has succeeded in making a Ukrainian woman subaltern's voice heard. As mentioned in the beginning of this chapter, the novel ruffled quite a few nationalist feathers in Ukraine and generated a number of hostile or simply dismissive reviews. Since the mid-1990s, however, *Fieldwork* has entered the canon of Ukrainian post-Soviet literature, which is evident from its adaptations for the stage and its place of prominence in textbooks on contemporary Ukrainian literature as well as university curricula.[28] Yet its position in the canon continues to be challenged from time to time by conservative functionaries from various institutions of Ukrainian culture.

A fairly recent example of such a challenge was the removal of actress Halyna Stefanova's faithful adaptation of *Fieldwork* from the list of three monodramas for which she was nominated for the Taras Shevchenko National Prize in 2008 ("Aktrysa Halyna Stefanova"). After the list of Stefanova's performances in the nomination was approved, the head of the Taras Shevchenko Prize Committee, Roman Lubkivsky, single-handedly crossed out the *Fieldwork* adaptation from the list – most likely so that "the word 'sex' would not appear next to the word 'Shevchenko,'" as one of the journalists quipped (Klymenko). Stefanova's letter of protest to Lubkivsky yielded no positive results, and the actress decided to withdraw her name from the list of nominees, stating that the circumstances surrounding her nomination had become "humiliating" to her (Klymenko). As this incident demonstrates, some individuals in the cultural establishment of Ukraine would prefer not to hear the female subaltern to whom *Fieldwork* gave a voice.

Zabuzhko's novel has specifically addressed not only Ukrainian readers but also Western audiences, which is most evident in *Fieldwork*'s construction of the authoritative first-person voice of the female intellectual. By means of this voice, Zabuzhko attempted to redress the invisibility of and lack of knowledge about Ukraine, Ukrainian women, and Ukrainian writing in the West, and to do it *in Ukrainian*, though by her narrator's admission, the choice to write in this language "is probably the most barren choice under the sun at present" (*Fieldwork* 36). As Oksana explains, this is so "because even if you did, by some miracle, produce something in this language 'knocking out Goethe's *Faust*,' as one well-known literary critic by the name of Joseph Stalin would put it, then it would only lie around the libraries unread ... just like your unsold books which gather dust somewhere at home and in bookstores" (*Fieldwork* 36). As we know, however, the novel that so lamented Ukrainian literature's and culture's invisibility in the world did find foreign readers via translations into many languages.[29] Nevertheless, *Fieldwork*'s constructed voice of the Ukrainian female subaltern received mixed reviews in the West, reviews which frequently refuted the novel feminist's credentials on the grounds of its nationalism.[30]

Such a reception not only ignores *Fieldwork*'s tension of ambivalent voices, as argued above, but also reopens the long-standing debate on feminism between the "First World" and the "Third World." Zabuzhko's contribution to this debate is that of a woman from the "Second World," which nonetheless appears close to the position of Third World feminists. In Yuval-Davis's summary of this (non) dialogue, "[o]ne side would call for women's liberation as the primary/only goal of the feminist movement. The other side would respond that as long as their people are not free there is no sense for them in speaking about women's liberation: how could they struggle to reach equality with their menfolk while their menfolk themselves were oppressed?" (117). Zabuzhko's focus on Ukrainian men's oppression under the Soviet regime in *Fieldwork* and her professed loyalty to Ukrainian culture were often deemed by Western critics as taking away from her feminist position, just as the Third World argument about men's oppression was frequently viewed by western feminists as not compatible with a "real" feminism. Yet, as Yuval-Davis points out, work by Third World scholars such as Kumari Jayawardena (*Feminism and Nationalism in the Third World*, 1986) demonstrates that "loyalty to one's national liberation movement does not necessarily mean that women do not fight within it for the improvement and transformation of the position of women in their societies" (118). Zabuzhko's *Fieldwork* is a good example of textual politics that does both – professes loyalty to the nationalist cause and critiques women's oppression at the hands of (formerly) oppressed Ukrainian men.

The denial of Zabuzhko's feminism by her Western critics, like the earlier denial of Third World feminism, demonstrates that many Western academics continue to reserve exclusively for themselves the right to define what "feminism" is and what it is not, or that, as Yuval-Davis put it, non–First World women continue to be assessed "in terms of their 'problems' or their 'achievements' in relation to an imagined free white liberal [Western] democracy" (118). Measured against such a yardstick, work by women like Zabuzhko comes up short, despite the fact that these women may self-identify as feminists. This peculiarity of *Fieldwork*'s Western reception does not allow one to conclude that the voice of the Ukrainian female subaltern, constructed by Zabuzhko, has been fully heard after all.

4
Rewriting the Nation: National Narratives by Maria Matios and Yevhenia Kononenko

While in the late 1980s and the early 1990s Ukrainian women's fiction addressed the very possibility of women's writing in late Soviet/post-Soviet Ukrainian culture, in the mid-1990s, with the publication and success of Zabuzhko's *Fieldwork*, this possibility was no longer questioned. Moreover, Zabuzhko's bestseller opened the floodgates of women's writing, writing that placed female characters in the very centre of their narratives and, in some cases, even created a new type of a female protagonist, dubbed by some literary scholars as "a thinking woman" (Filonenko). Prose by Kononenko, Matios, Sofia Maidanska, Svitlana Yovenko, Nadia Tubaltseva, Teodozia Zarivna, Maria Kryvenko, and other women authors began to appear in print more and more often in the second half of the 1990s, prompting critics to speak of a real boom in post-Soviet Ukrainian women's writing.[1] Yet it was not until the 2000s that the themes of the nation, especially of Ukraine's Soviet past and its lasting impact on the post-Soviet present, along with a continued focus on women protagonists, began to dominate – so much so that Matios called her 2001 collection of short stories *The Nation*.

Through its pioneering examination of national and gender identity in the post-Soviet Ukrainian context, Zabuzhko's *Fieldwork*, no doubt, paved the way for these early twenty-first-century narratives of women and/in the nation. Yet these later works are remarkably different from Zabuzhko's bestseller. While *Fieldwork*'s tortured exploration of the ambivalent loyalties of the autobiographical self zeroes in on the intersections of gender and national identity in an individual psyche, women authors' national stories present themselves as clearly more fictional narratives, and strive to cover a much larger terrain, writing of the nation as a collectivity and of women's positions, adventures, and roles within it at different historical moments. These narratives conjure up the simultaneous existence of different individuals embedded in their society, and thereby serve as vehicles for imagining a national community. I will call these works "foundational national narratives"; these are texts that, after the colonial Soviet period, strive to write the nation anew, producing more or less authoritative representations of the Ukrainian national community. This chapter discusses three such works: Matios's collection of short stories *Natsiia. Odkrovennia* (*The Nation. Revelation*, 2001, 2002, 2006[2]); her novel *Solodka Darusia* (*Sweet Darusia*, 2004); and Kononenko's murder mystery *Imitatsiia* (*Imitation*, 2001). The next chapter will explore the longest and most mythical among the recent foundational national narratives by Ukrainian women – Zabuzhko's novel *Muzei pokynutykh sekretiv* (*The Museum of Abandoned Secrets*, 2009) – and will briefly compare it to Kononenko's *Imitation*.

I borrow the term "foundational" from Doris Sommer's well-known study of Latin American "foundational fictions," that is, nineteenth-century "national romances," produced in the period after the Latin American wars of independence, which aimed to aid in their countries' projects of national consolidation by plotting charming romance stories, with happy endings, between lovers from the opposing political, racial, or economic camps.[3] By luring the readers with the passionate love of two attractive protagonists, these romances, Sommer claimed, popularized visions of unified national communities for the new independent states in Latin America. While only two of the above-mentioned Ukrainian texts may be seen, in one way or another, as Ukrainian "national romances," all four facilitate specific imaginings of the Ukrainian nation and attempt to redefine it through literary means. Significantly, the four works are also very women-centred, featuring complex, fully developed female protagonists and focusing on their life stories. This chapter and the one that follows explore this woman-centred poetics of the foundational national narratives by Zabuzhko, Kononenko, and Matios in an effort to understand the collective national identities these authors imagine for Ukraine and what role gender comes to play in their national visions.

The Poetics and Politics of a Foundational National Narrative

What exactly counts as a "national narrative" in fiction? What thematic preoccupations and formal literary means characterize it? Drawing on Anderson's argument about the realist novel's facilitation of national imaginings, literary scholar Cairns Craig offers a useful summary of the kind of ideological work on behalf of the nation that the traditional novel has done in the past, especially in the "nation-obsessed" nineteenth century:

> There is a profound similarity between the modern nation, with its implication of *all the people of a territory bound together into a single historical process*, and the technique of the major nineteenth-century novels, whose *emplotment enmeshes their multiplicity of characters into a single, overarching narrative trajectory*. (9; my emphasis)

Craig's summary points out three defining elements of any modern national imagining: its chief object of attention is (1) "all the people," (2) located within a delimited "territory," (3) and subject to "a single historical process." In the revised edition of *Imagined Communities*, Anderson included a chapter on the three modern "institutions of power" – the census, the map, and the museum – that helped various states in the past (especially colonial states, as he emphasizes) to fashion and popularize these three elements of national imaginings. The census, according to Anderson, not only sorted the population according to "the ethnic-racial classifications" invented by the state, but also operated on the fictional premise that it could count everyone ("all the people") ("Census, Map, Museum" 246). The map divided all those people groups, fashioned by the census, "by delimiting territorially where, for political purposes, they ended" (bounded "territory") (249). And the museum constructed out of the historical past and its artefacts a common "album of ancestors" for "all the people" ("a single historical process") (255).[4] The traditional novel, as Craig suggests, furnished its imaginative power and formal devices of emplotment to bind the three elements of people, territory, and history into one whole; it may be therefore seen as partly replicating and combining the ideological effects of the census, the map, and the museum.

The novel, in its more realist subgenres, has retained its nation-shaping functions in the twentieth and even the twenty-first century, especially in the new nation-states concerned with nation-building, such as the postcolonial Third World countries and the post-Soviet states. At the same time, however, many contemporary "national" novels, while still broadly engaging the questions of the nation's people, its territory, and its history/traditions, deconstruct, in a variety of explicit and subtle ways, the hegemonic ideological effects of the census, the map, and the museum – especially if the national imaginings were produced by these institutions under the former colonial regime.

How does a national narrative "emplot" its many different characters into "a single, overarching narrative trajectory" (Craig 9)? In other words, how does it transform a collection of individual stories into one collective story? One very popular way to accomplish this goal is suggested, once again, by Anderson, who ends *Imagined Communities* with an interesting discussion of what he calls "the biography of nations," comparing a modern person's (auto)biography and the biography of a modern nation (204). Both of these, through a complex interplay of remembering and forgetting, string together events into a narrative that imparts a sense of oneness and continuity, despite all changes and upheavals, to the person's or the nation's identity. Both are also "set in homogeneous, empty time," measured by the calendar, which in the case of a person is evidenced by the importance accorded to the calendar dates of his/her birth and death (204). Unlike individuals, however, nations have "no clearly identifiable births, and their deaths, if they ever happen, are never natural" (205). Because of this fact, Anderson insists, the only way to emplot a nation's biography (that is, a foundational national narrative) is to write it backwards, so to speak – from the present into the past. Crucially, this "archaeological" writing uncovers many deaths, but, as Anderson asserts, a nation's biography is interested only in the deaths "of a special kind": "exemplary suicides, poignant martyrdoms, assassinations, executions, wars, and holocausts," which, in order to become part of a nation's biography, "must be remembered/forgotten as 'our own'" (205–6). In this way, a national biography "transform[s] fatality into continuity," refiguring and remembering as heroic sacrifice for the sake of the nation's continued existence those deaths among its subjects that lend themselves to an ascription of a "national" meaning (11).

Anderson's ideas about emplotment of the nation are developed from the perspective of cognitive psychology by literary scholar Patrick Colm Hogan, who has defined three "narrative prototypes" dominant in nationalist thought: the heroic plot, the sacrificial plot, and the romantic plot.[5] Although Hogan does not emphasize the reverse emplotment that focuses on "national" deaths, it is clear from his analysis that such emplotment would usually rely either on the sacrificial plot, or on a combination of the heroic and the sacrificial plots. The romantic narrative prototype is what Sommer called "the national romance," and it stands somewhat apart from the other two. Yet, as my analysis of the four works by Zabuzhko, Kononenko, and Matios will show, all of these plots are utilized in their national narratives – often in combination with each other and sometimes in subversive ways.

Writing "true" biographies of nations has long been the province of professional historians; in fact, the kind of national narrative Anderson describes – focused on "assassinations, executions, wars, and holocausts" – is the stuff of conventional textbooks in national history, which many of us have read at school. Yet the view of history that exclusively focuses on "big" political events and historical macro-narratives has been criticized in recent decades by feminist historians.[6] They argued that in such historical narratives men figure as the chief protagonists and women are often excluded altogether.

For example, there has been a strong gender (and class) bias in the kinds of deaths that made it into the national narratives and were remembered as "our own." As historian John Gillis notes of the nineteenth century, "national commemorations were largely the preserve of elite males, the designated carriers of progress," and even though in the twentieth century "national memory practices became more democratic," women were still often assigned in them either "allegorical" or auxiliary roles, such as that of mourners of the dead (male) national heroes (10–12).[7] In a traditional national narrative then, a woman's death would either come to stand as symbolic of the nation (of the nation's perilous situation, for example, as in Shevchenko's *pokrytka* plot) or would not be remembered at all. One prominent example of such symbolization of a woman's death in Russian literature is Aleksandr Solzhenitsyn's 1959 novella *Matrionin dvor* (*Matryona's Home*) in which an old peasant woman's death prompts the male narrator to reinterpret her person as a symbol of the Russian nation and its traditional values, made almost extinct under the Soviet regime. In Ukrainian literature, the 1933 novel by Ulas Samchuk,[8] *Maria*, might serve as an example: in this first literary work about the Ukrainian Holodomor, the nation's tragedy is symbolically rendered through the starvation and eventual death of the eponymous female protagonist.[9]

In light of such gendered poetics and politics of a traditional national narrative, the four works by Ukrainian women writers seem unconventional, to varying degrees: while they mostly emplot their versions of Ukraine's national biography backwards – from the present into the past, as Anderson suggested is standard for national narratives – the deaths around which most of them are structured and in which they are especially interested are individual women's deaths.[10] Moreover, the authors of these texts make sure that the deaths of their women protagonists do not become allegorized as suffering Mother Ukraine. Instead, sometimes the writers (Matios in particular) allow the women characters themselves to speak about the meaning of their future deaths, and this meaning often turns out to be critical of the nation and of the roles assigned to women within it. In other texts, a woman's death prompts another (often female) character to investigate its circumstances, and this investigation becomes a simultaneous inquiry into a woman's unique life story and into the nation's bloody past or an unstable present. This inquiry shows, however, that in the national story, women play a multiplicity of different roles: some are victims, some are villains, some are heroes (even "national" heroes, but always on their own terms), and some are disconcerted observers; some willingly take on the roles of cultural reproducers and some reject these roles, preferring instead a position of cultural critique. In short, these women are independent actors in their respective circumstances, even if sometimes they only have a modicum of agency.

Equally importantly, as they portrayed and investigated women's lives and deaths in twentieth-century Ukraine, all four texts also engaged the "broad" national questions outlined above – the questions of people and their ethnic and cultural heterogeneity, of the land and its borders, and of the Soviet past. In this respect, women authors themselves took on the roles of cultural critics and made various interventions into the Ukrainian national imaginary of the 2000s. They confronted the fact that the ethnic composition and the post-Soviet borders of the independent Ukrainian nation-state were a result of the often brutal modernization policies of the Soviet regime as well as wartime annexation and ethnic violence. Such conditions accounted for the tension and disagreement on policies in the early post-Soviet decades between Ukraine's various constituent parts (sometimes simplistically conceptualized by observers as Western and Eastern Ukraine). As historian David Marples explained in his 2007 study, *Heroes and Villains: Creating National History in Contemporary Ukraine*, at the time Ukraine did not have one national narrative about its recent history, one which would be accepted by most of its population. According to Marples, it remained a point of contention whether Ukraine should be seen as a "descendant" of the Soviet Union and an inheritor of its fundamental historical myth of the "Great Patriotic War," in which Soviet citizens, at great personal and collective cost, defeated the Nazis, or whether it should be viewed as "the child of Ukrainian nationalists," who fought the Soviet regime's occupation of Western Ukraine during and after the Second World War and produced in the 1960s–80s many of Ukraine's dissidents.[11] Thus, a foundational historical myth of origins for independent Ukraine that would hold it firmly together was conspicuously missing from the Ukrainian national imaginary at the time of Zabuzhko's, Kononenko's, and Matios's writing of their national narratives.[12]

Because it is such an important issue for contemporary Ukraine and Ukrainians' identity, three of the four national narratives examined in this study go back to the events of the Second World War and especially to the Soviet annexation of Western Ukraine. In their works, Matios and Zabuzhko (who themselves hail from two different parts of Western Ukraine, although both now live in Kyiv) show the violence that accompanied this annexation. However, while Matios portrays it more as a clash between the ideology and policies of a ruthless modern state and the worldview of a premodern peasant society, and focuses on the lives of civilians, especially women, Zabuzhko creates a more heroic and mythical narrative in which Western Ukrainian guerrilla fighters figure prominently (although even this narrative is not devoid of complexity and ambiguity). By contrast, Kononenko, a native Kyivan, turns her attention to Ukraine's East and the internal cultural boundaries within Ukraine that separate the East from Kyiv and from the West. In their different ways, all four works intervene into the national imaginings produced by the ideological institutions of the census, the map, and the museum, and make women an essential part of this intervention.

Who Belongs to *The Nation*? Matios's Alternative National "Census"

Matios's *The Nation: Revelation* is a collection of ten stories (divided into two cycles), written between 1984 and 2006. Many of them were published in literary journals long before the collection first appeared in 2001 or took its final shape in the third edition of 2006. Nevertheless, its fullest edition does possess a degree of narrative unity, with stories arranged chronologically and describing events roughly from before the First World War to the times of independence. All stories take place in Matios's native region of Bukovyna. Before northern Bukovyna was annexed from Romania by the Soviet Union in 1940, and then, after intermittent German and Romanian occupations, incorporated into the Ukrainian Soviet Socialist Republic at the end of the Second World War, it was a truly multiethnic region – especially in the times of the Austro-Hungarian Empire, to which it belonged until 1918. According to historian Fred Stambrook, Bukovyna's population was "the most ethnically diverse" of all Austrian lands, with mixing and interconnectedness of ethnic groups in daily life and relatively peaceful coexistence at least until the beginning of the First World War (185).

However, as Matios notes in an introduction to one of her books of nonfiction, from 1914 to the end of the Second World War, her native Hutsul part of northern Bukovyna[13] had experienced regime changes almost twenty times (*Vyrvani storinky* 25). In the course of these political upheavals, especially the ones of the Second World War and the Soviet incorporation, the multicultural mosaic of northern Bukovyna disappeared, leaving behind a decimated and largely homogeneous Ukrainian community (in terms of ethnicity and class) and a Soviet administration, composed of ethnic Russians, Eastern Ukrainians, and some locals. The first cycle of stories in *The Nation* portrays this unravelling of the multicultural community and the ensuing political conflict between the representatives of the Soviet regime and the locals, some of whom join the guerrilla resistance forces – the Ukrainian Insurgent Army (UPA). The cycle does so, however, in micro-narratives about individuals, some having real-life prototypes. It depicts the perspectives on the dramatic events of those involved on all sides, including the perpetrators of violence, with considerable psychological nuance. The resulting picture is not black and white, but one with many shades of grey, a composition which moreover does not make claims of total knowledge or comprehensiveness.[14] The fact that *The Nation* is not a novel but a collection of stories, each of which captures only a tiny fragment of the great historical drama that unfolded in Bukovyna, a small region of Ukraine, underscores the author's efforts to position her text as only one of any number of national narratives. This kind of portrayal itself stands in stark contrast to the ideology and the governance of the Soviet regime, which Matios shows wreaking havoc and destruction on Bukovyna.

The story of the Soviet state's role in the transformation of cultural complexity and ambiguity into ethnic division and then ethnic homogeneity has been recently told by Kate Brown in *A Biography of No Place: From Ethnic Borderland to Soviet Heartland*. Brown describes how this process occurred in a different part of what is present-day Ukraine, beginning two decades before the Soviet occupation of Bukovyna with an all-Soviet drive to reorganize and modernize society, including through "counting national bodies," or a Soviet census (38). According to historian Francine Hirsch, such policies were implemented in an "effort to turn so-called backward peoples into nations – that is, to delineate new political boundaries and foster national-cultural distinctions – within the context of a unified state with a colonial-type economy and administrative structure" ("Toward an Empire of Nations" 204). As Brown poignantly demonstrates, the Soviet census imposed discrete "nationality" identities onto peasants, many of whom thought of themselves as "simply 'local'"; it had no tolerance for fragmentariness and ambiguity, striving to account for everyone and to disentangle the mix of cultures that existed in the first decades of the twentieth century in the borderlands between Russia and Poland (40). The Soviet census, just like the colonial ones in Southeast Asia described by Anderson, applied to its domain "a totalizing classificatory grid … the effect" of which "was always to be able to say of anything that it was this, not that; it belonged here, not there" ("Census, Map, Museum" 254). Brown shows that there was a connection between this search for absolute clarity and the invention of reified national categories on the one hand, and the later mass arrests, deportations, and exterminations of different population groups, both by the Soviet and the German administrations,[15] on the other. Both were part of the process of "creating distilled nation-space for modern governance" (230).

If in much of what is today's Ukraine the Soviet "census mentality" came first and the physical violence in the form of deportations and exterminations followed, after some time, to Bukovyna (as to other regions in Western Ukraine) the two came hand in hand. The local population was deemed suspicious by the new authorities from the outset. In a census-like move, the Soviet administration right away issued passports to the locals – for the sake of better control of the population (Musiienko 474). Thousands of individuals were arrested and deported from northern Bukovyna in just one year of the first Soviet occupation. Like Brown, although through fictional means, Matios portrays the local population's bafflement at the violence brought by the new administration. Trying to comprehend what was happening to them and to their world, the locals attempted to fit these events into their own "grid" of thinking – their religious beliefs, folk traditions, and cultural mythologies.

Thus, the collection's first story – about the dissolution of the ethnic mosaic and the gradual destruction of the Bukovyna Jews, told through the prism of the intertwined fates of a Ukrainian and a Jewish family – is named, from the locals' perspective, "Apokalipsys" ("The Apocalypse"). The pre–First World War Bukovyna village of Tysova Rivnia is described as a "human medley," with ethnically diverse families participating in each other's customs (Ukrainian neighbours joining a Jewish family for Purim or a Jewish man wearing a traditional Hutsul goatskin vest over his regular garment); yet we later see that the First World War brings with it the first pogroms, perpetrated by the regiments passing through the village. Soon after, the Second World War brings successive Soviet and Romanian occupations (a period which the story describes as the time "when the fish population in the rivers increased and the human population decreased"), and the Soviet annexation of 1945 brings an order to Jews, "the former Romanian citizens," to get out of the Soviet Bukovyna (*Natsiia* 7, 23).

This broader historical context is given by the omniscient narrator, whereas the villagers themselves comprehend it in more relational and mystical terms. Members of the different ethnic communities refer to each other's traditions and families as "our" and "your," but these terms are not exclusive of each other, as becomes especially obvious when a Jewish widow has a child with a man from a neighbouring Ukrainian family. At the same time, with the Soviet annexation, the new administration redefines all the remaining Jews as "foreign" [*chuzhi*], effectively depriving them of home (*Natsiia* 23).[16] Moreover, the story gives a mystical explanation of the destruction, grounded in folk belief: in an early scene that once again shows the mixing of ethnic traditions, the mother in the Jewish family warns the father from the Ukrainian family against using the wood from the aspen tree, which, according to a Hutsul superstition, brings misfortune. The father does not heed her advice and uses the wood to make the barn floor and a walking stick. At the end of the story, out of the two large neighbouring families – one Jewish and one Ukrainian – only the Ukrainian father and his daughter-in-law remain. The final scene shows the old father sitting with his walking stick near his house, mourning his dead wife and half-Jewish daughter. The latter stayed behind with the Ukrainian family after her mother and siblings had left Bukovyna, and later unexpectedly joined the local guerrilla movement that fought the Soviet administration. The story reverses traditional gender roles, showing the father as the mourner of the dead and giving the role of the resistance fighter to a woman (while her half-brother, as the old father says with contempt, "counts sheep droppings in the kolkhoz" [*Natsiia* 26]). It also works against the common historical narrative according to which the guerrilla forces in the UPA were ethnically all Ukrainian. Yet perhaps the greatest surprise of this story is the unresolved tension it sets up between the "external" historical explanation of the tragedy and the local mystical comprehension of it, which vividly dramatizes the encounter of the two worldviews, but also introduces ambiguity into the drama of the two families.[17]

Almost all of the texts in the collection are built around ambiguities. The story "Vstavaite, mamko …" ("Mother, Get Up …"), subtitled "Revelation of 1947," is a case in point. When a well-to-do Hutsul family is told by a sympathetic local member of the Soviet administration that the following day they will be deported to the Siberia as *kulaks*,[18] they decide to avoid deportation at any cost. With this goal in mind, they stage an elaborate performance of a Hutsul funeral for the mother of the family, who climbs into a casket and plays dead. The family's youngest son is told to run and hide in the forest, as he might inadvertently divulge the truth to the Soviet officials. When the administration representatives arrive, they find the family in mourning, engaged in the wake and funeral preparations, and are invited to join in. The officials remark that the family has turned out "lucky with death," which spared them from the deportation, but one of the local officials notes in passing that a cheek on the mother's face is flushed, which, according to a folk belief, is a sign that another death will soon strike the family (*Natsiia* 67). Having feasted at the wake, the officials leave, and the youngest son returns – only to find his mother actually dead in the casket. The abrupt, shocking ending sends the reader back into the story in search of some kind of explanation, which the text, however, does not give – beyond the ominous folk sign.

Contrary to one critic's suggestion,[19] this is not a narrative of the mother willingly sacrificing herself for her family because her death was supposed to be only a performance. The choice of the mother for this role was strategic, akin to the predominantly female participation in the peasant rebellions against the Soviet collectivization campaign and deportations in the 1930s in what is now central Ukraine. As Brown explains, "[w]omen went to the forefront of battles partly because they were conscious of the fact that they were considered too dark and ignorant to be held criminally responsible for their actions … The government responded more leniently to women rebels" (104). How is one to read this mother's real death then? As the fulfilment of the omen (which was not "real" anyway because the mother was still alive when her cheek became flushed)? As some cosmic punishment for playing with death, or for deception? Or as symbolic of the fact that while this particular family escaped deportation, many others in the community did not (which would then make the mother a figure for the nation's suffering)? The text does not contain any clues to be able to say one way or another with certainty.

Most of the stories in the collection are built upon an ambiguity of identity. "Self" [*svii*] and "the other" [*chuzyi*] are not obvious or stable categories in *The Nation*. This fact makes this work the exact opposite of the colonial census, the effect of which Anderson described as that of "always to be able to say of anything that it was this, not that; it belonged here, not there" ("Census, Map, Museum" 254). That is why Matios's collection may be read as an alternative "census," which deconstructs the Soviet "totalizing grid" and its reified categories, while at the same time deconstructing exclusionary national imaginings. Although on the whole the villagers in many of the stories perceive the Soviet administration as foreign, its representatives are not uniformly portrayed as villains. In fact, some of them turn out to be more merciful and understanding than some of the locals or the guerrilla fighters.

This occurs, for example, in the story "Prosyly tato-mama …" ("My Father Is Asking, My Mother Is Asking …"),[20] subtitled "Revelation of 1990," because, in keeping with Anderson's reverse poetics of a national narrative, it is told backwards – from the present into the past. When Kornelia accompanies her son to Chernivtsi, the largest city in northern Bukovyna, to help him choose a suit for his approaching wedding, she faints in the street after coming face to face with a man who carries a blue and yellow flag, now the national flag of

Ukraine, in his disfigured hand. Back at home, she tells her son the story from her past involving that man, named Koliay. In 1950, Kornelia and Koliay, with whom she was in love, were still part of by then minuscule guerrilla forces, fighting a clearly losing battle against the Soviet regime.[21] Ordered to disband by the commanders, Kornelia, Koliay, and another male fighter had to find a safe way to get to a different part of Bukovyna and "legalize" themselves in civilian life, under the watchful eye of the Soviet operatives from the Ministry of State Security (the MGB). Kornelia suggested that they walk in broad daylight, pretending to be a bridesmaid and groomsmen on a mission to invite people from the neighbouring villages to a wedding, which was really taking place at their final destination (hence the wedding invitation formula in the title of the story). The male fighters agreed, but in the morning, Kornelia found that they had already gone and left her to fend for herself. She walked through the countryside alone, pretending to be the bridesmaid, until in one village, she ran into the real wedding party that was going around issuing wedding invitations – and into the MGB officers. While the bride from the party, Kornelia's long-time friend, reluctantly agreed not to give her over to the MGB, Kornelia's life was ultimately saved by the MGB officer who chose to overlook her deception. As Kornelia's son finds out only forty years later, that officer eventually became Kornelia's husband and his father, helping Kornelia become "legalized" by getting her a forged identity document.

The story does not idealize the guerrilla fighters, showing both them and the MGB operatives embroiled in a vicious, self-perpetuating cycle of revenge, with both sides committing brutalities against the civilian population. After Koliay's girlfriend is killed by the MGB and her entire family is deported, Koliay, blind with rage, murders a schoolteacher, sent to Bukovyna from central Ukraine, disregarding all orders from his superiors. When Kornelia begs their unit's commander not to execute Koliay for this crime, the commander gives her a poignant answer:

> I don't want to walk around with a sin on my soul for the rest of my life. These times will pass – and someone, sometime in the future, will sort through our bones. I don't want them to be shaking with anger and cursing us. It would be good if white were white and black were black, but that's not the case. In this time, we've been deceived by so many from all sides that I don't want us to also deceive ourselves. (*Natsiia* 108)

The perspective of the MGB officers and of other Soviet representatives on the violent conflict in Bukovyna is given in another story from the first cycle, "Yuriana and Dovhopol." This text is based entirely on real events, with all central characters having real-life prototypes, including the Russian MGB operative Dolgopol and Matios's grandmother, who is the female protagonist in the story (*Vyrvani storinky* 282–4). The central motif is blood, which mediates the locals' and the Soviet representatives' understanding of who is *svii* [self] and who is *chuzhyi* [the other], but in the final scene, undermines the boundary between the two categories.

Although Yuriana is bleeding after yet another miscarriage, she shows up for work at her village's collective farm, fearful of being reprimanded by the strict supervisor from the MGB, Dovhopol. Called "Solomon" in the village for her sharp mind (including by Dovhopol himself), Yuriana nevertheless cannot understand what is happening in her community, with people "dying like flies": "Brother has gone against brother. All right, *these* are a different story, but brothers ... *Svii* is going against *svii*! Till they bleed to death!" (*Natsiia* 45; emphasis in original). Yuriana is referring to the local guerrillas taking revenge on their own villagers for not supporting them, but "not everyone can go to the forest," she reasons (51). She and her husband, Ulasiy, for example, have young children to support. When her husband is arrested though – ironically, on suspicion of having ties with the guerillas – Yuriana goes to Dovhopol rather than to anyone else to beg him to intercede for Ulasiy, and Dovhopol makes sure that Ulasiy is freed. As Yuriana's bleeding worsens, the Russian nurse Dusia, sent to Bukovyna with the Soviet administration, insists that Yuriana be taken to the regional hospital – in the same car as Dovhopol, who had been shot by the guerrillas. Dusia thinks to herself that Yuriana should have come to her earlier, but many Hutsuls do not want to see the nurse from Russia. "How do you explain to them that she wishes them well? ... Dusia has gone through war and the blockade, and she knows that blood doesn't have a nation" (*Natsiia* 54).

Dusia's pronouncement ushers in the last scene of the story, which is a stream-of-consciousness narration from the perspective of the MGB operative, Didushenko, who is the head of the convoy accompanying the bleeding Dovhopol and Yuriana to the hospital. Didushenko cannot comprehend why Dusia and Dovhopol himself begged him to take Yuriana with them. He notes that he can look at Yuriana's blood, but not at Dovhopol's. He begs Dovhopol not to die, "or I will shoot all of these mountains of theirs, and no one will stop me!" (*Natsiia* 56). But at the same time, he wonders why there has been so much merciless killing on both sides, and as he watches the two wounded passengers, he sees only blood and no difference between them.

In a tendentious reading of *The Nation*, critic Irina Zherebkina identifies in the collection, which she mistakenly calls a novel, "a rigid and uncompromising division of the world into 'the self' and 'the other'" (156). Such a reading is possible only if one completely ignores positive (real-life) characters, such as Dusia, and the poetics of many stories. In fact, one of Matios's chief goals is to undermine such a "rigid division," which the brutality of war and the Soviet annexation, as well as the "census" mentality, have brought about in Bukovyna. Yet Matios does not posit an inherently "good" local population, which was somehow "spoiled" by the Soviet regime. For example, throughout the collection, there runs a subtle parallel between the drive of the new administration to gain total knowledge, and therefore total control, of the people and the area, and the locals' desire to know everything about everyone and spread rumours through their well-established gossip networks. Both are shown to have similarly devastating consequences. Moreover, the collection's second cycle of stories, in which the action takes place in the peaceful times either before or after the Second World War and the ensuing Soviet incorporation of Bukovyna, establishes other parallels between the Soviet "census" mentality and the local attitudes towards life.

The story "Pryznai svoiu dytynu" ("Recognize Your Child"), for instance, which tells of an episode in one Bukovyna family's life at an unspecified time after the war, demonstrates the danger and folly of seeking a firm demarcation line between "the self" and "the other" – especially in physical or racial terms. A drunken villager, nicknamed Tataryn, blurts out to Dmytro, the father of a Hutsul family, that the latter's oldest daughter looks remarkably like himself. While Dmytro's wife dismisses the comment as absurd, her husband takes it to heart and begins to spend hours comparing the photos of himself and his daughter, Tania, studying his face in the mirror and hers when she is asleep. He also spies on Tataryn in order to examine his appearance, even stealing his photograph for this purpose. The more he looks at the photos, the more likeness he sees between Tania and his offender: both he and Tania have blond hair, unlike anyone else in Dmytro's family. No longer able to bear the sight of this difference from the self, Dmytro makes his wife and both daughters wear identical white kerchiefs when at home. He becomes withdrawn, loses interest in work, and finally slaps Tania on the face. The story ends with Dmytro's wife lamenting her husband's folly to his mother, as Dmytro himself once again peers into the mirror. This time, the only things he sees there are "pain and fear" (*Natsiia* 171). This story is thus reminiscent of "Yuriana and Dovhopol": both deconstruct the drive to fix the categories of "the self" and "the other," so that it would be possible to "say of anything that it [i]s this, not that; it belong[s] here, not there" (Anderson, "Census, Map, Museum" 254).

If the collection's opening story dramatized the utter loss of the interconnected community life of various ethnic groups in a Bukovyna village, *The Nation*'s final piece, "Ne plachte za mnoiu nikoly" ("Don't Ever Cry for Me"), shows that the very principle of interconnectedness – even after the polarizing war and violence – has survived and continues to function in the post-Soviet present. The story is one long conversation, in *skaz*,[22] between an old peasant woman, Yustyna, and the I-narrator, who elicits from the woman stories of the past while helping her air out the casket and other items, which Yustyna has been storing for many years in preparation for her death. Yustyna explains that, despite the villagers' mocking and their children's protests, both she and her husband had their caskets made decades ago, because of uncertain times. In over twenty-five years since then, they both have "lent" their caskets dozens of times to various individuals and families in the village for the burial of their relatives (all of whom died natural, not violent deaths). Yustyna's account thus becomes a mini-history of the village through stories of all the people who were buried in "their" caskets. Yet this history does not in the least sound morbid: it reflects Yustyna's very common-sense approach to life, of which death is a natural and important event. If anything, her account is amusing (chiefly because of the *skaz* narration) and instructive, as it turns out that "their" caskets became the final "home" for the bodies of all kinds of people: old and young, men and women, poor and well-to-do, Ukrainians and Gypsies, those working directly for the Soviet regime and those harbouring resentment towards it. In the story, the casket figures as the physical point of and the metaphor for interconnectedness. No one is refused the lending of the casket, not even the family of the deceased female head of the village council, against whom many in the village have a grudge for her toeing the Communist Party line – "for although she was the head, she was still a person" (*Natsiia* 178).

The stories of death told by Yustyna are nothing like Anderson's "exemplary suicides, poignant martyrdoms, assassinations, executions," which, according to him, make up a nation's biography, and which were more prominent in the first cycle of Matios's collection. These deaths are not and cannot be ascribed a "national" meaning in Anderson's sense – as sacrifices for the nation, for example. Yet in *The Nation*, they are shown to be no less important and worthy of remembrance than the first type.

In a positive review of Matios's book, written for the Ukrainian leftist website HASLO, reviewer Iryna Chebotnikova finds it "paradoxical" that the main protagonists of *The Nation* are women, yet does not elaborate on their roles in the stories or on Matios's women-centred vision of "the nation." What I see Yustyna and other women characters in Matios's collection doing is providing a vital corrective to the narrow, masculinist view of the nation's biography described by Anderson. As historian Yaroslav Hrytsak points out, and as *The Nation* poignantly shows with the example of Bukovyna, in Ukraine "the transition 'from peasants to a nation' occurred during wars and revolutions, and violence was among the main instruments of building a modern society" ("Tezy do dyskusii pro UPA" 94). This fact makes war an inevitable part of a foundational national narrative for modern Ukraine. Yet, as Yustyna's account shows, war does not make up the entire narrative.

In *The Nation*, women characters are also frequently the ones who reject the conception of national belonging in terms of a rigid and irreconcilable opposition between "the self" and "the other," especially in exclusivist ethnic terms. This rejection comes from the Russian nurse Dusia, for example, who makes the statement that "blood doesn't have a nation" (*Natsiia* 54). The collection itself shows women playing a variety of roles in their communities – from traditional to unconventional – and does not reduce its women characters to mere symbols of the nation. In Matios's "census," women do not belong to only one or two categories: they appear everywhere and sometimes critique the categories themselves.

Although Matios's *The Nation* is entirely set in Bukovyna and predominantly elaborates a sense of local identity (reflecting the way in which much of Ukraine's rural population continues to think of themselves), what makes it relevant for all of contemporary Ukraine are the frequently touchy subjects, such as the UPA, on which the author offers her own perspective. Matios depicts and validates most guerrilla fighters' desire to defend themselves and their families against the violent policies of the Soviet administration, but she does not gloss over their often brutal tactics and lack of tolerance for other points of view. In the end, *The Nation* does not suggest that we see the independent Ukrainian nation-state as "the child of Ukrainian nationalists" – one of the two lineage options mentioned by Marples. Neither, of course, does it approve the other option – that of "a descendant of Soviet Ukraine" (301). Instead, it elucidates the fact that the lineage of both was important in the process of making Ukraine what it is today – but so were many ordinary women, women whose voices Matios interjects into the national narrative.

Women on the Nation's Borders: The Map of Ukraine in Novels by Matios and Kononenko

If *The Nation*, through its subject-matter and the fragmentary form of a short story collection, engaged with and deconstructed the Soviet census imaginings and the polarized wartime opposition of the self and the other, the next two texts analysed in this chapter are novels that scrutinize the peculiarities of the Ukrainian map, which acquired its contemporary shape in the Soviet era. Matios's *Sweet Darusia* (2004), like *The Nation*, focuses on the incorporation of mostly rural Bukovyna into the Ukrainian Soviet Socialist Republic – a colonial map-making moment. By contrast, Kononenko's *Imitation* (2001) captures the Ukrainian elite's post-Soviet imaginings of the Ukrainian territory and its internal divisions, showing them to be an exaggerated reaction against the Soviet policies. Remarkably, both novels are built around a woman's death and tell their stories backwards, in agreement with Anderson's reverse poetics of a national narrative. In both, women's suffering and/or deaths are connected to the nation's borders, physically taking place on a boundary between two regions or in the liminal space of a railway station. These deaths also reveal much about how the real and imagined boundaries of and within Ukraine have come about, and the role that gender can play in such processes.

The National Map and Its Boundaries in Sweet Darusia

In many ways, *Sweet Darusia*, Matios's most celebrated novel to date, continues and develops the major themes and narrative techniques of *The Nation*. It portrays the violent transformation of peasant life as a result of the Second World War and the Soviet annexation of northern Bukovyna through the micro-lens of life in one village and through one family's history in particular. It revisits the brutal confrontation between the Soviet MGB forces and the UPA guerrilla fighters, and zeroes in on the fates and viewpoints of civilian peasants who are caught in the middle of this conflict. And it pays close attention to women's roles and voices in this dramatic moment in Ukrainian history. What appears to be a vital new element of this national narrative, in comparison with the collection of stories, is its intense focus on the borders and boundaries – physical, moral, and symbolic – as well as their breaking and their constitution.

As Francine Hirsch has detailed in her articles on the formation of the Soviet Union, the internal borders between the constituent Soviet republics were based on the census determinations of nationalities – not for the sake of nation-making itself, but "with the aim of consolidating the Soviet state" ("Toward an Empire of Nations" 209). Soviet government officials decided "that borders drawn along national or ethnic lines would be more durable than those established according to natural geographic boundaries or economic principles" (Hirsch, "The Soviet Union as a Work-in-Progress" 252). During and after the Second World War, however, the Soviet government aptly deployed the nationality rhetoric and presented itself as a "defender" of the national rights of its republics on the international scene in order to justify its territorial gains. The Soviet annexation of Western Ukrainian lands, including northern Bukovyna, in which ethnic Ukrainians constituted a majority, was externally presented as the historically just reunification of Eastern and Western Ukrainian brothers. As Matios shows both in *The Nation* and in *Sweet Darusia*, to simple peasants in the remote, mountainous regions of Bukovyna, this "reunification" looked just like another regime change – but this time a much more violent one. As the physical borders between states were redrawn, all kinds of moral boundaries were crossed and many people, especially women, were pushed to their limit.

Sweet Darusia tells a fictional story (but with some real-life prototypes) of one family deeply traumatized as a result of the Soviet takeover of Bukovyna. In the novel's centre stands Darusia, a mute woman who lives in the predominantly Hutsul village of Cheremoshne in northern Bukovyna. Darusia is nicknamed "sweet" by the villagers because of her pathological reaction to offers of candy: for days afterwards, she suffers from excruciating headaches and does not leave her hut. The text is a retrospective narrative in three parts (called "dramas"): the first two show Darusia's difficult daily life in her community in the unspecified present, with many mocking her and calling her dumb or crazy, and the last and longest part reveals the history behind Darusia's trauma. In 1940, just before the first Soviet occupation of Bukovyna and right on the then border between the Western Ukrainian regions belonging to Poland and Romania – along which the village Cheremoshne was located – a Ukrainian MGB officer captured Darusia's mother, Matronka. During the lengthy process of interrogation he tortured and raped her, releasing her only on condition that she would not say a word about what had happened. In the late 1940s, when the Soviet troops occupied the village the second time, Darusia was a ten-year-old child. Striving to find out whether Darusia's father had cooperated with the UPA guerrilla fighters, the officer who had earlier raped her mother extracted the truth out of Darusia by luring her with candy. Darusia told him how during the night her father, Mykhailo, was giving food to the UPA partisans, after which her family faced likely deportation to Siberia. Darusia's mother, who had recognized her torturer, finally confessed about the rape to her husband and hanged herself the next night out of hopelessness and despair. Darusia, who had witnessed her mother's suicide, became mute and terrified of candy and anyone in military uniform for the rest of her life.

The liminal physical setting of this tragic story – the banks of the Cheremosh River, which marked the border between Poland and Romania before the Second World War and divided two Hutsul villages, both named Cheremoshne – defines the novel's central preoccupation with boundaries. The redrawing of boundaries takes place first of all in the geographical and political sense. In the course of the Second World War, the two villages are occupied at different times by different forces, which, as the novel shows, brings confusion and much suffering to the civilian population. Darusia's mother is captured by the Soviet MGB and taken for interrogation across the border into the Soviet-occupied Cheremoshne on the Polish side, while her own village is still under Romanian control. With the first Soviet occupation of Cheremoshne on the other bank, all the Jewish businesses, such as the tavern and the mill, are forced to close, and several Ukrainian village activists are arrested and their families deported. With the beginning of the German-Soviet war, the Bukovyna Cheremoshne is occupied by Romanians, briefly by Germans, then their Hungarian allies, and finally by the Soviets again. In the chaos of these border redrawings, moral boundaries collapse. Some locals from the village participate in the looting of homes of the deported families and of those Jews who had managed to escape, and the Jewish taverns are all burnt down. Some villagers also prove adept at serving whatever regime is currently in power: as Matronka notices to her dismay, when the Germans enter the village, the local who comes out to greet them with the traditional Ukrainian bread and salt is the same man who had aided the Soviets in her capture. With the Soviet annexation of the Bukovyna Cheremoshne, one of the village's favourite pastimes – gossiping – is often put at the service of the MGB, which seeks to stamp out the guerrilla resistance. Thus, Matronka's husband, Mykhailo, gets in trouble with the MGB when a "kind" neighbour informs on him.

The personal drama of Darusia's family takes place against the background of this border dissolution and boundary collapse. However, Matios shows that while some boundaries disappear, others are constituted. National imaginings and brutal technologies of power, brought into Cheremoshne by war, draw sharp national fault lines, including right through women's bodies, which in this new discourse come to symbolically represent their community and its territory. In *Boundary Politics: Women, Nationalism and Danger*, political scientist Jan Jindy Pettman describes how the pervasive gendered imagining of the nation and its land as female endangers women especially during war, when they become "terribly vulnerable to rape in war, both as spoils of war and as ways of getting at 'other men's women'" (189). Such rape is both a technology of war and, because of the equation of woman with the nation, a symbolic act of taking control over the Other.[23]

Matronka's torture and rape by the MGB officer, some details of which Matios took from real life,[24] may be read in such terms: committed right before the first Soviet takeover of Bukovyna's Cheremoshne, it is meant both as a means of intimidation and an assertion of control over the territory across the bank. Later, it also makes Matronka a victim of her husband's suspicions and violence, when during the Romanian occupation the officials tell him that he is considered unreliable because of the dubious circumstances under which Matronka had disappeared, hinting that they suspect her of sexual contact with the enemy. The same day, Mykhailo for the first time in his life brutally beats his wife, tying her to the bench with her long, thick braid – the quintessential symbol of femininity in rural Ukraine. The narrator tells us that Mykhailo is guided in this violence by one thought – "that his wife has been in the hands of another – foreign – man" (*Solodka Darusia* 144). This explanation points to the fact that Matronka's supposed adultery is perceived by Mykhailo not simply as an affront to his own honour, but also to that of his community. As this episode shows, even the best among the Cheremoshne villagers, most of whom, including Mykhailo, do not appear to think in national terms before the war, adopt polarized national imaginings in its course. Women's bodies come to mark the symbolic boundaries between national communities in such imaginings.

Matronka is an innocent victim of this rapid constitution of gendered symbolic national boundaries. Through the character of Matronka, Matios reveals women's frequently complicated positioning in and vis-à-vis the nation. While the novel clearly suggests that the brutalities of war and the Soviet occupation were primarily to blame for Matronka's suffering, it also implicates Matronka's own husband and her community in it. In the end, after Matronka's rapist elicits from her daughter incriminating information against her parents, Matronka tells her husband about the rape and commits suicide. Her death may seem to qualify as one of Anderson's "poignant suicides" – those which become important for a national narrative – yet Matios makes it difficult to incorporate it into an unproblematic narrative of national martyrdom by showing the complicity of those closest to Matronka in her death. Significantly, the author does it in part by giving voice to Matronka herself and letting her interpret her suffering. The text features Matronka's last words in direct speech before she hangs herself. They take a form of a desperate verbal revolt against Mykhailo and the religious values of their village community, which Matronka now cannot reconcile with what had happened to her:

> What did I do to God that he sent my torturer today into my home? I thought that for my suffering my torturer has rotted away long ago, and today he made me an enemy out of my child? So where is God? Did he go blind, Mykhailo, when I so ardently prayed to him all my life, and he even took your sanity because you beat me as you would cattle, and I had to keep quiet? (*Solodka Darusia* 172)

Matronka's passionate speech reveals her utter despair, and her suicide becomes the only way she sees of escaping her position of a complete victim. She hangs herself using instead of a rope her braid – that symbol of Ukrainian femininity – as if to suggest being strangled by her gender. Her speech precludes an ascription to her death of a "positive" national meaning – that of a heroic or tragic sacrifice for the sake of the nation. Likewise, Matronka's speech, as well as the fact that her death is a suicide, makes it impossible to see this character as a mere symbol of her nation. Thus, despite sharing the name with Solzhenitsyn's Matryona, Matronka plays a very different role in Matios's narrative. If anything, Matronka's death appears to be a protest against the symbolic national order that is being constituted – in which her body is constructed as a symbolic boundary between national communities.

The novel's central character, Darusia, whose trauma is caused by her inadvertent betrayal of her parents and the witnessing of the horrific scene of her mother's suicide, seems to invite a more symbolic reading. As Myroslav Shkandrij suggested, "Darusia's muteness becomes a symbol of a traumatized generation unable, or unwilling, to relate its experiences" (*Jews in Ukrainian Literature* 226). This trauma thus can be seen as yet another boundary with roots in the wartime and post-war events in Bukovyna – a barrier between those who witnessed the colonial map-making process in Western Ukraine and their descendants, who knew nothing about the nature of this process until recently.[25]

Yet Darusia is also a highly individualized character, to whom Matios gives voice, literally, all through the first part of the novel: Darusia's present-day life in the village is narrated in free indirect discourse almost entirely from mute Darusia's perspective. As Elleke Boehmer notes, the figure of "the dumb, oppressed body" is ubiquitous in colonial as well as postcolonial literature, with the latter attempting to grant this body opportunities for "self-articulation" and "self-expression" (*Stories of Women* 127, 131). Matios's novel is a similar attempt, one in which Darusia gains a modicum of agency by reinterpreting her muteness as a voluntary decision on her part not to speak: "She doesn't know how to live among people *with her language*. The people themselves made her stop speaking. And now let them tolerate her muteness" (*Solodka Darusia* 31; emphasis in original). Darusia's interior monologue of the novel's first part is also a narrative technique that allows Matios to offer a defamiliarizing, non-national perspective on the Ukrainian past and present: to Darusia's childlike mind, there is no difference between the MGB officers who caused her trauma decades ago and her present-day villagers, many of whom taunt her and call her a fool. All of them are simply "people" [*liudy*] with whom she does not want to talk. Matios thus empowers Darusia's character by making her position one of valuable cultural critique. As in *The Nation*, the picture of the past that emerges from this position is far from being black and white.

As geographer Catherine Nash has theorized, using the example of Ireland, the "tension between the assertion of national identity in the postcolonial nation and the presence of the female subaltern can be paraphrased as a problematic relationship between the map and the body" (39). In *Sweet Darusia*, the story of the violent making of the Ukrainian map, which could be interpreted or refashioned as a narrative of national martyrdom, is disrupted by the presence of two female subaltern bodies – the traumatized one of Darusia and the dead one of Matronka. But the disrupting power of these two figures comes from the fact that Matios has given each of them a voice in the novel, each presenting a different perspective on the past. In the novel's reception, which has been very positive in Ukraine and beyond – with the novel earning the Taras Shevchenko National Prize in 2005 and being designated as "The Most Widely Read Book in 2007" in Ukraine – the authenticity of these voices, however, has not always been preserved. For example, in a stage adaptation of *Sweet Darusia* by the Chernivtsi Music and Drama Theatre, neither Matronka's protesting speech nor Darusia's inner monologues appear at all. The latter, of course, are extremely difficult to transfer to the stage, especially because the character is mute. Nevertheless, their absence and other subtle shifts of emphasis practically remove Matios's gendered critique of the nation from the work, making it into a national narrative that, in Anderson's parlance, "remembers/forgets" Matronka's suicide and Darusia's trauma as "our own."

Post-Soviet Postcolonial Desire and Ukraine's Internal Other in Imitation

Like *Sweet Darusia*, Kononenko's murder mystery *Imitation* (2001) examines the imaginings of Ukraine's national map and does it through a narrative that works its way backwards to discover the circumstances of a woman's death. However, if Matios's novel is an "archaeology" of a historical trauma that occurred in rural Western Ukraine, Kononenko's novel is a post-Soviet detective investigation of a Kyiv-based female intellectual's murder, which happened in a provincial town in Eastern Ukraine. While the two works could not be more different in setting or literary style, their similar thematic preoccupations and structural parallels make for a useful comparison and justify analysing them in the same section. In fact, reading *Imitation* right after *Sweet Darusia* brings into focus a telling and ironic reversal that took place in Ukraine when it gained independence in 1991. If in the 1940s the Soviet state sought to radically transform the consciousness of Western Ukrainians and "Sovietize" them, fifty years later the pro-democratic and pro-European post-Soviet elite attempted to Europeanize Ukraine's Eastern regions, which were perceived as the most Soviet. And if in *Sweet Darusia* the agents of change were military men who acted through violence and terror, in *Imitation*, the chief agent of change is a single-minded woman intellectual who works with the help of Western grants. Her murder and its subsequent investigation reveal deep internal fissures within Ukraine, but also invite the post-Soviet Ukrainian readers to critically examine their own national imaginings of contemporary Ukraine's territory.

Despite the post-Soviet boom in detective fiction by women writers, Kononenko's *Imitation* cannot be categorized together with the wildly popular murder mysteries by the Russian authors, such as Aleksandra Marinina or Daria Dontsova. Some critics have called *Imitation* a "bestseller for the 'elite,'" and Maksym Strikha even suggested that this work is a detective novel only to the degree that Nikolai Chernyshevsky's *What Is to Be Done?* or Umberto Eco's *The Name of the Rose* may be considered detective fiction.[26] Although Strikha's statement is an exaggeration, Kononenko's novel certainly puts the detective genre to a very special use. In *Imitation*, it serves as a literary device to paint a broad panorama of the Ukrainian post-Soviet era and to engage in a cultural critique of Ukraine's intellectual elite and their national imaginings. As I will explain below, the conventions of popular detective fiction – and even more so, the subversive modifications of these conventions – have greatly aided Kononenko in accomplishing these goals.

In *Imitation*, a smart, self-made Ukrainian woman from Kyiv, Mariana Khrypovych, who works for a Ukrainian branch of the non-profit Western foundation Gifted Child International, is run over by a freight train in a provincial town in the Donetsk region. Unlike Anna Karenina, however, whom the text playfully references in this and other aspects, Mariana is pushed under the train by an angry twelve-year-old boy – a boy who had failed to trick Ms. Khrypovych into sponsoring his supposedly talented handicapped sister. The boy shows Mariana a few paintings, which he created himself by imitating a young local talent, already supported by the foundation. He presents them as his sister's, but

Mariana rejects them as atrocious, laughable imitations. For this rejection, she pays with her life. On the surface of it, Mariana's death may look heroic. As a tireless worker for the advancement of Ukraine's talented younger generation, she "spends her days trying to pull her country out of backwardness and steer it onto a more progressive path," and perishes in the line of duty, so to speak (Andryczyk 91). Kyiv's intellectual circles mourn her death as a "national" loss. Yet the novel prevents the emplotment of Mariana's death as a heroic sacrifice for the nation. Instead, it subtly turns the investigation of Mariana's murder into a critical examination of post-Soviet Ukraine's prevalent national discourses.

Mariana's murder, motivated by fury at the "arrogant" lady from Kyiv, who works for "the rich Americans" but refuses to help the provincial boy's family out of their desperate poverty, occurs in the context of the transitional early post-Soviet 1990s, when the rise of new elites in Ukraine occurred at the same time as the majority of the population was plunged into destitution. In *Imitation*, Kyiv emerges as the base of Ukraine's new intellectual elite and the new centre, which replaces Moscow, the old colonial centre. However, as soon becomes obvious, most new ideas, programs, and cultural forms spreading in Ukraine originate not in Kyiv, but in the West. The novel identifies Kyiv's new elites, and Mariana as one of its unmistakable representatives, as the driving force behind Ukraine's Westernization. *Imitation* reveals that in their actions, these elites are motivated by what may be termed as the post-Soviet postcolonial desire. It is this desire which ultimately leads to Mariana's demise.

To Mariana, whose sudden death sets the novel's action in motion, there was absolutely nothing worse than imitation: she was a master at distinguishing between what was genuine and what was imitation, be it art, wine, or jewels, such as her pre-revolution emerald ring with which she never parted. Mariana's job at Gifted Child International consisted in finding real talents among Ukrainian children in the provinces and supporting their work as well as sometimes sending them to the West to get an education. Mariana's abhorrence of imitation stemmed partly from the "imitation epidemic" that had seized the post-Soviet Ukrainian society in which she lived: she saw most of the Kyiv elite as "pseudo-intellectual nobodies," capable only of pushing and shoving at various presentations and other social gatherings, lured there by the free refreshments (*Imitatsiia* 7, 14). In this vast sea of imitators, whose behaviour she viewed as a peculiar characteristic of *Homo Sovieticus*,[27] used to getting everything for free, Mariana prided herself on standing out as a real scholar, a genuine European intellectual, and a connoisseur of true talent.

Mariana's obsession with authenticity and the West as her model may be understood as a specifically post-Soviet desire that is also postcolonial. As David Chioni Moore suggested in "Is the Post- in Postcolonial the Post- in Post-Soviet? Toward a Global Postcolonial Critique" (briefly discussed in the introduction), this is a desire to claim as one's own "authentic source" of identity the Europe that was for decades inaccessible because of the Iron Curtain (118). In many post-Soviet countries, including Ukraine, this yearning resulted in the mimicry of the West – rather than the more usual postcolonial scenario in which, according to Moore, "subjugated peoples come to crave the dominating cultural form" (118). Moore saw in this total identification with Western Europe "a headlong westward sprint from colonial Russia's ghost or grasp" (118). Published in the same year as Kononenko's *Imitation*, the essay, like the novel, brought to light an important aspect of the psychological dynamics behind Ukraine's early post-Soviet transition. Twelve years later, the same (thwarted) desire for Europe and a European identity as an alternative to "colonial Russia's … grasp" would give initial impetus to the Euromaidan protests.

In the character of Mariana, Kononenko's novel points up the exaggerated nature and often dubious consequences of Ukrainian elites' actions, motivated by the post-Soviet postcolonial desire. The latter determines most of Mariana's behaviour, from her "super-Euro-apartment where Mariana decisively eliminated the kitchen as an element of the Soviet philistine subculture"; to her shocking pseudo-feminist pronouncements that love does not exist; to her choice of name for her son – Yuri – "so that even the sound of his name would usher him into the European context because in English that continent's name is pronounced 'Yurop,' *Europe*" (*Imitatsiia* 66, 107; emphasis in original). The post-Soviet postcolonial desire also explains Mariana's vision of the mission of Gifted Child International: unlike her friend and colleague, who wanted the foundation to support children's art and music institutions, "Mariana thought that such an approach would be Soviet-style levelling [*sovkova zrivnialivka*],[28] that the goal of the foundation was not to give social aid but to support the best of talents – that is, big grants for the most gifted, their personal exhibitions, concerts, their studies at prestigious schools" (76).

The reader gets Mariana's psychological portrait from her three friends – Ukrainian intellectuals from Kyiv – who are the novel's chief narrators and agents. They reminisce about Mariana as they write her obituaries, puzzled by her mysterious death, and finally decide to undertake a private investigation to learn what had really happened to their resourceful and tenacious friend in that remote provincial town in the Donetsk region. In the course of their investigation, readers gradually discover that Mariana's commitment to authenticity was in some cases less than principled, and that her desire for European values produced some doubtful results. For example, after many years abroad, her son Yuri had become what Mariana's friend Chekanchuk described as "a real specimen of *European upbringing*" (107; emphasis in original). He changed his name to George Moldanski, forgot his Ukrainian, and came to resemble, most of all, Mariana's pragmatic American boss and boyfriend with the telling name of Jerry Bist (Beast). "[I]f Yura-George is a real value, then I, in my forty years of life, haven't understood a thing about this world and its values," remarks Chekanchuk gloomily at one point (107).

Most importantly, what Mariana seemed not to notice, but what is revealed with increasing clarity as the investigation progresses, is that her "headlong westward sprint from colonial Russia's ghost," to use again Moore's formulation, led her to adopt a completely out-of-touch perspective from which she viewed her foundation work in the Eastern Ukrainian provinces. In fact, this was the perspective of her foreign boss, someone who cared about the local circumstances only as much as they could hinder the achievement of the foundation's goals. For instance, Mariana's friend Ryzhenko recalls her complaint about the difficulties in working out an efficient strategy for the foundation's work:

> Usually, in order to discover gifted children in the countries of *the Third World*, information on grants is sent to art and music schools, municipal councils and religious communities, and the data from there is sent to the Headquarters. But in Ukraine this strategy doesn't work because everyone is very clever and all are used to getting a free ride. They are flooded with absolutely irrelevant applications and were forced to take on two more employees who handle nothing else but rejections, after which they receive complaints and sometimes even threats. (10–11; emphasis in original)

Mariana's overwhelming concern for lessening the workload of the Headquarters and her own branch to the exclusion of local needs, which are dismissed with a disdainful characterization of her compatriots as "very clever" [*duzhe hramotni*] and used to "a free ride" [*na khaliavu*], speak volumes of her priorities. As the novel makes clear, the local needs in the provinces were usually very basic, and the foundation's goals were often a good match for these needs only by accident. Such was the case of the funeral the foundation had organized once upon the death of their young beneficiary from a provincial town: "Gifted Child International ... sponsored the funeral dinner in the town cafeteria, and there was a lot of food, and children got chocolate bars, and all the local inhabitants were very grateful to the young deceased boy because everyone ate their fill and took food home. The half-starved God-forsaken little town in the Kharkiv region hasn't had such a nutritious meal in a long time" (17–18).

Even Mariana's talent-scouting trips to the Eastern provinces, during which she had a chance to observe their life up close, did not alter her perspective. Her insensitivity to, and even contempt for, the horrifying conditions of life in these provinces ultimately led to her violent death. However, the readers get their own chance to become familiar with provincial life during the investigation, an investigation which takes Mariana's friends into the heart of a place ravaged by poverty and neglect. Setting a lot of her detective novel in the provinces of the Donetsk region was an important choice on the part of Kononenko; as literary scholar Stephen Knight writes in *Form and Ideology in Crime Fiction*, "[s]election of setting is a crucial ideological feature in crime fiction" (94). Knight uses the example of the Sherlock Holmes stories to demonstrate how the setting can be used for conservative ends: "The real threat to respectable life posed by the grim areas where the working-class and the 'dangerous classes' lived is thoroughly subdued ... When the plot needs to recognise such people and such areas, which is not often, Holmes goes among them, frequently in disguise, but the story does not go with him" (94). This omission allows the Holmes stories to preserve for their middle-class readership a comforting illusion of safety in their city. Kononenko, by contrast, takes a significant portion of her story to these "grim areas" of Eastern Ukraine and lets her readers see them, albeit through the eyes of the Kyiv elite. From their perspective, which is informed by their post-Soviet postcolonial desire and is also shown to have a strong class underpinning, provincial towns in Eastern Ukraine and their population look like the epitome of "Sovietness":

> Despite the fact that Novozhakhiv (New Horrorville) recently celebrated its 250th anniversary, no traces of its past as an old district town have been preserved. There were a few nondescript five-storied apartment blocks and your standard *miskvykonkom* (city hall), department store, and a recreation centre – all made out of concrete. The rest of the town consisted of village-type huts, varied in the level of shabbiness they displayed. From the bus station, Chekanchuk set out immediately for the NCAC – the New Horrorville Children's Art Centre, with the director of which, Maria Vasylivna, he was acquainted – she had come to Kyiv before to seek the support of the foundation. At the NCAC, they had already heard about the death in Kombinatne and didn't know how to react – whether to invite a priest to sprinkle the premises with holy water or to hold a moment of silence. So for now they haven't done anything – they were waiting for instructions [*chekaly vkazivky*]. (*Imitatsiia* 31)

Kononenko might have overdone it with naming the town Novozhakhiv (New Horrorville), but it is exactly how Mariana and her friends perceive it – as a surreal post-Soviet reality, depressing in its poverty, dirt, ideological confusion, and, as later scenes reveal, disease and crime. Through such scenes, given from the Kyiv elite's perspective, Eastern Ukrainian provinces emerge as Ukraine's still-Soviet, and therefore backward, internal Other. This becomes clear even from the humorous detail about the Centre employees' confused reaction to Mariana's death, when they hesitate about which ideological model to apply to the situation – the Soviet one or the Christian one (in fact, neither would be appropriate for Mariana). Tellingly, their default response is to "wait for instructions" from the authorities – a typically subservient Soviet reaction.

It is interesting that the Otherness of Eastern Ukrainian provinces in the eyes of the Kyiv elite is constructed in terms of "Sovietness," provinciality, and class rather than ethnicity. Eastern Ukraine (as well as Southern Ukraine and the Crimea), compared with Western and Central Ukraine, has a greater concentration of ethnic Russians and predominant use of Russian; however, language is not an issue in the novel. Characters from the Eastern region speak *surzhyk*[29] or attempt to speak correct Ukrainian for the sake of visitors, but this is not what makes them the Other in the Kyiv elite's perspective – most likely, because Kyiv itself is both Ukrainian- and Russian-speaking. In a paper from the mid-2000s, historian John Paul Himka called the "identity formation" he saw taking root in Kyiv at the time "the Euro-Ukrainian identity" (495). The name is very fitting for Kononenko's portrayal of the Kyiv elite in *Imitation*. Ultimately, the central object of Kononenko's critique is the tendency of some representatives of this identity position, who are motivated by the post-Soviet postcolonial desire, to construct the Eastern region as Ukraine's internal Other. Of course, the most recent political events in Ukraine, and especially the war in the Donbas, gave Kononenko's early critique of this trend special urgency.

Kononenko puts forth her critique in an unexpected way, making use of a special subgenre of detective fiction. Carl Malmgren, a scholar of murder fiction, subdivides this popular literature genre into three types – mystery fiction, detective fiction, and crime fiction – according to their "narrative dominants" (118). If mystery fiction focuses on "the investigation and solution of the mystery … generated by an initial crime" and detective fiction "foregrounds the actions and adventures of the investigating hero," the narrative dominant of crime fiction "is the character of its central protagonist," who is usually "implicated in the crime" and from whose perspective the narrative "unfolds" (121, 127). Because the readers are given no other perspective, they are forced to identify with "the problematic Self" of crime fiction, becoming "the narrative's accomplice" (129–30). This makes a work of crime fiction, as Malmgren explains, "more a subject to be experienced, less an object to be known" and creates a reading experience that "is decidedly disturbing, disquieting, even disorienting" (131).

Imitation is a subtle example of crime fiction, as defined by Malmgren. It gives almost all of the narrating authority to Mariana's three friends, Kyiv intellectuals who conduct the investigation. The reader has no choice but to identify with them and with the play of their post-Soviet postcolonial desire, which makes them see the Eastern provinces as Ukraine's internal Other. Although they see the poverty-stricken post-Soviet life in these provinces up close, they do not engage in any social analysis of these circumstances, which is something rarely done in conventional detective stories anyway. As literary scholar William Stowe explains, in classical examples of the detective genre, "crime is usually seen as a symptom of personal evil rather than social injustice," therefore a detective story "celebrates community by defining it as a relatively innocent 'we' over against a clearly guilty 'other'" (570, 574).

In the end, Mariana's three friends and colleagues interpret her murder as the result of the young boy's personal pathologies, caused in part by his poverty, which, however, they do not see as having much to do with "social injustice" (Stowe 570). The final scenes of the novel take place back in Kyiv, with their little investigative community gathered over a festive meal, celebrating the New Year and the successful conclusion of their so-called search for truth. As they discuss the disappearance of the little criminal and benevolently pronounce, "let him go on living, if he can" (*Imitatsiia* 179), there is no doubt that they see themselves "as a relatively innocent 'we' over against a clearly guilty 'other,'" as Stowe put it. It is at this point especially that the reader's identification with them feels most disturbing, jolting him or her out of the easy, escapist mode of reading, for which conventional murder mysteries are intended.

Ultimately, *Imitation* not only made visible the internal boundaries on the map of independent Ukraine, but also let readers experience the disquieting and indeed dangerous psychological dynamics of othering, which to some extent created and reinforced such boundaries.[30] Mariana ended up being murdered on an internal boundary partly of her own making – between "Euro-Ukraine" and the hopelessly backward and still-Soviet Eastern Ukrainian provinces. The liminal space of the train tracks, leading from New Horrorville back to Kyiv, symbolically represented this boundary in the novel.

In light of the recent events in the Donbas, Kononenko's 2001 portrayal of internal division within Ukraine appears to be remarkably – and sadly – prescient. It suggests that the main fault line between the Donbas region and Ukraine's centre is not due to ethnic or linguistic difference, but rather stems from a lengthy post-Soviet history of growing mutual alienation. This fault line was, of course, fully exploited by Russia and the local separatists in the wake of Ukraine's Euromaidan protests.

The novel shows Mariana to be at once a victim and a perpetrator – a complex female character who is an active, if misguided, producer of her national culture. It is, of course, profoundly ironic that Mariana's efforts on behalf of her nation turn out to be a rather poor imitation of Western models. In this respect, *Imitation* appears to present the post-Soviet Ukrainian equivalent of postcolonial mimic men (as first portrayed in *Mimic Men* by postcolonial writer V.S. Naipaul) – except it places at its centre a mimic *woman*. What this woman mimics, among other things, are Western feminist ideas about women's emancipation, career focus, and sexual liberation, but with them, she also adopts some of the elitist bias of Western feminism and the tendency to uncritically apply Western models to the post-Soviet space. Kononenko, who considers herself a feminist, is not poking fun at Western feminism in this novel. Instead, she simply underscores the foolishness of blind imitation of any kinds of behavioural models from elsewhere, without taking local circumstances into account. The national and gender aspects of the novel come together poignantly in the romantic plotline of *Imitation*. I will discuss it briefly in the next chapter while comparing Kononenko's novel to Zabuzhko's *The Museum of Abandoned Secrets*. Both works make use of the same narrative devices to emplot their national stories – a reverse national biography through women's deaths and a national romance – yet they do so to very different effect.

5
Excavating the (Gendered) Nation: Oksana Zabuzhko's Museum Novel

Of the four foundational national narratives examined in this study, Zabuzhko's 2009 novel, *The Museum of Abandoned Secrets*, is not only the longest and most ambitious, but also the most mythical. It comes closest to Anderson's definition of a national biography, which through an "archaeological" writing from the present into the past uncovers deaths and ascribes to them a national meaning, remembering them as "our own." Yet even this novel depicts some unconventional women's roles in the nation: as my analysis in this chapter demonstrates, the female characters whose deaths are investigated by the novel's protagonist are not mere symbols of Ukraine or its past suffering.[1] *The Museum of Abandoned Secrets* (hereafter *Museum*) may also be seen as a Ukrainian "national romance" – akin to the foundational fictions described by Doris Sommer in her study of Latin American literature. The novel's central plotline brings together a woman from Central Ukraine and a man from Western Ukraine in a happy and sexually fulfilling union (a far cry from Zabuzhko's *Fieldwork*!) that is clearly meant to cement in the reader's imagination a symbolic vision of Ukraine as a unified national community.

What makes this national narrative interesting is its critical inquiry into how history is produced, an inquiry achieved via the novel's engagement with concepts and institutions of the museum and the archive. In the process of telling a national story, Zabuzhko's text highlights not only the subjective and necessarily incomplete nature of history, but also the national imaginary's dependence on literature, especially if it is the imaginary of a postcolonial nation. The novel's other point of interest for the purposes of this study is Zabuzhko's construction of Ukraine's Soviet past and post-Soviet present as one continuous gendered history, a history in which many men have usurped and abused positions of power. This chapter will explore each of these aspects of *Museum* in turn, and will briefly contrast it with Kononenko's *Imitation*, which was analysed more fully in the previous chapter.

Unearthing Ukraine's "Album of Ancestors"

By her own admission, Zabuzhko conceived *Museum* as a novel about "the connection of the times" (Teren). Indeed, this 820-page text weaves together several storylines that unfold in Ukraine between the 1940s and the early 2000s, and bridges the Soviet/post-Soviet divide through a focus on its characters' daily lives, their perceptions of the present, and their memories and explorations of the past. To a great extent, *Museum* combines most of the historical and present-day themes of the three previously examined national narratives: wartime and post-war conflict between the UPA and the Soviet MGB in Western Ukraine; Ukraine's ethnic and regional diversity, and its divisive past; the historical role of women as subjects; Kyiv's Euro-Ukrainian identity, and so on. It also adds many other themes. In this sense, Zabuzhko's text is truly a monumental and "national" work – in what may be seen as a hybrid genre of a museum novel.

In *Stalinist Cinema and the Production of History*, Slavic studies scholar Evgeny Dobrenko theorizes the museum's handling of history and argues that "[t]he museum is above all not a collection but a composition – a conception of the past, an ideological montage. The fundamental characteristic of all the functions of the museum is the appropriation of history" (8). By its very title, Zabuzhko's novel claims the museum's appropriative power regarding the past, and because it is a self-proclaimed "museum," the novel accesses and constructs history primarily by meditating and commenting on various real objects from the past – especially photographs. In so doing, it strives for "authenticity," appearing to subscribe to Walter Benjamin's famous maxim that "History does not break down into stories but into images." However, because it is, after all, a novel, it uses the photographs and other artefacts, which it "puts on display," as starting points for storytelling. Out of them, through her characters' accounts and their explanations of how these stories were or could not be unearthed, Zabuzhko fashions for contemporary Ukraine what Anderson called a common "album of ancestors," which, however, is necessarily – and explicitly – fragmentary (255). This is the chief difference between Zabuzhko's *Museum* and conventional historical museums, especially those of the Soviet era: while the latter tend to present a comprehensive narrative, with gaps disguised by what Dobrenko calls "ideological montage," the former underscores both the gaps and many of the techniques of putting a narrative together.

Museum focuses on the stories from three generations that lived in Ukraine between the mid-twentieth and early twenty-first centuries, and in most of these stories women are the central characters. These narratives are pieced together by the novel's protagonist – the Ukrainian television journalist Daryna Hoshchynska, who is on a personal mission to uncover various buried and abandoned secrets of her own and of her nation's past. Among the more important mysteries is the personality of Daryna's deceased father, a talented Kyiv architect who was placed in the Soviet psychiatric clinic as punishment for his staunch defence against the authorities in Moscow of the initial project of the Kyiv concert hall known as Palace "Ukraine."[2] Another key mystery surrounds the circumstances behind the car accident that killed Daryna's lifelong female friend Vladyslava (Vlada), a famous Ukrainian painter, in the late 1990s. Yet another important secret is linked to a curious photograph from the 1940s portraying a group of the UPA partisans and prominently featuring a woman among the male insurgents. In the novel's various chapters, dubbed "halls" (as in "museum halls"), some of the mysteries get solved, some receive only hypothetical or even mystical explanations, and some remain locked forever, to the chagrin of the curious and enterprising Daryna.

What Zabuzhko's "museum" then strives to put on display is not a totalizing knowledge of the past, but rather the very process by which partial knowledge of the past may or may not be discovered. The point of access to this knowledge is seemingly insignificant objects, memories, and scraps of writing. Thus, when Daryna finds the single word, "This!!!," followed by three exclamation points, scribbled in the margins of one of her father's books, next to a sentence that speaks of Hamlet's indecisiveness in the face of evil, she feels that this word gives her a tiny glimpse into the personality of her father and into his assessment of his own position vis-à-vis the Soviet regime. Small things like this one word in the margin of a book, which, incidentally, is turned into the name of this museum novel's first "hall," become the narrator's clues to the past:

> Since then I have more faith in misplaced trifles than in rehearsed stories, which always feel like something gutted, stuffed, and roasted before being served for me to gobble up … I know that these excavated remains of vanished civilizations, the many, many civilizations that had once existed under people's names, do not lie. If we have any hope of understanding anything about another's life, this *this!!!* is it. We've heard all the other stories before, thank you very much, and we're sick of them. (*Museum* 34–5; emphasis in original)[3]

At the same time, Zabuzhko's heroine is perfectly aware that her own uses of these clues result in nothing other than stories. As a journalist, she understands the alluring power of the story, yet is also committed to the truth. Thus, when her friend and famous painter's tragic death in an automobile accident causes unsubstantiated rumours to spread among the Kyiv elite, Daryna both passionately fends off suspicions and realizes wherefrom they are coming:

> … and it took me more than a few months … to learn not to blush like a ripe tomato and screech mean things, quite without composure, every time someone asked me the question, with its probing emphasis, "Are you sure it was an accident?" – more than a few months to grasp that it was not truth people asked for, whatever it ultimately turned out to be, but a story. Amen. And who am I, who makes a living manufacturing such stories, to judge them? (78)

Drawing attention to the mechanisms by which stories, including stories of the past, get constructed is a strategy Zabuzhko uses throughout the novel in order to deal with the anxiety about making the leap from objects to narratives, which is the conventional museum's standard operation. As Dobrenko explains, "museumification is the process of selection of what has been constituted as 'history' (collection), the assembly from this selection of a coherent picture of the world (conservation), and the advancement of this picture into the space beyond the museum (exhibition)" (12). At one point, Zabuzhko shows the related work of selection/collection and exhibition in the ideological medium of television, in which her principal character works. One of the "halls" includes a description of Daryna's television interview with her friend Vlada (not long before her death) from the point of view of the camera-eye, so to speak. This objectifying description of the two young women in conversation differs considerably from what Daryna herself perceives as a participant of this interview. Such a contrast lays bare the process in which the TV camera, not unlike the museum, produces power: according to the museum studies scholar Kevin Walsh, this is "the power of the gaze, an ability to observe, name and order, and thus control" (32). In addition, the interview account contains a number of parenthetical comments, presumably made mentally by Daryna to herself, indicating the parts of the interview that will be later edited out. This element of the narrative, of course, highlights the process of ideological montage typical both of documentaries and museums.

Zabuzhko's own, final, narrative in *Museum* is a similar montage, although one self-consciously constructed and full of gaps. This becomes apparent in the way the novel's most important mystery – that of an elegant-looking young woman portrayed on a photograph from the 1940s among a group of Ukrainian male insurgents – gets solved. Because none of those pictured in the photo are alive, Daryna goes on a wild goose chase all over Ukraine to find any surviving relatives of the insurgents or archival evidence of them. Daryna's attempts to obtain any information about these partisans from the archives of the Ukrainian Security Service (formerly the KGB) in Kyiv fail because the records she needs were either transferred to Moscow or burned in the summer of 1991, when the KGB was hastily destroying the incriminating evidence of the Soviet liquidation of the Ukrainian Insurgent Army's units in Western Ukraine. The story that she finally pieces together from interviews with the young woman's surviving relatives, from chance conversations with a former KGB agent, and from her own conjectures is full of unknowns.

However, the most important part of the story – its imaginative, emotional portrayal of and inner perspective on events – comes to Daryna through the mysterious dreams of her boyfriend, who is the nephew of the woman in the photograph. Adrian (Daryna's partner) repeatedly sees coherent, vivid dreams about the underground existence of his aunt and her male colleagues, pictured in the photograph. In these dreams, Adrian "is" one of the male partisans. The dreams seem so real that he actually speculates about the possibility of an existence somewhere "out there" of an enormous virtual archive containing the filmed experiences of everyone who ever existed – from their point of view. It seems to him that what he sees are not dreams, but rather the "film reel" of that one male partisan's life.

The archive is an important topos in postcolonial literatures and cultures. Literary scholar Julie Mullaney explains that the "interest" of postcolonial writing in both "history" and "'metahistory,' the analysis of processes of historical inquiry informing the 'writing' of history" come together in "the image and idea of the archive" (38–9). The topos of the archive in Zabuzhko's narrative serves exactly this function. On the one hand, the unavailable or burnt archives of the Soviet era underscore the impossibility of uncovering the history of some controversial episodes in Ukraine's colonial past. On the other hand, Adrian's phantasmatic concept of the complete, unedited dream/film archive of every person's life from their perspective (which would be a perfect archive, if it existed!) points up the existing archives' shortcomings. Mullaney identifies them as "the selective, contradictory and powerful technologies embedded in the construction and maintenance of the archive as a repository of knowledge" (39). The fact that Daryna and Adrian actually make use of this "dream archive" to fill in the blanks in the story of the female insurgent makes this story highly subjective and fictional. Yet it also highlights what an important role imagination – and imaginative literature as one of its sources and products – plays in the making of the national imaginary: because none of us have access to the "dream archive," we inevitably rely on our own imagination and on fiction to help us conjure up the many past and present lives of individuals in the nation.

The story about the female insurgent Helia, which Daryna uncovers, and some missing pieces from which she imagines with the help of Adrian's "dream archive," is a violent story of death and betrayal. In 1947, the commander of the little group of insurgents in the photograph, whose child the female insurgent was carrying, gave out the information about the group's location in the forest to the MGB – in exchange for his life and the life of pregnant Helia. When the MGB came to arrest the insurgents, the entire group, including Helia, refused to surrender and came out of the bunker with hand grenades, blowing up themselves and some of the MGB operatives. It is significant that Zabuzhko herself undertook detailed historical research and collected some oral histories from the surviving UPA veterans both to plot this story and to write Adrian's dreams for the "dream archive." There is little doubt that the story of Helia and her insurgent group is a plausible one, true to the ethos of the UPA and the historical circumstances of those times. Women were active participants in the armed resistance, and although less numerous than the men, they were nevertheless a significant presence. In *The Nation*, Matios also includes female guerrilla insurgents, but Zabuzhko's narrative, unlike Matios's stories, shows a woman in combat. Helia's death does acquire a "national" meaning in the novel: unlike the remaining male insurgents in her group, who have only two choices – to die in battle or to be arrested and tortured in a Soviet prison – Helia has the option of being freed because of the commander's deal with the MGB. Yet she chooses to die rather than betray her ideals. This death, however, is a conscious choice of an active subject in the nation rather than a symbol of the victimized nation. Moreover, what Helia chooses in these extreme circumstances is a decidedly "unfeminine" role – that of a fighter rather than a mother.

What the "dream archive" adds to this story is mostly an internal perspective on these events of another male insurgent, which allows the reader to better understand the motivations, ideals, and problems of the UPA, and this, in turn, humanizes the insurgents, but does not idealize them. These dream sequences show, for example, the cruelty and abuse of power by the group's commander, the daily witnessing of death, the internal disagreements, and the frightening realization that if the brutal conflict with the MGB continues for much longer, there will be few civilians left to defend. *Museum* also offers the perspective of the opposite side through Daryna's long conversation with a former KGB agent, who is an adopted son of an MGB operative. He is not portrayed as a villain in the novel, but rather a product of his time and a strict, sometimes abusive upbringing by his father. His tale also allows the reader to understand the motivations and the reasoning of those serving in the MGB.

Museum's mythical national narrative thus emerges mostly not from the "historical" dream sequences or the present-day discussions about the past by the novel's characters, but rather from the way in which Zabuzhko emplots these figures and events from the past into the present-day narrative. She does it through the tropes of the family and family genealogy, both biological and "spiritual." As Anne McClintock points out, "nations are symbolically figured as domestic genealogies" ("No Longer in a Future Heaven" 262). *Museum* takes full advantage of the symbolic potential of such a figuring: on its very first page, it features a three-generation family tree of Daryna and a similar family tree for Adrian. As these two characters form Zabuzhko's national romance couple, they bring two different regional histories – those from the West and the East of Ukraine – into a unified romantic and familial plot. The female insurgent Helia is Adrian's aunt, and Daryna meets Adrian through her professional interest in Helia's story. When at the end of the novel Daryna finds out that she is pregnant, she and Adrian think of their child as a "spiritual" heir to Helia's unborn child. In a further twist of Zabuzhko's convoluted national family plot, it turns out that the former KGB agent with whom Daryna spoke was the biological son of another female insurgent fighter, who had died in prison, and of the male partisan whose life Adrian "saw" in his dreams. Thus, through the symbolism of family genealogy, Zabuzhko suggests that independent Ukraine really is "the child of Ukrainian nationalists," as Marples put it, denying any lineage connections between it and Soviet Ukraine. This kind of symbolic dynamic in the novel may be understood as a form of ideological montage in itself, and this is the kind of montage which Zabuzhko's *Museum* does disguise – by figuring the author's preferred political affiliations as "natural" family filiations.

The "album of ancestors," which Zabuzhko constructs for postcolonial Ukraine as an alternative to official Soviet history, also includes Daryna's late father and her recently deceased friend Vlada. As in Helia's case, many pages in the novel detail Daryna's attempts to comprehend these individuals' stories by discovering the meaning behind their deaths. Such a focus is paramount for Zabuzhko's alternative history project, which may be understood in one sense as a search for an articulated and heroic history of Ukraine – rather than one of silence and continuous victimization. In the novel, it is Daryna who expresses the need for a reconsideration of history when she thinks about her father's seemingly ignoble end in a provincial psychiatric clinic as one of countless, hidden victims of the Soviet regime. The ordinary causes of death, indicated in the Soviet death certificates of so many Ukrainians like Daryna's father, disguised their lives of heroic, even if ultimately failed, resistance to the colonial system. Daryna's passionate desire to piece together her father's real-life story stems from a belated realization that this system had robbed her of her own history and honourable memory about her father.

In contrast to both Helia and Daryna's father, Vlada at first appears to have died a random, if tragic, death that cannot possibly have any kind of "national" meaning. Through discussions with Vlada's boyfriend and in the process of her search for her friend's paintings, which had disappeared from the site of the car crash, Daryna gains glimpses into possible reasons for the crash. Yet Vlada's death eventually receives another hypothetical explanation, suggested by people who live near the crash site. They tell Daryna that many decades earlier that stretch of the highway was the site of a mass grave for the victims of the Holodomor, and that many car accidents occur there every year. Daryna, in turn, remembers that Vlada's parents were rumoured to have participated in the collectivization campaigns in Central Ukraine during the famine. She also sees a strange dream in which the deceased Vlada reappears and complains to her about "very many deaths." Thus, Vlada's death appears to be connected to the national past after all by some mystical ties of familial retribution. As Vira Aheieva writes about contemporary Ukrainian literature that restores the memory of the past, "[t]he sins and crimes of the parents unexpectedly turn into curses for the children, and an otherworldly cold wind blows from the black holes of history" ("Pislia karnavalu" 346–7).

In a recent analysis of *Museum*, Tamara Hundorova denies Zabuzhko's novel any "mythogenic" capacity because, in her view, it does not link the family histories it recounts to "national myths" ("Uiava i pam'iat'" 138). Yet a focus on how Zabuzhko's novel makes sense of the three main deaths investigated in it – those of Helia, Daryna's father, and Vlada – permits one to see that *Museum* does connect these individuals and their family stories to important historical phenomena that have acquired the status of foundational national myths in independent Ukraine. These are the UPA, the Holodomor, and dissidence in Soviet Ukraine. In fact, Zabuzhko very consciously emplots *Museum* in a way that would lay mythic foundations for a nation that has not been in a position to write its own history until very recently. "The Museum of Abandoned Secrets" of the novel's title therefore refers to all of Ukraine – a nation with many little known or yet unresolved historical traumas, which continue to haunt its often unsuspecting present-day subjects and influence their daily lives in profound ways. This central metaphor is what links all of *Museum*'s characters, even minor ones, who are not incorporated into the symbolic national family plot. The novel's protagonist, Daryna Hoshchynska, is not only the chief figure in Zabuzhko's symbolic genealogies, but also an investigator and an analyst of the nation's Soviet past. And despite her awareness and frequent laying bare of the ideological montage involved in composing narratives, the stories she uncovers and imagines come together as a national narrative of mythical proportion.

National Romance and Gendered History

The picture of Ukraine that Zabuzhko paints in *Museum* would be completely grim were it not for the novel's heroic figures and its romantic plot. In depicting in the present the positive love relationship between Daryna and Adrian, and by emphasizing its strength and potential, Zabuzhko counterbalances the bleak and bloody Ukrainian past with a hope of a better national future. She thus endows this love story with the elements of a foundational national romance. This type of romance is a fairly new development in the literature of the independent Ukrainian nation-state. The plotline surrounding Daryna and Adrian's egalitarian relationship is a utopian narrative that embodies the idealized imagining of the nation as a unified and "horizontal" community of equals, to use Anderson's term (*Imagined Communities* 7). Hogan also sees in the romantic emplotment of nationalism clear democratic implications "in favor of individual freedom and choice" (307).

In this respect, it is interesting to juxtapose Zabuzhko's *Museum* with Kononenko's *Imitation*. Both novels are plotted as reverse national narratives and as national romances, yet to completely different effect. The investigation of Mariana's murder in *Imitation* reveals profound internal divisions within Ukraine, divisions which cannot be symbolically mended even through what appears to be the most genuine of national romances. Kononenko utilizes an interrupted national romance plot to underscore the depth of this internal boundary in Ukraine. Mariana, who has an American boyfriend in Kyiv, falls in love with a poor music teacher, Anatoliy, from a provincial town in the Donbas region. Their brief love affair ends when Mariana perishes on the train tracks in a small Donbas town. Anatoliy himself dies a violent death because of his involvement with Mariana: suspecting him of secretly pocketing the foundation's money supposedly given by Mariana to support the music school, one of the schoolteachers sends her drunk husband to confront Anatoliy. In a moment of panic, the man kills Anatoliy. Mariana and Anatoliy's love relationship – which is, ironically, the most genuine aspect of Mariana's life – briefly gives the reader the hope of symbolically unifying Donbas with Kyiv, but quickly takes that hope away. Unlike Zabuzhko's national romance, a utopian one that supplies a unifying egalitarian myth for the Ukrainian national imaginary, Kononenko's only points up the regional and class-based internal divisions within the nation.

This is not to say that *Museum* ignores divisions and conflicts in Ukraine's post-Soviet present. Zabuzhko's utopian portrayal of Daryna and Adrian's romance is set against the background of a realistic depiction of Ukraine's past and present society, in which gender inequality is shown to be a major factor. In the course of the novel, Zabuzhko's female protagonist gradually realizes that there exist numerous parallels between Ukraine's Soviet past and its post-Soviet present, and a crucial one is the continued usurping of political power by men. *Museum* demonstrates how history has been made by men, particularly through their abuse of power.

Such a portrayal in *Museum* comes through in three structurally similar conversations that Daryna has with different men in power during both the Soviet and the post-Soviet eras. In fact, Daryna is able to successfully navigate the later, post-Soviet conversations because she can draw on her experience in a similar situation in 1987 with a captain of the KGB.[4] Her memory of how the captain attempted to recruit her to inform on her university friends helps Daryna in new, ethically questionable post-Soviet situations. Relying on that memory, she is able to stand up to the director of the independent television station where she works, when in the early 2000s, amid partial return of mass media censorship under Leonid Kuchma's presidency in Ukraine, the channel is bought by some rich members of the new post-Soviet economic elite. When Daryna's boss gives her a long and vague speech about the channel's new format and her chance to become its "face," promising her a prime time slot and a salary unheard of in post-Soviet Ukrainian television, Daryna recalls how similarly the KGB captain "prattled about who-knows-what for two hours straight, like wind blowing sand at her from all sides at once, and then offered her an opportunity to 'cooperate'" (222). This recollection prompts Daryna to be cautious and ask more questions about the sources of the channel's future financing. When her boss finally mentions the plan of the channel's owners to launch a TV beauty pageant, Daryna suddenly intuits from his veiled explanations that this beauty pageant is meant to recruit girls to be used later in a sex-trafficking scheme, and that the high salary he promised her would be coming out of its profits.[5] Like the KGB captain, the channel's director asks that their conversation remain between them, but Daryna not only rejects his offer of "cooperation," but also vows to interfere in her boss's despicable scheme.

Distrusting police officials, Daryna turns to Vlada's former boyfriend, Vadym, who is a member of the Ukrainian parliament and the only individual with real political power whom she knows. Yet her conversation with Vadym suddenly begins to follow the pattern of the previous two. Vadym dismisses Daryna's story about the sex-trafficking scheme, responding that he has "more important affairs to attend to" – business "of the state" (355). And when Daryna retorts in anger that she could not care less about a state in which sex trafficking becomes "the norm," Vadym replies that she should be more "realistic" (355). Then, like the KGB captain and the channel's director, Vadym gives Daryna a long, confusing lecture (this time the topic is "successful" state politics) and makes her an offer of "cooperation." He invites her to work as his public relations agent in the upcoming electoral campaign, which would mean implementing some of the questionable PR techniques he had advocated earlier in the conversation.

Very similar meetings with men in power (the KGB) are also depicted by Andrukhovych in *The Moscoviad*. The encounter between the (Soviet) state and the people in post-Soviet fiction seems to be habitually emplotted as a confusing "cooperation conversation" – a modern equivalent of the traditional "deal with the devil" motif.[6] However, if Andrukhovych and other writers use this motif in depictions of the Soviet state only, Zabuzhko, through the parallelism between the Soviet and post-Soviet conversations with men in power, suggest its applicability across the Soviet/post-Soviet divide.

Zabuzhko's heroine comes to think of men's abuses of power in Ukraine as characteristic only of a certain category of men (and, theoretically, of women as well, although *Museum* does not show such female characters). These are men who seem "strong" when, in fact, they are just unscrupulous opportunists, quickly adjusting to any change in regime for their own benefit. *Museum* puts together a mini rogue gallery of male characters from different historical periods and regions of Ukraine, and from different professions and political affiliations.

Significantly, Daryna also attributes some of the blame for the deaths of Helia and Vlada to such men. From conversations with Vadym, she gathers that the couple had conflicts and that Vlada had left their common apartment in a terrible emotional state on the day of the crash. Daryna ends up blaming Vadym for inadvertently causing Vlada's death, and she considers it to be Vlada's fatal mistake to have trusted Vadym in the first place. Daryna also reads Helia's death in similar gendered terms – as a result of Helia placing her trust in a seemingly powerful yet ultimately cowardly and unworthy man, one who ended up betraying their insurgent group.

These powerful, yet corrupt, men stand in contrast to Adrian and other positive or neutral male characters, who, however, are not in positions of power. The plot of *Museum* ends several months before the Orange Revolution, and its final note is one of anticipated positive change: political power in Ukraine may be in the hands of unscrupulous men, but its main characters display hope that there are enough honest and politically engaged people in Ukraine to resist these men's most egregious abuses of power.

Zabuzhko also writes strong and positive women characters into her foundational national narrative. In Daryna and Vlada, she creates complex heroines who take an active part in the making of their society. Daryna and Vlada represent a fairly new type of female character in Ukrainian literature. They are outspoken women intellectuals and independent cultural producers, who through their work (television journalism for Daryna and experimental visual art for Vlada) attempt to critique and remake their nation and its culture from within. The women are very aware of the impact of their cultural roles: as Daryna says to Vlada during the interview, Vlada's art as well as the fact of its international recognition help transform Ukrainians' imaginings of themselves.

Daryna's and Vlada's worldviews and life choices differ radically from those of the previous generation of women. For instance, Daryna notes that her mother harbours a profound mistrust towards "political concepts": she "still doesn't know the difference between liberalism and democracy, or what a civil society is – they're all men's games for her, only relevant to her own life inasmuch as they can one day ruin it" (*Museum* 245). The comment about "men's games" is telling: on the one hand, it supports Zabuzhko's portrayal of men's power struggles, and on the other, it reveals why women by and large have not intervened into these "games." By contrast, Daryna does attempt to interrupt some of the men's corrupt political and economic plots, as her conversations with her boss and Vadym demonstrate. And even though Vadym at first declines to do anything about the sex-trafficking scheme, Daryna's intervention does produce a positive result in the end – ironically, when Vadym spreads information about the scheme as part of the negative PR campaign against his political opponents. Yet Daryna, much like Zabuzhko herself, does not enter the political arena, preferring the role of a cultural producer and critic.[7]

As my exploration of Zabuzhko's *Museum* demonstrates, this museum novel was constructed as a national romance; an "archaeology" of (mostly) women's deaths, considered in light of both national and gender concerns; and a gendered history of abuse of power. By combining all these plots, Zabuzhko strove to maintain a double, simultaneous focus on gender and the nation, as she also did in *Fieldwork*. This standpoint was dubbed "national feminism" by Tatiana Zhurzhenko.[8] One of several strands of feminist critique in contemporary Ukraine, national feminism is concerned with both gender equality and the process of post-Soviet democratic nation-building. Yet national feminism, Zhurzhenko points out, is not a fusion of feminism and nationalism. It "emerge[d] as a result of a demarcation between the nationalist mainstream and its inevitable thrust of women into private life on the one hand, and on the other, the Western feminist tradition with its cosmopolitan trajectory" ("Feminist (De)Constructions" 176). The discourses of Western feminism, which tend to distance themselves from "the national question" altogether (with the exception of the postcolonial feminist critique), have not been seen by national feminists as entirely applicable in Ukraine, where democratic nation-building is still such a pressing problem (176).

In a society where, according to Marian Rubchak, "feminism remains largely an elite concern" ("In Search of a Model" 158) and gender inequality often goes unrecognized, Zabuzhko has managed to popularize national feminism, especially through her fiction.[9] This has been possible, in part, exactly because she does not only focus on women's issues, but also links them to what would be considered "significant" national problems, such as Ukrainians' provincial complexes, inherited from the Soviet era, and the corruption of the state. The risk of such a double focus is, of course, that the national issues will eclipse the gender issues in the works themselves or in their public reception. Zabuzhko has written about this particular problem in her essay "Zhinka-avtor u kolonial'nii kul'turi," where she diagnosed it as a specific challenge for a Ukrainian woman author both in the past and in the present.[10] In Zhurzhenko's summary of Zabuzhko's argument, "[b]y focusing exclusively on women's themes, she [a woman writer] avoids [what are seen as] the most urgent problems of the nation and thus marginalizes herself. Assuming the role of a [national] fighter, she finds herself repressed by a brutal masculine system of values" ("Feminist (De)Constructions" 181).

Museum has been usually read as a novel mostly about the nation, with much less attention devoted to its portrayal of gender roles or analysis of gender issues, thereby confirming the reception pattern outlined above. To what extent, however, does the novel's text itself justify such a reading? It is clear that Zabuzhko assigns to two of her principal women characters, Helia and Daryna, the role of a national "fighter": Helia fights, in the literal sense, as a UPA insurgent, while Daryna's struggle is more on the cultural and historical front. By investigating her nation's past, Daryna attempts to endow herself and her nation with a meaningful history. Both of these roles are somewhat unconventional for women. Daryna also takes up a more specifically feminist cause with her efforts to undermine her boss's sex-trafficking scheme. Yet at the same time, *Museum* presents both Daryna and Helia, as well as women more generally, in the traditional role of national reproducers.[11] In fact, Helia's and Daryna's pregnancies are linked to an explicitly articulated argument about motherhood being a special national "front" occupied by women. In this instance, Zabuzhko reiterates the conservative *Berehynia* plot, which somewhat undermines her efforts elsewhere in the novel to articulate new roles for women in the nation. Thus, to a certain degree, *Museum* mythologizes both women and Ukraine, even if it does not use women as mere symbols of the nation.

Laying Foundations for the Nation and National Writing

The four "national" works by Zabuzhko, Kononenko, and Matios analysed in this chapter and the previous one have garnered much attention from critics and readers in Ukraine and beyond, and have propelled their authors to the forefront of Ukrainian literary life, while carving out space for them in Ukraine's literary canon. Three of them received prestigious literary prizes,[12] all four have been translated into other languages, and two (*The Nation* and *Sweet Darusia* by Matios) have been adapted for the stage and/or the screen. Thus, it might be safe to say that these texts did make a contribution to Ukraine's national imaginary, even if their reception did not always take into account all the key meanings embedded within these texts. What foundations, then, do these foundational national narratives attempt to lay down?

First and foremost, all four works show, even by the very fact of their reverse, "archaeological" narration, that the clues to Ukraine's modern identity are to be found in its Soviet past, and especially in its most traumatic aspects, such as the Holodomor, the violent incorporation of Western Ukraine into the Soviet state, and the large-scale social transformations set into motion by the Soviet regime. All four texts also suggest that this past produced and continues to sustain internal divisions within Ukraine, divisions which the three authors attempt to address or resolve in a number of ways. Matios and Kononenko do so by revealing and critiquing the dynamics of othering involved in the creation and maintenance of such boundaries. Zabuzhko tries to help readers overcome the fractures in their national imaginings by resorting to the symbolic plot of a national romance. Matios and Zabuzhko also strive to create "bridges" over internal boundaries by presenting perspectives from both sides of the UPA-MGB confrontation. In addition, Matios holds up Bukovyna's pre–First World War legacy of multiculturalism and inter-ethnic connectedness as an example of unity in diversity.[13] These representational strategies ultimately show that these women writers consider Ukraine's national community in its pre-2014 borders to be a value absolutely worth preserving – despite the fact that the borders themselves were forged by the Soviet regime. At the same time, through their interventions in the national imaginary and their critique of hegemonic perspectives, writers like Kononenko and Matios advocate for more inclusive conceptions of a collective national identity – based on civic rather than ethnic models of the nation.

By focusing on complex, well-developed, and individualized women characters of all ages and social strata, the four texts often challenge the exploitative use of women as mere symbols of the nation. Through the character of Matronka, Matios critiques the role of symbolic national border guards ascribed to women, and shows how such conceptions endanger women's lives. Both Kononenko and Zabuzhko shift the standard nationalist narrative based on male heroes to one based on activist heroines (even if Zabuzhko also casts these heroines into the more traditional role of national reproducers). And all three authors not only attempt to make the nation "more hospitable to women's presence," to use Boehmer's formulation, but also present women's perspectives on the national past, present, and future, sometimes even giving their female characters the positions of cultural critics of the nation (*Stories of Women* 12).

The latter role is what the three writers have taken on by authoring their national narratives. It is telling that in all three cases, this move is exactly what gained these authors recognition as Ukrainian writers rather than "only" women writers. Zabuzhko's first novel on the subject of the nation – *Fieldwork* – despite its hostile reception, earned the author all-Ukrainian literary fame. Matios, who has been writing poetry and short stories for decades, only gained national popularity and acceptance into the Ukrainian literary canon after her publication of *The Nation* and *Sweet Darusia*. Similarly, although Kononenko was known in the narrow literary circles by her masterful short stories, a truly national literary reputation came to her when she turned to writing novels. This fact, of course, points up Ukrainian culture's continued, if perhaps decreasing, misunderstanding of and bias against women writers, as well as its obsession with all things national at present, but at least, the contemporary situation with women writers in Ukraine is a far cry from the late 1980s and very early 1990s, when both Kononenko and Zabuzhko wondered in their texts how a Ukrainian woman can write at all.

6

New National Chronicles: Women (Writers) on the Euromaidan

Arguably, since the collapse of the USSR the greatest changes in the Ukrainian national imaginary have been wrought not by texts, but rather by two waves of mass protests, the Orange Revolution and the Euromaidan, or the Revolution of Dignity. The kind of conceptual, abstract imagining of the national community that Anderson saw as being facilitated by novels and newspapers pales in comparison with the emotional and psychological bonds forged by the physical experience of standing together with hundreds of thousands of one's compatriots – in the same place, at the same time, and in the very name of one's community. As protesters themselves attested, participating in Kyiv's Maidan gave one "the feeling of special tactile connection – joined hands, simultaneous smiles, the feeling of incalculable importance of what was happening. Here we are all together, and all of us are the people of Ukraine, and it is we who are the country" (Dukhnich 8).

In the context of protests over issues that affected Ukrainians as citizens, this unforgettable experience of Maidan *communitas* transformed the collective consciousness of Ukrainians and brought various changes to Ukraine's public culture.[1] Analysts of the impact of the Orange Revolution wrote of Ukraine's "vibrant civil society" and "unprecedented media pluralism" (Wilson 322), whereas observers of the Euromaidan emphasized how the latter fostered widespread acceptance of the civic model of national identity in Ukraine. Marko Pavlyshyn as well as historian Marci Shore, among others, noted that the Euromaidan brought about a "civic turn" in the Ukrainian national imaginary.[2] This is evidenced by the fact that "except for part of the Donbas, the predominantly Russian-speaking parts of the country rejected secessionist initiatives inspired by the ethno-cultural ideology of the 'Russian World,' while the volunteers who enlisted in self-organized military formations to combat the Russian-backed separatists were as likely to speak Russian as Ukrainian" (Pavlyshyn, "Literary History" 77).

While there seems to be a consensus among scholars about the democratizing impact of these recent events on Ukrainian national identity, their effect on societal beliefs about gender and "appropriate" gender roles is less clear. In fact, according to some commentators – including Yevhenia Kononenko herself – these beliefs have become markedly more traditional. In a newspaper interview in 2014, Kononenko asserted that the Euromaidan protests and the ensuing events in the Donbas had once again marginalized Ukrainian women and their contributions by giving centre stage to men – as the chief protesters and later defenders of Ukraine's territorial integrity (Koniaieva). Kononenko was not alone in commenting on what she perceived to be the society's renewed emphasis on more traditionalist gender roles during and after the Euromaidan. In September 2014, a panel of Ukrainian women writers and journalists discussed women on the Euromaidan as an "(in)visible force," whose vital contributions were rarely acknowledged (Iankovs'ka). The idea to organize such a panel discussion was prompted by instances of sexism encountered by these and other women during the protests in Kyiv: as the panel moderator explained, someone persistently took down the stickers with the slogan "Heroiniam slava!" ("Glory to the Heroines!"), which she would sometimes put up next to the ubiquitous posters with the more conventional "Heroiam slava!" ("Glory to the Heroes!") (Iankovs'ka).[3] The moderator also mentioned seeing a sexist announcement in one of the Maidan kitchens, which appealed to women to clear away dirty dishes and thereby do something "pleasant" for the male revolutionaries (Iankovs'ka).

Anthropologist Sarah Phillips interpreted this particular announcement and other manifestations of sexism during the Euromaidan as attempts to cast women participants into a "support role" deemed "'appropriate' for (women) protest action" (415–16). Many women participants in Ukraine's previous Maidan, the Orange Revolution, had viewed their role in the protest as secondary to that of men. Ukrainian activist Maria Dmitriieva stated in one of her recent blogs: "Men talk about how they 'made the revolution'.... Women, by contrast, talk about how they 'helped'.... [In] reality men also brought food to the Maidan and women also served as picket-guards. But in accounts about their experience people for some reason reproduced the traditional, patriarchal division of roles – an active role for men and an auxiliary one for women" (Dmitriieva).

In analysing women's presence on the Euromaidan, Phillips linked such politics of representation to what she termed, following Yuval-Davis's gender/nation analysis, "the maternalist-nationalist discourse" (416). This discourse, which also underlies the Ukrainian independence-era *Berehynia* model discussed in the introduction, assumes that a woman's most natural role vis-à-vis the nation is that of a mother, including, symbolically, Mother Ukraine. It is therefore the men's job to protect women as the symbolic embodiments of the nation from any outside threat, and it is the women's job to carry out typical duties of a caring mother: offer emotional support, meet physical needs for food, shelter, and medical care, and so on. Needless to say, the former role becomes the central one in times of national upheaval, such as war or even mass protests, and the latter role, no matter how dangerous it can actually be, takes second place. This is exactly what happened time and again on the Euromaidan, Phillips points out. When the protests turned violent, men asked women to leave "the barricades," but this did not mean that women protesters were out of danger. As Phillips writes, "[a]way from the barricades, women continued to serve in roles that placed them in harm's way. They were on-site doctors and nurses, volunteer medics, couriers of emergency medical supplies, on-the-scene journalists, advocates of wounded protesters in city hospitals ... and lawyers for arrested protesters" (416). Yet these roles were often perceived as secondary.

The majority of women on the Euromaidan not only performed duties that were seen as "motherly" or "womanly"; according to historian Olesya Khromeychuk, they also "spoke out ... as mothers, protecting their children, or as wives, standing by their husbands," thereby only feeding the popular opinion about their auxiliary roles in the protests (126). Khromeychuk regrets that women protesters usually "did not speak for men or the community as a whole," and fears that their lack of a direct public voice will contribute to a skewed memorialization of the Euromaidan as exclusively a story of heroic men (126).

This chapter strives to counterbalance the rather pessimistic conclusions of the women scholars cited above by analysing the literary interventions of two women authors, Oksana Zabuzhko and Maria Matios, into the rapidly developing process of memorializing the Revolution of Dignity and its impact on the Ukrainian national imaginary. Both Zabuzhko and Matios took a very active part on the Euromaidan, and within a year of its conclusion, each of them published a book of (mostly) non-fiction about the protests as well as the ensuing Russian takeover of the Crimea and the beginning of the war in the Donbas. In their representation of women protesters' voices and actions, including their own, these women writers created a considerably different picture of women's participation in these historic events – and consequently, a somewhat different story about the events themselves. While both books give evidence of the presence of maternalist discourse on the Euromaidan, they also frequently underscore its limits – showing a number of women deploying this discourse strategically and subversively, or emphasizing other ways in which women themselves understood and actively shaped their roles during the protests and afterwards.

Several factors played a role in making these alternative stories of women on the Euromaidan possible. Surprisingly, the first factor had to do with the nature of the event itself. Because the impetus for the Euromaidan, as for the Orange Revolution before it, was the violation of Ukrainian citizens' rights and interests by a corrupt government, joining the protests was symbolically an assertion of one's status as a citizen, regardless of gender. While some, mostly older, women chose to go to the Maidan to "support" others' acts of civil disobedience, many women, especially younger ones, protested as citizens directly affected by the government's actions. Zabuzhko and, to some extent, Matios give clear evidence of such self-perception by numerous women protesters. Moreover, the government's subsequent engagement with the protesters, including the passing of anti-democratic laws and the violence of the riot police, impacted both men and women present on the Maidan. In a sense, the entire ordeal may be viewed as a *sui generis* training in active citizenship – significant for women especially because it occurred in the public sphere. Writing about the Orange Revolution, political scientist Alexandra Hrycak remarked on the potential of mass protests to impact women's consciousness: "[w]omen … who participate in such solidarity-building protests might one day find themselves in a better position to achieve a new sense of solidarity through the mutual recognition of their confinements to a 'separate sphere' that renders them second-class citizens. … ironically, before they can think of themselves as second class-citizens, they have to become mutually aware of themselves as citizens" ("Orange Harvest?" 177). As this chapter demonstrates, the developing awareness of oneself as a Ukrainian citizen, with an important, direct role to play in the protests, is one of the strong themes in the book about the protests contributed to and published by Zabuzhko.

Another factor that enabled the telling of unconventional stories of women's participation in the protests is the genre chosen for the two books. In this respect, the two works may be seen as an artistic reaction springing from a general "desire to document" the dramatic events of the Euromaidan. The wish to capture history unfolding and to represent the protests faithfully and effectively both on the Ukrainian and the international stage found expression in documentary cinema and various non-fiction literary genres – preferred modes of representation because of their objectives of sustaining historical truth and authenticity.[4] *Litopys samovydtsiv. Dev'iat' misiatsiv ukrains'koho sprotyvu* (*The Chronicle of Witnesses: Nine Months of Ukrainian Resistance*, 2014), a compilation of mainly social media posts, with some poems, speeches, and articles – by a variety of Ukrainian activists, protest participants, and witnesses of both genders – was conceived by Zabuzhko and compiled by journalist Tetiana Teren as a document of Ukrainian history-in-the-making and a record of the emotional ebb and flow of the Revolution of Dignity. Similarly, Matios's *Pryvatnyi shchodennyk. Maidan. Viina …* (*Private Diary. Maidan. The War …*, 2015) attempted to document, often day by day and in part through Facebook posts, the revolutionary events of 2013–14 in which the writer actively participated, including in her new role as a member of the Ukrainian parliament.

The two books are thus considerably different from any of the works analysed in previous chapters. Both make a special claim to authenticity by including only participants' or eye-witnesses' testimonies: while Matios herself is the chief subject of her book, *The Chronicle* gives direct voice to hundreds of

Russian- and Ukrainian-speaking protesters of various ethnic and social backgrounds and from all regions of Ukraine. Both books also convey a sense of immediacy of the protesters' experiences by utilizing texts written at the time of the protests: *The Chronicle* consists entirely of such entries, and *Private Diary* combines memoir with online posts and newspaper articles written by the author at the time of the events. In Matios's words, her book presents "truth ... [w]ithout make-up" (*Pryvatnyi shchodennyk* 15). *The Chronicle* appears to adopt the same approach, evidenced, among other things, by the fact that all testimonies are printed unedited, even with language errors left intact.

Finally, both books are identified as unfinished chronicles, using dates of events and of online text publication as the chief organizing principle. As such, these works fit Hayden White's definition of "chronicles" as opposed to "history" proper: they lack narrative closure and a unifying overarching plotline ("The Value of Narrativity" 16). While the individual entries in each of the books do often tell stories, these stories are not tied together into a coherent whole with "a well-marked beginning, middle, and end," which is the defining feature of a plot (6).[5] Such purposefully weak overall emplotment, coupled with the stylistic characteristics described above, allows Zabuzhko and Matios to avoid telling the story of the Euromaidan as a conventional national narrative focused entirely on male heroism – which is how it has been frequently told. Since the Euromaidan culminated in horrific killings of protesters, who became known as "The Heavenly Hundred,"[6] and since most of them were male, the final account acquired the familiar contours of Hogan's heroic and sacrificial narratives, and of Anderson's national biography, in which the men's deaths were assigned utmost significance and were emplotted as a heroic sacrifice for the sake of the nation.

Although *Private Diary* and *The Chronicle* acknowledge and mourn these tragic losses, the books' chronicle structure prevents these deaths from overshadowing the rest of the events described. Narratively speaking, the killings occur under specific dates in late February 2014, and while they impact the entries that follow, they do not affect the texts that precede them – as they inevitably would in a plotted story about the Euromaidan. A fictional account of the Revolution of Dignity, written by a relatively unknown male author, Marko Rudnevych, can serve as an example of the latter and a point of contrast to Zabuzhko's and Matios's books. Rudnevych's novella, *Ia z Nebesnoii sotni* (*I Am from the Heavenly Hundred*, 2014), which, interestingly, pays homage to the civic ethos of the Euromaidan by being released in a bilingual Russian-Ukrainian edition, tells the story of how a young male student became a hero of the Revolution of Dignity. The account's main focus is the student's heroic death on the Euromaidan, which is detailed in the narrative twice: in the prologue and in the final chapter. The title itself makes it clear that this death organizes and structures the entire narrative. Although the story of the student's participation in the protests is told in chronological order, the titles of the chapters are a literal countdown to the student's death: "Six days before," "Five days before," and so on. Such emplotment turns the male student into the central subject of the story marching towards an inevitable heroic end. Even though this first-person account (presumably from beyond the grave) features many other individuals, including women, and is self-effacing in tone, the plotting of the story places the characters within a clear hierarchy of significance. It is therefore not surprising that women in this narrative function fully in accordance with the maternalist discourse or with other traditional supportive roles that exist only to underscore the heroic sacrifice of the male protagonist.[7]

Besides the absence of such plotting, what differentiates Zabuzhko's and Matios's books from Rudnevych's novella is their privileging of women's voices. Matios achieves this more obviously in the *Private Diary*, making herself both the central actor in and the chief commentator on the events described, with much attention devoted to her unique positioning as a woman protester, a woman politician, and a woman writer in Ukraine. *The Chronicle* is not as woman-centred, but a simple count of the number of entries by women versus those by men demonstrates that women's voices predominate (117 entries were written by women authors and 77 by men). Moreover, this book is a collaboration of two women (Zabuzhko and Teren) and contains a foreword by a third – the Belarusian writer Svetlana Alexievich, who was awarded the Nobel Prize in 2015 in recognition of her own books of documentary prose. Thus, it may be said that in selecting and organizing the entries in *The Chronicle* in the way they did, the authors have conveyed something of their own the perspective – the perspective of women writers – on the events of the Euromaidan. In a brief preface, Zabuzhko states that the book serves as evidence of the fact that "[w]e are learning to speak about ourselves by ourselves" ("Zamist' epihrafa"). While it is clear from the context that by "we" she means Ukrainian citizens, the emphasis which *The Chronicle* places on women's testimonies (as well as on testimonies in Russian) suggests a desire on the part of the compilers to prompt a reconsideration of who counts as "we."

Matios's *Private Diary*: Maternalist Performances of Power

Despite its loose chronicle structure, Matios's *Private Diary* underscores one theme that runs through the book: it is the author's gender and the ways in which it has impacted her role in the protests and the ensuing events. Matios emphasizes this theme by beginning her book with a "Prologue" consisting of several poignant scenes. In each, men from either side of the conflict – be they the so-called *titushky* during the Euromaidan protests[8] or officers in the Ukrainian armed forces fighting in the Donbas – point to Matios's gender as the main reason why she does not belong where she is at the moment. "This is not a place for women!" yells an athletic-looking young man with a baseball bat to Matios when she attempts to enter a building in central Kyiv where a group of wounded protesters are hiding from the riot police (*Pryvatnyi shchodennyk* 4). Similarly, in a later scene taking place at a military airport close to the frontline in the Donbas, a Ukrainian army general bellows at his subordinates: "What is a woman doing here?" (7). In each of these scenes, the story develops in a way that problematizes these sexist remarks, the entire discourse about women's "proper" place in violent situations, and Matios's particular positioning vis-à-vis this discourse. In the latter scene, one of the officers responds: "This is not a woman, this is a member of the parliament," eliciting laughter from the soldiers present (7). In the former scene, having taken in her truly dangerous surroundings and especially the baseball bat over her head, Matios recalls the bravest women characters from her fiction books and launches into a verbal attack against her adversary, cleverly deploying the maternalist discourse to her own advantage: "If you are this brave, then begin with me! … Go on! Here I am, a hundred and fifty-five centimeters including the hat! But you must surely have a mother. Remember her and just imagine that right now you are going to strike your mother" (5).

These scenes serve as a leitmotif to the entire book, which makes visible both the constraints and the unique opportunities afforded to Matios by her identities as a well-known writer, a politician, and a woman during the Euromaidan protests. Matios's response in the latter scene also illustrates her keen awareness of literature's ability to offer role models and behavioural scripts. In the book's preface, Matios explicitly acknowledges this ability with a somewhat religious formulation – as the "material" power of the "Word" (11, 16). It thus seems entirely fitting to consider her *Private Diary* in this study – as a continuation of her literary efforts, first evidenced in *The Nation* and *Sweet Darusia*, to renegotiate women's places and roles in the nation. If in her fiction she created women characters who often undermined stereotypical woman/nation plots with their actions and their critical voices, in the *Private Diary* Matios herself finds inspiration in their behaviour and power when she embarks on unconventional actions.

Undoubtedly, much of Matios's power during the protests stemmed from her status as a high-ranking politician. Because she was a Ukrainian parliament member who belonged to the opposition to President Yanukovych, Matios was frequently at the epicentre of activity throughout the protests. Early on, the presence of parliamentary deputies[9] often granted rank-and-file protesters a measure of protection, deterred provocations, and opened doors that would have otherwise remained closed. Matios describes how she and other women deputies joined their male colleagues in expeditions to hospitals and police stations where arrested and wounded protesters were held; at the frontline barricades surrounding the Maidan to prevent their storming by riot police; and in various marches and picketing lines in strategic, yet dangerous locations. As one among only a handful of female members of the Ukrainian parliament, in which the ratio of men to women was about ten to one at the time,[10] Matios met with a variety of reactions at protest hotspots, reactions which she meticulously documented.

In keeping with the maternalist discourse, her male colleagues in parliament nicknamed her "our mom" – a designation which she grudgingly accepted and a role which she proceeded to diligently fulfil through acts of motherly care directed at the protesters, the recruits in Ukraine's internal troops,[11] and even the hated Berkut riot police (*Pryvatnyi shchodennyk* 18). She bought and distributed food, made sure the wounded received proper medical care, and, drawing on her reputation as a popular writer on national topics, struck up conversations about the values needed to lead Ukraine out of the crisis. Yet actions that did not fit the maternalist discourse elicited resistant attitudes and sometimes desperate measures from men on both sides of the barricades. For instance, as soon as there was word that a situation might turn more dangerous, her male deputy colleagues would try to force Matios to leave. They pleaded and argued when she refused to go, and on one occasion, when they anticipated a storming of the Maidan, they tricked her into leaving by sending her on some urgent mission to a different part of the city. "I went outside the perimeter of the Maidan, and now I am powerless," posted Matios on Facebook when she discovered their ruse (*Pryvatnyi shchodennyk* 86).

What her male colleagues did not understand and what comes through clearly in Matios's diary is that she felt most empowered, and was in fact able to accomplish tasks which men could not, when facing danger. This often became possible when Matios would turn the maternalist discourse to her advantage, exploiting the stereotypes of gendered behaviour or capitalizing on the symbolic power of the mother figure in Ukrainian culture. On occasion this strategy permitted her to pass through multiple police cordons when her deputy's identification had no effect. In some instances, Matios and other female deputies would even ask their male colleagues to step back in order to achieve their goals in negotiations with the police. The riot police, it turned out, would much rather heed a woman's pleading not to open fire on the protesters than honour the same request from a member of the parliament. Because Matios was both, she was once even turned away by a police commander, who told her: "if in our country one could trust at least one politician, you and I could continue our conversation" (*Pryvatnyi shchodennyk* 140).

Yet in many instances, reported in the *Private Diary*, Matios was able to accomplish what she set out to do through sheer perseverance, bravery, and willpower – as well as through clever deployment of the maternalist discourse on her own terms. What she did so effectively again and again was to insert herself into the militarist scenario in a consciously performed motherly role, a role accorded some authority in traditional Ukrainian culture.[12] By refusing to leave the scene of potential violent conflict and by forcing the men around her to see her *as* a woman and to listen to her *as* a mother, she was often able to prevent or interrupt a violent confrontation.[13] To return to the scene in which Matios was threatened by a *titushka* with a baseball bat, in response to her demand he see in her a mother figure, the man shouted back: "Woman! Go away, woman! I don't like this moral pressure, woman!" (*Pryvatnyi shchodennyk* 5). Matios concludes this scene in her book with a self-satisfied recognition that her strategy was successful: "That's it! This means he is not entirely a hopeless case. Let's bring on the pressure" (5).

Matios, of course, was not the first to deploy maternalism in protest for political ends. Mothers' movements have been active in many countries at various times, and most have been criticized as traditionalist precisely for the premise of their mobilization – motherhood. However, Matios's maternalist performances of power differ in several ways from those of many such movements, including the mothers' group that protested on the Euromaidan.[14] They also depart from the motherly *Berehynia* model embraced by some contemporary Ukrainian women's organizations and described in the introduction. A brief comparison of Matios's strategic behaviour with one influential mothers' movement will make these differences clear.

In her analysis of the Madres, who protested against the Argentine Junta's "Dirty War" in the late 1970s and inspired other mothers' movements around the world, performance studies scholar Diana Taylor argues that "[w]hile consciously performing 'motherhood,' the Madres were trapped in a bad script" (299). They came out onto the central square in Buenos Aires to accuse the military regime of "'disappearing' their children" (286) and to demand their return home and the punishment of the leaders. The Madres variously underscored the non-threatening and apolitical character of their movement: they marched in sorrowful silence, wore slippers and kerchiefs to symbolically indicate that their "proper" place was the home, and aimed to elicit the audiences' sympathy and outrage through their displays of powerlessness vis-à-vis the cruel authoritarian regime. They were successful in producing the desired effect and achieving visibility for their cause worldwide, but their performative protest did not change, nor did it seek to change, the traditional perceptions of women's roles in the public sphere. As Taylor explains, "[t]he Madres won significant political power, but they claim not to want that power, at least not for themselves but only for their children" (291).

By contrast, Matios often performed the role of the mother as a moral and benevolent authority figure, juxtaposing herself with the repressive Yanukovych regime, not in her powerlessness but in her competing claim to power and legitimacy. She also did so vocally, speaking on behalf of all Ukrainians, and making no apologies for commanding the public sphere. For example, in an effort to prevent violence against the protesters, she frequently went to speak to the internal troops standing near protest areas and government buildings. She addressed these young men as sons, told them to call their parents and reassure them that they were safe, and, in warning them not to attack the protesters, appealed to their moral conscience as "our children," children who have a duty before their parents and not before the criminal regime (*Pryvatnyi shchodennyk* 25).

This is not to suggest, however, that such deployment of the maternalist discourse was available to all women on the Maidan, or that it was always effective. Obviously, Matios's age (she was fifty-four at the time of the protests), the sheer force of her personality, and her shrewd understanding of behavioural scripts available to women in Ukrainian culture greatly aided her in her successful performances of maternalism. Moreover, once the Euromaidan protests entered their most violent phase, with Molotov cocktails and sniper bullets flying across the protest space, no amount of maternal pleading, yelling, or moral pressure could stop them. Yet in the early Euromaidan days, when there was still hope that the conflict could be resolved relatively peacefully, Matios's strategy provided an interesting and effective example of subversive female behaviour during the protests.

While some may still interpret this behaviour as traditionalist (essentializing mothers/women as peacemakers), it is crucial to remember that this was a strategically deployed performance. In contexts where a more confrontational style promised greater returns, Matios did not hesitate to adopt it and use whatever leverage she could muster as a politician, well-known writer, and/or "motherly" figure to achieve the desired outcome. In combining authoritative performances of maternalism and her role as a member of the parliament, Matios showed that it is possible, despite the cultural bias described by some scholars, to integrate motherhood as the Ukrainian ideal for women with political leadership.[15] In fact, one may even say that by authoritatively performing maternalism in the public sphere, Matios reinserted the "matriarchal implication" into the *Berehynia* model of feminine behaviour, which had been conveniently de-emphasized in the independence-era public discourse (Kis, "(Re)Constructing Ukrainian Women's History" 158).

At the same time, her experience of "making revolution," which involved developing this rich repertoire of strategies in real-life, dangerous circumstances, has been transformative for Matios. She writes in the preface that it had revealed to her new, unexpected sides of herself and others around her. The diary entries capture Matios's developing confidence in her ability to make a real difference in the protests and the ensuing events, and the simultaneously growing dissatisfaction, even exasperation, with the lack of courage, commitment, and enterprise on the part of many Ukrainian male politicians at a time of national crisis. These sentiments are evident in a social media post which

Matios wrote in early February 2014 and which is mentioned in the *Private Diary*: "My Facebook post and the photos of four women defence ministers in Norway, Sweden, the Netherlands, and Germany, as well as my assertion that a fifth one – a Ukrainian one – is missing, generated enthusiastic comments and support" (*Pryvatnyi shchodennyk* 101). These feelings are reiterated in a Facebook post written half a year later, which reports that five women have been appointed to key positions in the new Japanese government, including ministers of defence and national security (268). Perhaps a culmination of these sentiments occurs in June 2014, when Matios reports receiving a phone call from a Ukrainian general in charge of the border troops in Ukraine's Eastern region – at a time when the Russian-backed separatists in the Donbas were on the offensive. Matios had met the general during one of her trips to Ukraine's eastern *oblasts*, which she began to make regularly after the Euromaidan, and the general reached out to her with a desperate plea to interfere when no help was forthcoming from Ukraine's Ministry of Defence. In a Facebook reaction to the phone call, Matios minces no words in her characterization of the Ukrainian military leadership in Kyiv and rhetorically asks the newly elected President Poroshenko whether time has come to transfer all the key defence posts in the Ukrainian government to women – "[b]ecause they are more responsible" (*Pryvatnyi shchodennyk* 217).

At first glance, it may seem that these entries are very different from many others in the *Private Diary*, ones which detail Matios's more conventionally maternalist efforts on behalf of the critically injured protesters and soldiers: locating resources for their medical care, visiting them in hospitals, providing aid to their families, and so on. Yet in fact, the former are a logical continuation of the latter. It is Matios's strong sense of "maternal" concern for the well-being of her fellow citizens that prompts her to declare women "more responsible" – and therefore allegedly more fit to occupy key government posts. Although this argument is based on an essentialist premise, it counteracts several of the enduring stereotypes about women's roles and place in the nation: it represents them as strong rather than weak, as capable of effective defence rather than needing to be defended, and as belonging to the public sphere as key agents rather than being only "helpers" whose "proper" place is in the home.

The Chronicle of Witnesses: Citizenship, Nation, and Revolution through Women's Voices

In its representation of women's participation in the protests, *The Chronicle of Witnesses* portrays a much greater variety of female roles and perspectives than Matios's *Private Diary*. This is due to the fact, of course, that *The Chronicle* features testimonies by multiple male and female protesters and witnesses. Because the vast majority of the authors included do not possess Matios's experience of involvement in top-level politics, they mostly do not attempt to reimagine Ukraine's political order in terms of gender and sometimes depict women's roles on the Maidan in traditional ways. A number of pieces by women protesters show evidence of their having internalized the maternalist discourse: some women, for example, speak of their "mission" to care for the male heroes on the Maidan and some give gender-based explanations for what they perceive to be their inability to join men on the barricades (*Litopys* 67–8, 78). In several pieces by both male and female bloggers and journalists, women's service in the Maidan kitchens is taken for granted, whereas men's participation in kitchen duty merits a special mention, as something extraordinary.

Nonetheless, *The Chronicle* also includes pieces that portray women's participation less conventionally. Most of these entries are posts by women protesters who document a growing awareness of themselves as Ukrainian citizens with an active role to play at a time of national crisis. Early in the protests, this role usually meant simply leaving the safety and comfort of their home and coming to the Maidan to declare their disagreement with the government's actions. In many of these posts, written in either Ukrainian or Russian, women speak not as mothers or wives, but as citizens, and on behalf of their national community: "no one has the right to beat us, no one has the right to intimidate us, and no one has the right to take our freedom away. my [sic] stance as a citizen demands that I take to the streets. I WILL COME OUT TOMORROW TO SAY: I AM A UKRAINIAN [*ukrainka*]. AND I AM FREE!" (*Litopys* 16). A significant number of posts by women are addressed to friends or relatives in the Crimea, in the Donbas, or in Russia, explaining what is taking place and spelling out their positions as active protesters. These pieces also speak on behalf of the Maidan community and often the nation. For example, in a post titled "to those who don't understand, but want to understand, what I have forgotten on the Maidan," a Russian-speaking female protester from the Luhansk region, Lena Samojlenko, writes: "You understand, in my country they are killing people. To death. People become irreversibly dead. This shouldn't happen. … To force, one responds with force. This is how we do it in the Donbas. This is how we do it in the Carpathians. This is how we do it in Ukraine" (*Litopys* 87–9).

Written already after the first deaths on the Euromaidan, Samojlenko's piece conveys her sense that the protests have reached a point of no return and that she "cannot leave," in spite of the danger (89). Entries of this kind, in which women as well as men communicate readiness to stand their ground even when facing potential arrest or even death, begin to appear in *The Chronicle* from 16 January 2014 – the day when the Yanukovych-controlled parliament passed the infamous series of anti-democratic laws.[16] Several pieces by women indicate that the government's brutal actions actually compelled female protesters to take on roles that are unusual for them. As journalist Yulia Babych put it, "very peacefully a Revolutionary grew in me out of an Evolutionary [sic]… Probably,

I am ready … And you know, when you realize this, you couldn't care less about any 'anti-laws' because you are filled with FREEDOM!" (56). While commenting on the forced radicalization, some women underscore the fact that assuming this role goes hand in hand with symbolic masculinization. For instance, in the poem "The Extremist" by a female protester, the lyrical heroine ironically introduces herself to her mother as an extremist, purposely using the masculine gender form of the noun (57). While this new masculine identity marker is repeated in every stanza, one line of the poem reveals the actual gender of the lyrical heroine in passing – when she uses the feminine grammatical ending on a past-tense verb. The poem makes it clear, however, that the extremist status, coupled with a symbolic maleness, is bestowed upon the woman participant by the draconian laws of Yanukovych's regime. According to these laws, almost everyone on the Maidan is considered an extremist – and the actual feminine gender of the lyrical heroine only serves to underscore the absurdity of this label when applied to peaceful protesters like her.

As the protests evolved from the peaceful to the more violent stage, some women insisted on performing the traditionally male, militarist roles on the barricades. Phillips and several other scholars, such as Tamara Martsenyuk and Olesya Khromeychuk, have recently described the participation of women in self-defence units on the Maidan, including as members of the so-called women's squads. The Ukrainian word for "squad," *sotnia* – literally meaning a hundred – was adopted by protesters for self-defence brigades, comprising anywhere from 70 to 150 activists. At the height of the protests, there were 42 squads, most of them all-male, although several included women, and three were all-female *sotnias*.[17] The phenomenon of female participation in self-defence has been criticized by some feminist scholars as misguided. For example, Maria Mayerchyk opined that this strategy endorsed what she called, in somewhat essentialist terms, "the principle of male military confrontation that has … become widely authorized" ("Seizing the Logic").[18] Mayerchyk and critics like her pointed out that women's participation in the military formations of the Euromaidan sometimes had unintended and undesirable results. At one extreme, female protesters in military grab frequently became the subject of sensationalized and/or sexualized depictions in the media.[19] At the other extreme, in their eagerness to fit in and prove that they could do the dangerous work of self-defence as well as men, many female squad members willingly adopted a "masculine" persona.[20]

The Chronicle features only one piece by a woman protester who participated in self-defence, compared with several by men. However, this is an interesting text because it shows a person seamlessly combining what are traditionally perceived as "masculine" and "feminine" roles, thereby undermining their conventional polarization. On 9 April 2014, Russian-speaking female protester Aliona Stadnik, who was part of the 38th self-defence squad, which included men and women, wrote a piece in which she reminisced about the most frightening days on the Euromaidan and their squad's mourning of several male comrades, killed by snipers' bullets. On the one hand, her testimony gives evidence of her participation in the activities of self-defence together with the male activists, and does so without any special emphasis: she mentions putting on the uniform, living in one of the administrative buildings occupied by the protesters, and taking turns with others "to be on the frontline" or to rest after sleepless nights (Stadnik 201). She wrestles with survivor guilt, asking why it was her comrade who was killed and not her, and discusses how taking apart and reassembling a gun calms her nerves. On the other hand, her entire piece describes and performs mourning, as well as communicates sympathetic identification with the killed protesters' mothers, in ways that are conventionally thought of as "feminine." She takes great pains to portray her own and her friends' conflicting feelings of grim decisiveness and utter despair; she describes in detail the grief of the mothers of the killed men and her own unbearable emotional pain from witnessing and identifying with this grief. Stadnik's "masculine" and "feminine" personas are completely intertwined in her text, making it difficult to say which one influenced the other, and in what ways. Her example therefore challenges the theoretical arguments about the consequences of women's participation in the military formations on the Euromaidan.

Nonetheless, the emphasis on a mother's mourning in Stadnik's text is in itself quite traditional. After the killings of protesters on the Euromaidan, the theme of mothers grieving the loss of their sons becomes prominent in women's texts featured in *The Chronicle* – especially in poems. Kononenko, who has studied Maidan poetry as a general phenomenon, singles out this theme as a major one for women poets and goes so far as to argue that female poets hardly wrote of women's active experiences of protest violence. According to Kononenko, "[i]f female poets of Maidan speak about the feminine, it is on the topic of the Mother" ("Ievanheliie vid poetiv" 22). While this statement also seems to be largely true of the poetry by women included in *The Chronicle*, the poetic entries – by both male and female witnesses – are generally the most conventional in their portrayal of gender roles on the Euromaidan. Perhaps this is partly due to lyric poetry's general tendency towards "omnitemporality" and "timelessness" of address, as noted by Rory Finnin and summarized in the introduction to the present volume.[21] However, poems constitute only a small portion of the work by women featured in *The Chronicle*. Many other entries by female authors, as argued above, show women performing a variety of roles in the protests, identifying as citizens, and speaking on behalf of the protesters' community or even the nation. Some female authors do indeed focus on women's experiences of the protests in their violent stage. Several pieces, for instance, describe women authors' thoughts and feelings about having to wear bulletproof vests on the Maidan and their reactions to being in the middle of violent standoffs with the riot police. They write about being chased and beaten, but also about coming to the aid of others, finding shelter for themselves and fellow protesters, and returning back to the Maidan, despite their fears. One female protester writes in a rational, measured way about the need to continue protesting, but also about the need to stay alive, implicitly arguing against the cult of heroic death: "Right now there are water cannons and a smell of death on the Maidan. I put on a new warm pair of pants because the other ones are torn and stained with blood, and I keep going. Though I understand that right now the main task is to stay unharmed and alive, for why does my country and the world need my corpse in the morgue, with a label on my big toe, or a young cripple?" (*Litopys* 108).

Generally speaking, however, what predominates in *The Chronicle* is an overall sense that in these critical circumstances, the participation of every person in the protests – no matter the gender or the role performed – is an essential act of civic courage, and it amounts to "making revolution."[22] The status of a revolutionary is bestowed upon everyone who shows up on the Maidan for the right reasons, and even on those who become involved in the causes of the Revolution of Dignity without being present on the Maidan itself. In this respect, the words "witness" and "resistance," used in the title of the book, stress the compilers' conscious decision to expand the conceptual reach of what is usually understood by the term "Euromaidan" or even the more capacious "Revolution of Dignity." What is meant by "resistance" is not only the mass protest itself or even Ukrainians' mobilization to defend their country in the war that followed. It is also the formulation and the voicing of Ukrainians' changing understanding of themselves and their nation. This understanding was often articulated not only by direct participants but also by "witnesses" of the events – observers, journalists, bloggers, and writers, many of them women. A multitude of voices are featured in *The Chronicle of Witnesses*, the compilation and publication of which is to be taken in and of itself as an act of the "resistance" referred to in the title. The fact that this book is a product of two female writers' work, and that Zabuzhko and Teren made women's direct voices such an important part of *The Chronicle*, attests to another crucial role played by women in the events of the Euromaidan – that of shaping the future memory of these events and thereby impacting the national discourse in Ukraine.

Largely owing to their inclusiveness and the peculiarities of the chronicle genre, the *Private Diary* and *The Chronicle of Witnesses* offer a rich representation of women's roles in the Euromaidan. The women's participation in the protests often defied a simplistic explanation, as seen in the variety and nuance of responses to the constantly changing situation. The individual women's portrayals of their own and other women's roles complicate the argument that the

Euromaidan only reinforced traditionalist gender imaginings. Although it is true that the powerful discourse of maternalism impacted many of the women's actions and the ways in which their roles were perceived, it neither wholly determined these roles nor was immune to subversive deployment. By featuring female participants who speak directly about their protest experiences, the two books show women often acting and thinking beyond this discourse, or using it strategically. These works also underscore women's agency and creativity – rather than their powerlessness or adherence to traditional roles – in navigating the challenging circumstances on the Euromaidan. This representation provides a corrective to the conclusions of a number of scholars who have argued that the Euromaidan merely reproduced "[s]ocially accepted patriarchal views on the role of women in Ukrainian society" (Onuch and Martsenyuk 120).

Such pessimistic conclusions are unwarranted especially when one considers that the Euromaidan protests "facilitated the processes of modernization in Ukraine," as some scholars have pointed out (Hundorova, "Ukrainian Euromaidan" 176). The most remarked upon aspect of this modernization has been the reimagining of Ukraine as a civic nation in the process of what some commentators considered to be "the first postcolonial revolution" in the post-Soviet space (Gerasimov). Ukraine was powerfully imagined as a civic nation when "[i]ndividual people with active civic positions stepped forward to protest the abuse of their rights by the tyrannical regime" (Gerasimov 27). As I have tried to show, many of these people were women, women who came to realize and articulate their own "active civic positions" as a result of participating in the protests. Moreover, in some cases, their understanding of women's roles evolved in the course of the protests, as evidenced, for instance, by Matios's posts about the need to have more women in top-level governmental positions. Thus, it is possible to say that the protests also modernized at least some women's perception of their place in the public sphere and in the nation more generally. The conservative *Berehynia* model of Ukrainian womanhood, which consigned women exclusively to the private sphere, or, even worse, to the symbolic plane outside real life altogether, did not fit the actual circumstances of the Euromaidan, which required protesters to be active, mobile, and daring in the very public spaces of active protest. Thus, the Euromaidan may be thought of as an example of a social situation in which female activists, while seemingly struggling exclusively for *national* liberation, also made some gains in breaking the boundaries between the "separate spheres." That events like mass protests or war can result in such opportunities for women has been acknowledged more than once. For instance, in a recent interview, Oksana Kis noted the changes for women that have been occurring in Ukraine since the protests and the beginning of the war, stating that this is "a time when the tight social fabric that used to keep women away from certain domains tears, and the gender barriers become more porous" (Lazurkevych).[23]

That the protests became a key moment of opportunity to attempt a renegotiation of the relationship between women and the nation is also evidenced by unprecedented activity of feminist groups on the Euromaidan. They included peaceful marches, rallies, and performance art, as well as participation of women in the militarist initiatives such as self-defence – especially through the formation of all-female squads. While commentators agree neither about the ideological usefulness of these activities nor about their impact on women or the society at large,[24] there is no doubt that the gender/nation intersections received much more attention in this mass protest than in Ukraine's earlier Orange Revolution. The larger academic and popular debate on women's roles in the Revolution of Dignity and in Ukrainian society in general, which has been sparked by the protests, also confirms the validity of Hrycak's argument, mentioned above, about the capacity of protests to affect women's consciousness in positive ways.

Finally, as the very existence of books like the *Private Diary* and *The Chronicle* implies, women writers have themselves intervened in the debate, carving out for themselves and for other women another vital role with respect to the Euromaidan. In writing and compiling these works, Matios, Zabuzhko, and Teren took it upon themselves to document women's participation in the Revolution of Dignity through first-hand accounts by the participants themselves. Their focus on direct women's testimonies allowed them to bring to light not only female protesters' actions but also their reflections on the events, documents that often evaluated and critiqued various roles, practices, and behaviours. In so doing, these women writers brought greater visibility and value to women's multifaceted roles in the protests, and, crucially, endowed women with a stronger public voice in which to speak on their own behalf, as well as on behalf of their nation.

Conclusion

As shown in the many examples explored here – ranging from Bichuia's narrator, who cannot utter a single word in her recurrent nightmare, and the mute child whom she encounters in another dream; to the gagged woman poet in Kononenko's "On Sunday Morning"; to the struggles of Oksana in Zabuzhko's *Fieldwork* to find a place from which she could speak; to Matios's mute Darusia, who is nevertheless given a critical voice in the novel; to Kononenko's Mariana in *Imitation*, who is murdered because of her cruel, mocking words and all too forceful a voice; to Daryna's attempts to uncover the voices from the past in Zabuzhko's *Museum*; to the women's voices of protest in the non-fiction chronicles of the Euromaidan – much of Ukrainian women's prose since the collapse of the USSR has displayed a fundamental interest in speaking as self-expression, as a form of power, and as a basic way to signal one's presence in the world. While gaining a voice has long become a commonplace of feminist theorizing, it remains a vital first step, and it has been a very important one for independence-era Ukrainian women prose writers. As Rosi Braidotti has stressed, "[i]n order to announce the death of the subject, one must first have gained the right to speak as one" (169).

Yet these authors have been searching for a voice not only for and as women (writers), but also for and as Ukrainians. In their case, Braidotti's dictum has to be coupled with a similar statement about the nation: before one can even consider announcing the decline of the nation as a paradigm (as some nationalism scholars have done in the last three decades),[1] one must first have gained the right to try to use it "as a viable space for political self-expression" (Boehmer, *Stories of Women* 191). Because Ukraine became independent only in 1991, and because the writers whose work I examine have all lived a part of their lives under the Soviet system that organized and policed literary production in Ukraine differently and more stringently than in the Soviet metropole, they have deemed an independent nation-state a precondition for being able to speak, write, and publish as Ukrainian women authors – including on previously forbidden topics. The explosion in Ukrainian women's prose writing that followed the collapse of the Soviet empire suggests that these authors were right in this respect.

Nonetheless, as I have argued throughout this study, the works by Zabuzhko, Kononenko, and Matios have often been critical of the nation, and an important part of this critique stems from a focus on women characters and their lives. Through such a focus, these authors have often pushed against the boundaries of the heavily circumscribed women's (and women writers') roles vis-à-vis the nation, or have criticized other aspects of the Ukrainian national imaginary, sometimes eliciting hostile reactions. Still, the very fact that they addressed crucial national issues in their fiction has allowed them to gain significant literary recognition in Ukraine. Through their writing, Zabuzhko, Kononenko, and Matios have been able to successfully position themselves as critics of their culture and lead the way for the younger generations of Ukrainian women prose writers.

Present-day visibility of women authors in Ukraine suggests that important changes have taken place since the disintegration of the Soviet state and its gender order – at least, in the domain of literary production. This study has traced a trajectory of gradual gains – from the forced as well as self-imposed silence of a rare prose writer in the Soviet stagnation period (Bichuia) to the multiple and varied voices of both established and unknown women authors, journalists, bloggers, and so on, whose pieces were included in *The Chronicle of Witnesses*. Certainly, the democratization of the very process of literary production, partly enabled by the increasing availability of Internet publishing, has contributed to these gains. Yet one cannot discount the active role of Ukrainian women authors themselves. In particular, the women of the eighties generation, who started by writing themselves onto the literary scene and reconstructing the pre-Soviet women's literary tradition, later responded to each other's work and the work of other women writers, publicly criticized discrimination against female authors, and published anthologies of women's writing.[2] Zabuzhko's conception of *The Chronicle of Witnesses* as a democratic collection of voices, including those of women who directly speak about themselves and their nation, is only the latest logical step along this forward path.

The trajectory from Bichuia to *The Chronicle* and the *Private Diary* may also be described in terms of the collapse of the Soviet discursive monopoly. While Bichuia's "The Stone Master" ended with the image of the female writer-narrator swallowed up by a crowd that was fully controlled by the authoritarian regime, both non-fiction books about the Euromaidan protests testified to the complete reversal of that image in much of Ukraine in the winter of 2013–14. The hundreds of thousands of protesters who gathered on the Maidan came out to rally against the repressive regime, and they included many female participants and women writers/commentators, some of whose voices are featured in *The Chronicle* and the *Private Diary* – and often speak powerfully about women "making revolution."

In their national narratives that predated the Euromaidan, Zabuzhko, Kononenko, and Matios had already written about women's multiple and varied roles in the nation. This study has analysed these writers' use of different national plots for their woman-centred national stories. The two main types of plots that they utilized are Anderson's reverse national biography, which transforms individual deaths into national continuity, and the national romance. In particular, I traced how women authors often undermined the conventional gender patterns in these plots, such as the symbolization of the nation through a woman's death, or the portrayal of men as the only true national heroes. Even though in many cases the three women writers changed the gender dynamics of these plots, by using such forms of national emplotment in the first place, they still affirmed the nation – because they gave it, in Boehmer's terms, an "enabling" form (*Stories of Women* 11).

For example, although Kononenko's *Imitation* put a female activist in the centre of the narrative and refused to ascribe a heroic or sacrificial national meaning to her death (as well as critiqued the construction of the East as Ukraine's internal Other), it still "enmesh[ed]" a "multiplicity of characters … into a single, overarching narrative trajectory," to refer back to Craig's formulation (9). Granted, this narrative revealed conflict and internal division within Ukraine, yet it still brought characters from Kyiv and Ukraine's East onto the pages of the same text and into the twists and turns of the same national story – and thus staged that very simultaneity of coexistence which Anderson considered to be the novel's major "national" function.

Of course, there is a significant difference between such narratives and a conventional nationalist plot – not only in the dynamics of gendering, but also in how they conceive of a collective national identity: while the latter might imagine a monolithic, ethnically exclusive national community in which women symbolize the nation, Kononenko's novel conceives of Ukraine as a country in which citizens with different conceptions of their identities attempt to coexist – and where various national and gender discourses collude and collide. Nonetheless, *Imitation* still allows readers to imagine Ukraine as a distinct national entity and therefore still helps produce the Ukrainian national imaginary. Paying attention to emplotment and its effects reveals the extraordinary power of novelistic plots to project imagined national worlds.

Yet narrative plotting usually comes at a cost: by emplotting individuals into a single story, a narrative by default places them into a hierarchy of significance. A novel must have heroes and sidekicks, protagonists and minor characters, agents and objects of action. Until recently in Ukrainian literature, narratives of all kinds, but especially national stories – with rare exceptions – tended to place men in the former and women in the latter positions. In their fiction, women *visimdesiatnyky* sought out various means to rectify this situation. At times they simply reversed the hierarchy, at times they portrayed it and allowed their women characters to critique it, and occasionally they attempted to fashion an "egalitarian" plot, in which male and female characters would be more or less equal partners. Zabuzhko experimented with such a plot by crafting *Museum*'s national romance story of Daryna and Adrian, in which she gave to each a narrating voice, agency, and a vital presence in the novel.

Ukraine's recent mass protests made women's roles in the nation the subject of a broader discussion. The common tendency to describe men's participation in terms of "making revolution" and women's in terms of "helping" clearly demonstrated that narrative plotting is at work not only in literature. By giving up an overarching plotline and featuring direct women's testimonies recorded at the time of the protests, Zabuzhko's and Matios's Euromaidan chronicles maximized women's opportunities to figure as heroines and agents in this nonfictional national story. Their choice of form allowed them to bring greater visibility and value to women's multifaceted roles in the protests and in the nation more generally.

In my attention to emplotment and other literary devices in works by Zabuzhko, Kononenko, and Matios, I have followed the call made by several scholars of postcolonial literature to "return to a focus on literariness and literary form" after decades of ignoring it or treating it with suspicion (Sorensen xi).[3] One of these scholars, Eli Park Sorensen, argues that such a return "may lead to an alternative appreciation of the more constructive aspects at stake in the literary work – rather than merely focusing on literature's deconstructive qualities" (xiv). Although their writing has sometimes resorted to deconstruction, the "constructive aspects" of literary form have been very important for women *visimdesiatnyky*. The capacity of literature to imagine and depict new ways of being and acting has allowed these women writers to put forth their own visions of Ukraine's past and present. It has also enabled them to write women, including themselves, into the national story – often in roles heretofore uncommon.

Notes

Introduction

1 See Khruslins'ka, *Ukrainskyi palimpsest*, p. 227; my translation. All translations hereafter are mine unless otherwise indicated.

2 The strong presence of women prose writers among the finalists and winners of important prizes in contemporary Ukrainian literature serves as one type of evidence for the post-Soviet explosion of women's prose writing in Ukraine. For instance, the jury committee of the prestigious BBC Book of the Year, which has been awarded since 2005 in Ukraine to authors of prose, shortlisted twenty-two books by women and twenty-six by men between 2005 and 2014 (the year of the Euromaidan's conclusion, which serves as a cut-off point in my study). Out of thirty-six single-author books of prose that won the title "Book of the Year" in an all-Ukrainian national rating between 2000 and 2014, one-fifth were books by women authors. Perhaps the most impressive evidence comes from the results of the international literary competition *Koronatsiia slova* (Coronation of the Word), whose aim is to support contemporary Ukrainian culture and the discovery of new names in a variety of cultural genres, including novels. Between 2001 and 2014, 134 novels were recognized in this competition, receiving the first, second, or third prizes, or a diploma. Seventy-one of these novels were written or co-written by women authors, and out of the fourteen first prize winners, the majority (eight) were women writers.

3 See, for instance, the final chapter of Aheieva's monograph *Zhinochyi prostir*, and Taran, *Zhinocha rol'*. Chernetsky also acknowledges the trend and examines some works by Zabuzhko in chapter 8 of *Mapping Postcommunist Cultures*. Michael M. Naydan introduces a number of new Ukrainian women's voices to the Western reader in "Emerging Ukrainian Women Prose Writers." Finally, in her 2018 monograph, *Ukraine's Quest for Identity*, which is a broad mapping out of dominant themes in contemporary Ukrainian writing, Rewakowicz includes one chapter on women writers of various generations.

4 On the last Soviet generation, see Yurchak. For more on the *visimdesiatnyky* vis-à-vis the previous generations of writers, see Andryczyk, especially pp. 10–12.

5 Other well-known Ukrainian women writers from this generation include Halyna Pahutiak, Liubov Ponomarenko, Liudmyla Taran, Teodozia Zarivna, Sofia Maidanska, and Valentyna Mastierova. For more on them, see Gabor, *Neznaioma*.

6 On who counts as a "literary oligarch" in Ukraine and the difficulties of being a full-time professional writer in Ukraine, see Klymenko.

7 See, for instance, Kuehnast and Nechemias, *Post-Soviet Women Encountering Transition*, and Johnson and Robinson, *Living Gender after Communism*.

8 A Belarusian journalist and non-fiction writer of partial Ukrainian descent, Svetlana Alexievich was awarded the 2015 Nobel Prize for Literature for her non-fiction book cycle, *Voices of Utopia*.

9 See Holmgren, "Writing the Female Body Politic (1945–1985)."

10 See, for example, Sutcliffe, *The Prose of Life*.

11 On the exceptions from this tendency, such as the figure of Iryna Vilde, see chapter 1 of this book.

12 See my analysis of Kononenko's and Zabuzhko's early prose that thematizes women's writing in chapter 2.

13 Vitaly Chernetsky applies this term to both Ukraine and Russia in the preface to *Mapping Postcommunist Cultures*, p. xiv.

14 For more on *Let My People Go*, as well as other writings about the Orange Revolution by women authors, see Tytarenko, "Women's Voices."

15 Vitaly Chernetsky and Maria G. Rewakowicz were the first among the literary scholars based in the West who discussed the presence of the gender/nation nexus in early independence-era Ukrainian literary scholarship and writing, and particularly in Oksana Zabuzhko's work. See Chernetsky, *Mapping Postcommunist Cultures*, chapter 8; and Rewakowicz, "Women's Literary Discourse," "Feminism, Nationalism, and Women's Literary Discourse in Post-Soviet Ukraine," and *Ukraine's Quest for Identity* (especially chapter 3). As Rewakowicz notes of independence-era Ukrainian women's writing more broadly, "[t]he link between feminism and national identity … is subtle but, at the same time, pervasive" (*Ukraine's Quest for Identity* 108).

16 As recently as 2011, a scholar of women's history, Oksana Kis, wrote: "The history of Ukraine in the twentieth century abounds in events that have altered the country's political, social, and economic landscapes, yet the part that Ukrainian women played in that history during the past hundred years is only marginally visible" ("Biography as Political Geography" 89).

17 On the concept of "nationalized" history and its distinguishing features of essentialism, ethnic exclusivity, linearity, etc., see Kasianov, "'Nationalized' History."

18 For an explanation of such attitudes to women's writing in Russia, see Goscilo, *Dehexing Sex*, especially pp. 16–18. On the very limiting expectations for women's literature in Soviet Ukraine, see Khruslins'ka, *Ukrainskyi palimpsest*, p. 215.

19 In her discussion of Nathaniel Hawthorne's literary engagement with the meanings of "America," Lauren Berlant uses the term "the National Symbolic." Although similar to "the national imaginary," this term has Lacanian provenance and emphasizes the legal order in which citizenship constitutes the relationship between individuals and the state. Berlant sees the Statue of Liberty as the key symbol in this National Symbolic order. The Statue "represents the promise of the nation … to provide a passage for the individual subject to the abstract identity of 'citizen'" (24). Because Ukraine was stateless for much of its modern history, I find the term "the national imaginary," which foregrounds conceptions rather than such material objects as national monuments, more useful for this study.

20 See Kuzio, "History, Memory and Nation Building." Some other cogent discussions of Ukraine's language issues as national issues include Riabchuk, *Vid Malorossii do Ukrainy*, and Wilson, *The Ukrainians*, esp. chapter 10.

21 On nation as utopia, see Berlant as well as Gourgouris.

22 Paul Ricoeur writes about this duality of what he calls "a socio-political imaginaire" of a society (and of its dependence on narrative): "the imaginaire operates as an 'ideology' which can positively repeat and represent the founding discourse of a society, what I call its 'foundational symbols,' thus preserving its sense of identity. After all, cultures create themselves by telling stories of their past. The danger is, of course, that this reaffirmation can be perverted, usually by monopolistic elites, into a mystificatory discourse which serves to uncritically vindicate or justify the established political powers" ("The Creativity of Language" 29).

23 As Paul Gilbert argues in *The Philosophy of Nationalism*, a "myth may incorporate history, true or false," but its function is usually not to reflect history in all of its complexity, but to illuminate and communicate "national values": "mythic use of national history … sets before us national values that only this history can convey in their specificity and relevance to national life" (163–4).

24 See Smith, *National Identity* and *Ethno-Symbolism and Nationalism.*

25 Besides Anderson, see Brennan, "The National Longing for Form," and Carey-Webb, *Making Subject(s).*

26 See Pavlyshyn, "Literary Canons and National Identities in Ukraine." "Iconostasis" is the term ordinarily used for the wall of Christian icons – a traditional architectural element in an Eastern-Rite Christian church.

27 Bu-Ba-Bu is the name of a literary performance group, founded in 1985 and consisting of three Ukrainian male writers of the eighties generation: Yuri Andrukhovych, Viktor Neborak, and Oleksandr Irvanets. The group's name stands for "burlesque," "farce," and "buffoonery," three terms that reflect its emphasis on carnivalesque laughter as a cultural force of resistance and innovation.

28 Pavlyshyn gives the example of the poem "Love Oklahoma," written by the Bu-Ba-Bu member Oleksandr Irvanets as a spoof on the poem "Love Ukraine" by the Soviet Ukrainian poet Volodymyr Sosiura. The poem's calculated effect was to provoke "the patriotic audience which might find the older poem moving and its political sentiments

appealing" ("Literary Canons" 16). On the same poem as an example of "a biting critique of the national imaginary," see Shkandrij, "The Shifting Object of Desire," p. 81.

29 One of the very few Russophone writers in Ukraine of that generation who belonged to the new canon is Andrey Kurkov.

30 See Pavlyshyn, "Literary History."

31 See Lynch and Warner, "Introduction: The Transport of the Novel."

32 For more on the different, but equally essential, contributions of poetry and prose to Ukraine's national project, see Pavlyshyn, "Literatura i modernist'."

33 This argument has been made by many postcolonial historians and literary scholars. See, for example, Chatterjee, *The Nation and Its Fragments.*

34 For general theoretical discussions, see, for example, "Empire, Union, Center, Satellite," "On Colonialism, Communism and East-Central Europe – Some Reflections," and Chari and Verdery. For more specific applications of postcolonial theory to various postsocialist nations and their cultures, see, for example, Pavlyshyn and Clarke; Cavanagh; Kelertas; and Korek.

35 Moore points out, for instance, that a journey from Moscow to Tashkent, "until the opening of the colonial Central Asian railroads in the nineteenth century," would be much "rougher" than the sea voyage from London to Cairo. The distance that separated the imperial centre from the periphery was thus comparable to the "classic" colonial cases (119).

36 The Organization of Ukrainian Nationalists (OUN) was created in 1929 in Vienna as a response to the failure of the Ukrainian liberation struggle in 1917–1920. Its ideology of militant nationalism and terrorist activities were not supported by the majority of Ukrainians, but gained influence in the chaotic and violent times of the Second World War in Ukraine. In 1940, the organization split into a more moderate and a more radical faction, the latter led by Stepan Bandera (1909–1959). The OUN's controversial legacy, including the collaboration of both factions with the Nazis, is still a subject of much debate in contemporary Ukraine. Myroslav Shkandrij's *Ukrainian Nationalism* offers a most comprehensive and balanced account of the OUN ideology, mythology, and political struggle.

37 See Pavlyshyn, *Kanon ta ikonostas* and "The Tranquil Lakes of the Transmontane Commune"; Shkandrij, *Russia and Ukraine*; Chernetsky, *Mapping Postcommunist Cultures*; Romanets, *Anamorphosic Texts and Reconfigured Visions*; and Hundorova, *Tranzytna kul'tura.*

38 See, for instance, Zabuzhko, "Zhinka-avtor u kolonial'nii kul'turi" ("A Woman Writer in a Colonial Culture"); Kononenko's both serious and sacrastic references to imperialist projects and postcolonial syndromes as features of Ukrainian history, for example, in *Rosiis'kyi siuzhet* (*The Russian Plot*); and Matios's bitter commentary on Ukraine's colonial legacy in *Vyrvani storinky z avtobiohrafii* (*Pages Torn Out of My Autobiography*).

39 The argument about literature's greater freedom in handling archival lacunae, as compared with history, is made by Assmann in "Canon and Archive."

40 See Watkins, *Doris Lessing*.

41 Despite Hayden White's analysis of emplotment in narrative history (for instance, in *The Content of the Form*), its role in history writing often goes unacknowledged.

42 As Tamar Mayer summarizes in "Gender Ironies of Nationalism," theorizations of the gender/nation nexus, informed by feminism, have begun to appear in the West since the late 1980s (5). In thinking through the issues of gender and nationalism, I have benefited from reading Jayawardena, *Feminism and Nationalism in the Third World*; McClintock, "Family Feuds" and "No Longer in a Future Heaven"; *Dangerous Liaisons*, edited by McClintock, Mufti, and Shohat; Yuval-Davis, *Gender and Nation*; and *Between Woman and Nation*, edited by Kaplan et al. For the gender/nation nexus in postcolonial fiction, see Shultheis, *Regenerative Fictions*, and Boehmer, *Stories of Women*.

43 On the depiction of Ukraine as a *pokrytka* in Shevchenko's poetry, see Grabowicz, *The Poet as Mythmaker*, esp. pp. 110–11.

44 Murav, "Engendering the Russian Body Politic," p. 43.

45 For more on Lesia Ukrainka's and Kobylianska's reception in Ukrainian culture, see Pavlychko, *Dyskurs modernizmu v ukrains'kii literaturi*; Aheieva, *Poetesa zlamu stolit'*; and Zabuzhko, *Notre Dame d'Ukraine*.

46 For an analysis of women characters in Shevchuk's prose, see Hrabovych, "Kokhannia z vid'mamy." See also Buhaichuk, "Zhinochi mifolohichni obrazy u tvorchosti Valeriia Shevchuka."

47 On what Pavlyshyn has aptly described as "phallic frenzy" of Ukraine's early postcolonial literature by male writers (122), see his article, "Ukrainian Literature and the Erotics of Postcolonialism."

48 This occurs, for example, in an early short story by Kononenko, analysed in chapter 2. The author uses irony and intertextual play to deconstruct the myth of the Ukrainian folk poet Marusia Churai, which has been used to buttress the claim about unquestioned valorizing of women's poetic expression in Ukrainian culture. Both strategies – ironic or parodic figurations of woman/nation myths and realistic portrayals of women's multifaceted lives – have been described by Murav in "Engendering the Russian Body Politic," p. 43.

49 See, for example, Bahri, "Feminism in/and Postcolonialism"; George, "Feminists Theorize the Colonial/Postcolonial"; and Boehmer, *Colonial and Postcolonial Literature*, p. 216.

50 Based on pioneering historical work on nineteenth-century Ukrainian women's movements by Bohachevsky-Chomiak (see *Feminists Despite Themselves*), feminist scholar Tatiana Zhurzhenko formulated this term to describe a standpoint that combines concerns about oppression of women and issues of postcolonial nation-building (see *Gendernye rynki Ukrainy* and "Feminist (De)Constructions of Nationalism").

51 For a critique of national feminism, see, for example, Kis, "(Re)Constructing Ukrainian Women's History," pp. 162–4. For a more sympathetic analysis of

national feminism, including how it manifests in Zabuzhko's work, see Hrycak and Rewakowicz, "Feminism, Intellectuals and the Formation of Micro-Publics in Postcommunist Ukraine." For my comments on national feminism in Zabuzhko, see chapters 3 and 5.

52 Hrycak and Rewakowicz, "Feminism, Intellectuals and the Formation of Micro-Publics in Postcommunist Ukraine."

1 On the Invisibility of Ukrainian Women's Writing in the Soviet Empire

1 Besides Kobylianska and Lesia Ukrainka, there were many other Ukrainian women authors writing in this period. The most well-known among them were Olena Pchilka (1849–1930), Natalia Kobrynska (1855–1920), Liubov Yanovska (1861–1933), Hrytsko Hryhorenko (1867–1924), Yevhenia Yaroshynska (1868–1904), and Liudmyla Starytska-Cherniakhivska (1868–1941). For brief biographies and some of their works translated into English, see Franko. For a recent analysis of the limited entrance of women's writing into the Ukrainian literary canon of high modernism, see Hnatiuk, "Zhinoche oblychchia ukrains'koho modernizmu."

2 The statistics that I have compiled based on the series *Pys'mennyky Radianskoi Ukrainy* (*The Writers of Soviet Ukraine*, 1987) are instructive in this respect. The series included thirteen volumes of essays on more established Soviet Ukrainian writers working in all genres (with a stronger focus on older writers) and was published between 1955 and 1987 by the publishing house of the Union of Writers of Soviet Ukraine, *Radianskyi pys'mennyk*, with an average of three volumes per decade. Out of 127 writers covered in these volumes, there were only four women writers. Out of these four, two were children's writers, one stopped publishing in the 1930s, and only one (Iryna Vilde) wrote fiction for adults through much of the Soviet period (Petrosiuk 232–6). This is not to say that there were virtually no women writing in this period. If one examines the list of members of the Soviet Ukraine's Union of Writers, one will find many more women's names, but only very few of them achieved a position of prominence in Soviet Ukraine.

3 The Stalin Prize for literature was awarded yearly between 1941 and 1954. In 1966, it was revived and renamed the State Prize of the USSR. While this dubious honour has never been bestowed on any of the Ukrainian women writers, their male colleagues in the Union of Soviet Writers of Ukraine received it many times, most notably Oleksandr Korniychuk (in 1941, 1942, 1943, 1949, and 1951), Mykola Bazhan (in 1946 and 1949), Volodymyr Sosiura (in 1948), and Oles Honchar (in 1948 and 1982). It was also awarded three times (in 1943, 1946, and 1952) to a Polish Bolshevik woman writer, Wanda Wasilewska, who escaped from Hitler-occupied Poland into Ukraine, joined the Communist party, married the Ukrainian writer Oleksandr Korniychuk, settled in Kyiv, and wrote propagandist novels in Polish, some of which were commissioned personally by Stalin. Thereafter they

were quickly translated into Russian and Ukrainian and awarded prizes already in translation (Vasyliv). For more on Wasilewska, see Leshchenko.

4 In 1965, at the very tail end of the thaw period in Ukraine, Vilde received the Taras Shevchenko Prize for her novel *Sestry Richyns'ki* (*The Richynski Sisters*, 1964) – a lesser literary award specific to the Ukrainian Soviet Republic, which was nevertheless a sign of her work's official recognition. Another prominent Ukrainian woman author from this period – the poet Lina Kostenko (b. 1930) – did benefit from a Soviet education, received at the Maxim Gorky Literary Institute in Moscow, which may have contributed to the success of her early poetry in official Soviet culture. Yet she experienced many difficulties in her subsequent literary career in Soviet Ukraine. For more on Kostenko, see page 29 and note 9 in this chapter.

5 For more on Vilde's struggles to navigate the Soviet-era literary world, see Horak.

6 Zinaida Tulub (1890–1964), a Ukrainian author of historical novels, plays, film scripts, and literary translations, was arrested in 1937 on false charges of counter-revolutionary activity. She spent many years in prison and exile, and was allowed to return to Kyiv only in the mid-1950s. Nadia Surovtsova (1896–1985) worked for the government of the short-lived independent Ukrainian state, the Ukrainian People's Republic, in 1917–1918. After years of exile in Austria, she decided to return to (Soviet) Ukraine, where in 1927 she was arrested and spent the next thirteen years in prison, followed by sixteen years in exile. After she was rehabilitated, she attempted to write and publish short prose and extensive memoirs, various parts of which were confiscated from her at different times by the Soviet authorities. Her memoirs and letters were never published during the Soviet era.

7 The practice of the "internal reviews" of manuscripts, which were commissioned by publishing houses from politically loyal literati, existed through much of the Soviet period as an additional mechanism of control over the literary process. Bichuia had suffered much more from this form of Soviet censorship than from any other in the course of her literary career (Bichuia, Personal interview).

8 See Yekelchyk, *Stalin's Empire of Memory*, p. 130; and Risch, p. 124.

9 Kostenko did not stay, and although her early collections of poetry, published in Ukraine at the height of the thaw period (in 1957, 1958, and 1961), gained her much acclaim and immediate popularity, Ivanov was ultimately right. As early as in 1963, she was severely criticized for formalist experimentation, together with fellow poets Mykola Vinhranovsky and Ivan Drach, even though in comparison with them, Kostenko favoured much more traditional forms (Briukhovets'kyi 22, 80–1). Her subsequent collections were banned from publication, and Kostenko disappeared from the official literary scene until the late 1970s.

10 In his memoir of Soviet-era literary life in Lviv, Mykola Ilnytsky describes various repressive measures used by the local party bosses against the leadership of the Lviv branch of the Writers' Union and the editors of Lviv's thick journal *Zhovten* (*October*), including threats to send troops to the journal's editorial office (*Drama* 88).

11 For more on the role of the journal *October* in the literary politics of Soviet Ukraine, see Risch, *The Ukrainian West*, esp. chapter 5. In his discussion of literary life in Lviv between 1945 and the late 1980s, Risch mentions dozens of male writers, editors, and other members of the Soviet Ukrainian literary establishment and only one woman – Iryna Vilde. This fact gives additional confirmation to my argument about a virtual absence of prominent Ukrainian women authors in this period.

12 After the favourable reviews of Bichuia's first collection of stories (see especially Adel'heim, as well as Il'nyts'kyi, "Vyvorozhy"), Ivan Dziuba's thoughtful overview of Bichuia's work, initially published in the journal *Kyiv* in 1984, is one of very few careful assessments of this writer's prose by a literary critic from the Ukrainian capital ("Palitra 'mis'koi' povisti"). Even this article appeared only in the 1980s. Other detailed Soviet-era critical pieces on Bichuia were written almost exclusively by her Lviv colleagues (see, for example, Ivanychuk, "U poshukakh" and "Tema liuds'koi tvorchosti"). At the same time, through much of Bichuia's literary career, there appeared occasional short reviews of her works by non-Lviv-based Ukrainian critics that were more or less standard Soviet-era fare and gave little true insight into Bichuia's writing (see, for example, Donchyk, "Dokument i poetyzatsiia," p. 146; Lomazova; Panchenko; Hordasevych).

13 See Gabor, *Neznaioma*, p. 63; book description on the inside front cover of Bichuia's 2003 collection *Zemli romens'ki*; Khudyts'kyi; Levkova, etc.

14 Western Ukrainian writer Halyna Pahutiak is one notable exception.

15 This understanding, or rather misunderstanding, seemed to imply that women's prose was much narrower in scope than the prose written by men, and in Hordasevych's rather Soviet interpretation, it was also meant to be exclusively realistic so that the average female reader could easily identify with its characters (116–17).

16 Ivanychuk even formulated a theory about fighting the regime from inside, i.e., serving the interests of one's own people from various positions of power within the Soviet system of cultural production (*Blahoslovy* 141–4).

17 Bichuia has published no new fiction since the fall of the Soviet Union, although many of her earlier pieces have recently come out in new editions.

18 All quotations from "The Stone Master" come from my translation, published in *Herstories*, an anthology of Ukrainian women's prose edited by Michael M. Naydan.

19 Yurchak gives numerous examples of the performative shift occurring in various spheres of life, from pro forma voting in Soviet elections to almost automatic production of formulaic party speeches. For a full explanation of the performative shift, see *Everything Was Forever, Until It Was No More*, chapter 1.

20 The latter is another important aspect of the Soviet regime's discursive monopoly, one which Oushakine does not emphasize in his analysis because of his primary focus on political rather than artistic dissent. The subject position of a writer in the Soviet Union, as defined by Soviet authoritative discourse, has always privileged writing that reflected directly on the regime itself and its leaders.

21 For a detailed analysis of Donna Anna's masculine behaviour, see Krys.
22 The relationship of Bichuia's narrator to the traumatic experiences of her father and his generation fits Marianne Hirsch's conceptualization of "postmemory" – a form of profound connection which the "descendants of survivors ... of mass traumatic events" establish "to the previous generation's remembrances of the past" (105–6).
23 Spivak, "Can the Subaltern Speak?"
24 The portion of the story that describes this dream and the circumstances that led to it illustrates very well the provincialization of cultural production in Soviet Ukraine – an aspect of Soviet cultural politics mentioned earlier. The reason why the narrator comes in touch with the peasant women is because at the theatre where she works, they are in need of authentic props from the village for the performance of a humorous nineteenth-century populist play about Ukrainian village life. This play fit the Soviet bill for acceptable cultural expressions of diverse Soviet nationalities: its focus on folk costumes and other ethnographic details purportedly showed what Ukrainian culture was all about. The bitter irony captured in Bichuia's story is that while the Soviet Ukrainian urban theatre audiences enjoyed the politically correct "performances" of village life on stage, the real traditional culture of the Ukrainian countryside was being destroyed by collectivization, deportations, the man-made famine, and so on.
25 Bichuia told me that in her own career, she had at least one definite opportunity to increase her visibility as an author in exchange for glorifying the Soviet regime in her writing. In the early 1980s, she was issued an invitation by the secretary responsible for ideology of the Lviv Regional Committee of the Communist Party to write a play based on one of Leonid Brezhnev's alleged memoirs for a Lviv theatre. She was promised a literary prize for doing it, as well as awards for the theatre and the actors. Needless to say, she declined the offer (Bichuia, Personal interview).
26 In many of her works, Bichuia attempted to write beyond the regime's discursive field, choosing topics to her own liking that usually simply ignored the existence of the Soviet state. Likewise, she opted for a style that eschewed the transparency and plainness of socialist realist sloganeering, experimenting instead with fragmentary, non-linear, and often evasive narration, and with complex imagery.
27 Naydan, "A Conspicuous Blossoming" and "Emerging Ukrainian Women Prose Writers," p. 16; Rewakowicz, "Women's Literary Discourse," p. 275.

2 How Can a Ukrainian Woman Write?

1 Naydan, "Emerging Ukrainian Women Prose Writers," p. 15.
2 Zabuzhko's formulation is quoted in Hrycak and Rewakowicz (326). Although Kostenko wrote a lot of superb lyric poems, which were and continue to be very popular in Ukraine, her civic poetry and especially her historical novel in verse, *Marusia Churai* (1979), secured her status as one of Ukraine's foremost poets. For more details on Kostenko's early literary career, see chapter 1, p. 29 and note 9.

3 As Ukrainian historian and writer Olena Stiazhkina explained, works by Ukrainian women poets of the 1960s and the 1970s created "the lyrical heroine" as a new type of female character in Ukrainian literature; she was not interested in "the building of utopia or the struggle against this utopia" and focused instead on "the minutiae of the private sphere" (81, 83). Such a focus was often criticized or dismissed as trivial by both the Soviet literary officialdom and the ideologues of the new Ukrainian literary movement of the sixties generation. This was despite the fact that the emphasis on the private and the individual could be seen as a form of resistance to the prescribed public and collectivist ethos of socialist realist literature. Stiazhkina called the unenviable position in which the "lyrical heroine" found herself "a trap of the discourse on 'woman's destiny'" (83). It is therefore not by accident that the prolific Ukrainian woman poet of the sixties generation Iryna Zhylenko, who wrote predominantly lyric poetry and published numerous volumes of it since 1965, frequently faced a mixed reception and did not receive the Taras Shevchenko prize for her poetry until 1994.

4 Among authors of children's literature, Zabila and Oksana Ivanenko were rare exceptions, becoming full-time writers for children and youth as well as functionaries in charge of children's literature in the official Soviet culture.

5 Clark, *The Soviet Novel: History as Ritual*, p. xiii.

6 For more on the repressions against Ivanchenko, see Kozulia (246–8).

7 One well-known example is the reaction of Ukraine's Communist Party ideologues to Roman Ivanychuk's 1968 historical novel *Mal'vy* (*Hollyhock*), which "was confiscated from libraries and bookstores" (Risch 176).

8 It seems that this attempt was successful. As one Soviet-era review of *It Is Not Easy to Love* euphemistically (and condescendingly) states, this collection by Ivanchenko "demonstrates the young writer's more rigorous effort as compared with her previous work" (Diachenko 207). A year after the publication of this collection, in 1977, Ivanchenko was permitted to join Ukraine's Union of Soviet Writers.

9 While the number of female writer awardees has considerably increased with independence, most of them have still been awarded the Taras Shevchenko Prize for novels, especially those that deal extensively with national and historical topics. Like Iryna Vilde, who received this prize in 1965 for her monumental novel *Sestry Richyns'ki* (*The Richynski Sisters*), and like Lina Kostenko, Soviet-era Ukraine's most famous female poet, who was nevertheless awarded this prize in 1987 for a novel, albeit in verse (*Marusia Churai*), independent Ukraine's women writers receive this recognition predominantly for their works in the same genre: Raisa Ivanchenko in 1996 for a tetralogy of historical novels, Maria Matios in 2005 for *Sweet Darusia*, Liubov Holota in 2008 for the novel *Epizodychna pam'iat'* (*Fragmentary Memory*), and Halyna Pahutiak in 2010 for *Sluha z Dobromylia* (*The Servant from Dobromyl'*). It is only in the 2010s that this trend seems to be shifting, with the Shevchenko Prize recently going twice to women authors of non-fiction books: in 2010 to Oksana Pakhliovska for a collection of articles, essays, and

interviews, *Ave, Europa!* (2009), and in 2019, to one of the heroines of this book, Oksana Zabuzhko, for a collection of articles, essays, interviews, and memoirs, *I znov ia vlizaiu v tank ...* (*And Once Again I Am Climbing into a Tank ...*, 2016).

For detailed information on the Taras Shevchenko National Prize of Ukraine and its awardees, see *Komitet z Natsional'noi premii Ukrainy imeni Tarasa Shevchenka.* Of course, as an originally Soviet institution, the Shevchenko Prize may be expected to exemplify some continuity with the previous era in cultural forms, if not in ideology, and it has been frequently criticized for this continuity. However, because it remains the nation's most prestigious official literary award, it cannot be discounted as a significant cultural mechanism, one that both reflects and shapes current trends in literature.

10 On the development of and approaches in feminist literary studies in Ukraine, see Aheieva, *Zhinochyi prostir*, esp. pp. 309–15; Chernetsky, *Mapping Postcommunist Cultures,* esp. pp. 238–48; and Rewakowicz, "Women's Literary Discourse" and *Ukraine's Quest for Identity*, pp. 21–9.

11 A 2001 dissertation about the literary reworkings of the folk ballad about Marusia and of her legend examines over a dozen literary works on this theme, from Bohdan Zaleski's ballad written in the 1820s to Lina Kostenko's 1979 historical novel in verse, and mentions many more. See Dakh, "Literaturne zhyttia narodnoi ballady 'Oi ne khody, Hrytsiu ....'"

12 A leader of Ukrainian Cossacks, Bohdan Khmelnytsky, led a major uprising against the Polish Commonwealth in 1648–57, which turned into an all-out Cossack-Polish War, and led to the creation of the Cossack state (The Hetmanate) in what is present-day central Ukraine.

13 Hundorova, *Femina Melancholica*, p. 198.

14 *Vechornytsi* was a traditional peasant youth party that was the primary Ukrainian village site for courtship in traditional Ukrainian culture.

15 See, for instance, Hundorova, *Femina Melancholica*, p. 197.

16 Kononenko, "On Sunday Morning," translated by Svitlana Kobets, pp. 152–3.

17 Kis', *Zhinka v tradytsiinii ukrains'kii kul'turi*, pp. 162, 164.

18 Grothe, "Medusa, Cassandra, Medea: Re-Inscribing Myth in Contemporary German and Russian Women's Writing," p. 18.

19 Although it may seem that Zabuzhko's personal confidence would prevent her from experiencing "anxiety of authorship," her own testimony proves otherwise. In an autobiographical sketch that accompanies her 2003 collection of prose, *Sestro, Sestro* (*Sister, Sister*), she confesses that she has been writing prose as well as poetry since a very early age, but "did not have the courage to publish it: I was tortured by a realization that there was 'something wrong' with how I wrote it [prose], that I had no previously thought-out structure for it, but wrote it as I would write poetry – from a feeling that by itself, from 'inside,' creates its own composition" (235).

20 In *Notre Dame d'Ukraine*, Zabuzhko emphasizes this link even more by calling Cassandra Ukrainka's alter ego and using the writer's letters to demonstrate the

metaphysical nature of Ukrainka's gift: "no sooner do I start some more mundane project than some inescapable, despotic dream literally 'seizes' me, torments me in the night, simply takes the life out of me. Sometimes I am even scared of it – what kind of a mania is this?" (qtd in Zabuzhko, *Notre Dame d'Ukraine* 71).

21 Although the Lacanian theory of language is often justly criticized for being ahistorical, it suits my purposes here because both Ukrainka and Zabuzhko, in *Cassandra* and *The Alien Woman* respectively, deal with a myth, the timeless and universal insights of which they test and rewrite.

22 Of course, not all women authors in fact occupy such a liminal position: many of them adopt a masculine position for a variety of reasons. In this sense, it is not by accident that Zabuzhko chose Ukrainka for her literary ancestor. As several Ukrainian feminist scholars noted, the poetry of the most distinguished Ukrainian female poet of the Soviet period – Lina Kostenko – has often been written from a masculine position. This idea has been expressed well by Vira Aheieva: "In this poetry, there is very little room for a genuinely *feminine* voice … These poems are convenient for quoting (incidentally, they are frequently used as didactic material in schools …). Maxims and sayings, apt, sharp, but *hopelessly univocal* [*odnoznachni*] – these are texts that you would search in vain for *insights into psychic experiences, for semantic multiplicity, which are important, perhaps, not so much in and of themselves as for what one gains along this path of exploration*" (*Zhinochyi prostir* 264; my emphasis). Aheieva concludes that in comparison with the feminist motifs in the work of Ukrainka, the poetry of Kostenko is marked by a regression from a feminine stance (269).

23 See, for example, Tebeshevs'ka-Kachak, "Avtobiohrafizm"; Hrabovych, "Kokhannia z vid'mamy"; and Rewakowicz, *Ukraine's Quest for Identity*, pp. 113–16.

3 Voicing the Self

1 As Hrycak and Rewakowicz point out, in 2006 Zabuzhko's *Fieldwork* was named "The Most Influential Book for the 15 Years of Ukraine's Independence" (325). The novel has been translated into many languages, including Polish, Russian, Czech, Bulgarian, Romanian, Hungarian, German, Swedish, Dutch, Italian, and English. For more details, see Zabuzhko's official website: www.zabuzhko.com.

2 For more on the scandal caused by the novel, see Taran, "Lantsiuhova reaktsiia" and Zabuzhko's own essay, "Zhinka-avtor u kolonial'nii kul'turi," esp. pp. 190–2.

3 The criticisms voiced by *Ukrainske slovo* are cited in more detail in Monakhova's essay, "'Pidporiadkovane' v ukrains'komu konteksti," p. 124.

4 See Hrycak and Rewakowicz, "Feminism, Intellectuals and the Formation of Micro-Publics in Postcommunist Ukraine," as well as Rewakowicz's recent monograph, *Ukraine's Quest for Identity*, pp. 102–5.

5 Chernetsky, *Mapping Postcommunist Cultures*, p. 228; Monakhova, "National Identity in the Postcolonial Situation," pp. 182, 186, and "Pidporiadkovane," pp. 127–9, 131.

6 In Spivak's retelling, the young woman, Bhuvaneswari Bhaduri, was a member of a local group of fighters for Indian independence that assigned to her the task of a political assassination. Agonizing over her inability to carry out this task, Bhaduri decided to kill herself, but since she knew that everyone would most likely interpret her suicide as the result of an illicit pregnancy, she waited to commit her desperate act until she was menstruating. She thus sent a message, "in the physiological inscription of her body," to her family and the conservative culture at large (Spivak 308). Nevertheless, when Spivak made inquiries about Bhaduri's death from those who knew the young woman, she was told that the reason for the suicide was "illicit love" (308).

7 Hereafter all quotations are from Zabuzhko, *Fieldwork in Ukrainian Sex*, translated by Halyna Hryn.

8 For a similar argument in the context of Central Asia, see Ol'ga Zubovskaia, "Primenima li i kak zapadnaia postkolonial'naia teoriia dlia analisa postsovetskogo feminizma?" Zubovskaia writes of the construction of what she calls "'the voice' of Central Asian feminism" as a position "between various discourses on gender" – the discourse of Western aid donors, the Soviet discourse on "the women's question," and the discourse of Central Asian nationalism (178).

9 See Blacker, "Nation, Body, Home," p. 490. See also Rewakowicz's recent commentary, in which the author briefly describes Zabuzhko's national feminist stance in the novel, yet does not distinguish between the different voices and the narrator's personas, which results in the familiar argument about the deficiency of the heroine's feminism: "one is surprised that the heroine longs to form a union with a man who has clearly interiorized imperial abuse but whom she perceives (at least initially) worthy of her attention and worthy of fathering her child. One can almost surmise that her old-fashioned yearning (as radical feminists would put it) to have family entails dependence rather than freedom and equality" (*Ukraine's Quest for Identity* 115).

10 The use of language in the novel has been remarked upon by Kobets, briefly analysed by Monakhova, and studied in more detail by Amy Elisabeth Moore in her comparative doctoral dissertation on Nicole Brossard and Zabuzhko, although the latter work includes many misinterpretations, in my view. In this chapter, I go beyond this previous analysis of language(s) in *Fieldwork*.

11 Nila Zborovska sees *Fieldwork* as a "love" novel that deals with "the death of love" (*Feministychni rozdumy* 113, 119). Maryna Romanets focuses on the dynamics of masochism in the narrator's love affair and in the Soviet society at large ("Erotic Assemblages"). Chernetsky's reading of *Fieldwork* focuses on its depiction of bodies and its "critique of colonial masculinities" through its image of Oksana's lover, although it does briefly discuss the novel's "working through a virtual palimpsest of traumas" (*Mapping Postcommunist Cultures* 258–9). In her 2009 essay, Rewakowicz dismissed the novel's thematic preoccupations as "anything but new, … a typical story of 'boy meets girl,'" attributing novelty only to *Fieldwork*'s subversive blending

of autobiography and fiction ("Women's Literary Discourse" 286–7). In her recent monograph, she gave *Fieldwork* more credit and acknowledged the existence and innovative treatment of other important thematic concerns in the novel, but did not analyse them in detail (*Ukraine's Quest for Identity* 102–5, 113–15).

12 For more on the general function of displacement in *Fieldwork* and in other contemporary Ukrainian novels, see Chernetsky, "The Trope of Displacement."

13 This mini-dialogue appears in English in the original text.

14 This question is asked in English in the original.

15 Volodymyr Vynnychenko (1880–1951) was a prolific Ukrainian modernist writer and politician. Because of his political activity, including his active involvement in the establishment of an independent Ukrainian state, the Ukrainian People's Republic, in 1917, his opposition to the Bolsheviks, as well as the substance and style of his writings, his works were banned in Soviet Ukraine.

16 While Mykola's behaviour fits the more general image of post-Soviet masculinity in crisis, widely examined in the fiction and films of the 1990s, Zabuzhko identifies specifically "Ukrainian" features of this postcommunist phenomenon.

17 This analysis demonstrates the Ukrainian specificity of what has been generally described in academic literature as the "unmaking" of the Soviet man (see, for example, Lilya Kaganovsky, *How the Soviet Man Was Unmade*). It thus offers a response to an argument made by scholars like Madina Tlostanova, who maintains that Zabuzhko's Ukrainian man does not differ in any way from the generalized Soviet man, with his characteristic "complexes of inferiority and symbolic castration as well as unimaginable egocentrism and moral immaturity" (Tlostanova 174).

18 For instance, in Hryn and Zabuzhko: "prior to the appearance of *Field Work* [*sic*] the voices heard in our literature were predominantly male, and misogyny, either overt or latent, became part of a fashionable writer's make-up – all those guys playing the role of 'eternally young' macho boys, to the cheers of the same 'eternally young' macho critics." The male protagonist of the novel, "'the genius painter' … belongs, undoubtedly and recognizably, to the same type" (21).

19 Written in 1970, Erofeev's "poema" was first published in 1973 in Israel. In the Soviet Union, it was officially published only in 1989.

20 Since Andrukhovych and Bu-Ba-Bu in general gave primacy to sound and reading out loud (Hundorova, "Bu-Ba-Bu"), it makes sense to decipher this name on the basis of its phonetics. In Ukrainian, "Otto von F." sounds like the beginning of the phrase "Ото фанфарон!" (*What a braggart!*). Coming into Slavic languages from the Spanish *fanfarrón*, the word denotes someone who is "conceited, prideful, arrogant blabbermouth; a braggart," which would make it a fitting ironic name for any and all of Andrukhovych's buffoon characters (*Etymolohichnyi slovnyk ukrains'koi movy*, vol. 6, p. 73; *Slovnyk ukrains'koi movy*, vol. 10, p. 562).

21 All quotations are taken from Vitaly Chernetsky's English translation (Andrukhovych, *The Moscoviad*).

22 See Hundorova, *Pisliachornobyl's'ka biblioteka*; Chernetsky, *Mapping Postcommunist Cultures*; Pavlyshyn, several essays in *Kanon ta iconostas*; Hnatiuk, *Proshchannia z imperiieiu*, p. 482, among many others.

23 While Otto seems to closely resemble Venedikt Erofeev's Venichka, the two characters actually represent distinct, if related, types – the Ukrainian buffoon and the Russian holy fool. For the differences between the two, see Shavokshyna, "Typolohiia smikhovykh personazhiv v ukrains'komu, ches'komu ta rosiis'komu postmodernizmakh (blazen' – pabitel' – iurodyvyi)." For the function of the holy fool in Russian culture and especially in Dostoevsky's works, see Murav, *Holy Foolishness*. For Venichka's use of irony, which is very different from Otto's, see Ready.

24 This exchange appears in English in the original.

25 "The Ballad of Misfortunate Captives" is a well-known Ukrainian folk ballad dating back to the seventeenth century. In it, the Zaporozhian Cossacks captured by the Turks lament their fate and long to return to Ukraine.

26 See Monakhova, "Pidporiadkovane," and Amy Elizabeth Moore.

27 In her perceptive review of *Fieldwork*, Svitlana Kobets argued that Zabuzhko employed "the technique of defamiliarization" in the novel, meaning for her "ladies and gentlemen" audience to "serve as a collective mediator through the eyes of whom the Ukrainian reader is forced to take a fresh look at himself and his world" (183). This insight underscores the potential of *Fieldwork* to have performative effects for its Ukrainian reading public, serving as a catalyst for their reconsideration of their own Ukrainian identity.

28 There have been at least two adaptations of *Fieldwork* for the stage: a monodrama by the Ukrainian actress Halyna Stefanova, which premiered in Kyiv in 2003, and an adaptation by the Polish theatre Polonia in Warsaw, which premiered in 2006 (see Zabuzhko's official website). A college handbook on contemporary Ukrainian literature, *Suchasna ukrains'ka proza*, by Roksana Kharchuk devotes a separate chapter to *Fieldwork*.

29 The English translation, however, did not come out until 2011, when the translator was finally able to secure a publisher.

30 For a critique of the position of one Russophone Ukrainian commentator, who also found Zabuzhko's feminism not feminist enough, see Chernetsky, *Mapping Postcommunist Cultures*, p. 248.

4 Rewriting the Nation

1 See Naydan, "A Conspicuous Blossoming," but also Stiazhkina, *Zhinky v istorii ukrains'koi kul'tury*, pp. 70–1; and Rewakowicz, *Ukraine's Quest for Identity*, pp. 10–11, 99–100.

2 The contents of the collection were gradually expanded and revised by the author from the first to the third edition of the book. In this chapter, I use the fullest, third edition.

3 See Sommer, *Foundational Fictions.*
4 As Anderson explains, the colonial state carefully managed the functions of the "museumized" past it constructed: the foreign colonial ruling elites clearly did not share the native populations' "albums of ancestors," but eventually were able to present the colonial state as a benevolent "guardian of the local tradition" (253).
5 See Hogan, *Understanding Nationalism.*
6 A foundational text containing such a critique is Joan Scott's seminal *Gender and the Politics of History* (1999).
7 These roles, of course, fit well into the framework of women's roles in the nation, elaborated by Yuval-Davis and discussed in the introduction.
8 Ulas Samchuk (1905–1987) was a Ukrainian writer and journalist who lived much of his life in exile, in Czechoslovakia, Germany, and Canada, travelling back to Soviet Ukraine in the early 1930s to witness the Holodomor. On the connections of his writing to Ukrainian nationalist ideology, see Shkandrij, *Ukrainian Nationalism*, chapter 10.
9 Although Maria is an individualized character and her early life is somewhat unconventional for a Ukrainian peasant woman, her *death* is made into a symbol of collective, national suffering. This becomes clear, for example, when Hnat kisses her hand towards the end of the narrative, referring to it as "the hand of the mother" (*Mariia* 272). Tellingly, Samchuk dedicates his novel to all Ukrainian mothers who perished in the famine.
10 Sadly, Anderson's poetics of a national biography, with its overwhelming focus on death, works particularly well for Ukraine, which had a staggering death toll in the Stalinist repressions and the events of the Second World War (but also in the First World War and the Bolshevik Revolution). The term "bloodlands," coined by Timothy Snyder to refer to the human suffering in the space and time "between Hitler and Stalin," is especially applicable to Ukraine.
11 These terms come from a 2005 *Kyiv Post* editorial, which Marples quotes, p. 301. Yaroslav Hrytsak made a similar point more recently in a *Slavic Review* piece, "Postcolonial Is Not Enough," where he emphasized "Ukraine's two roles – as the core of the Russian and Soviet projects, on the one hand, and as the center of anti-imperial and anti-Soviet resistance, on the other" (733–4).
12 This situation has been rapidly changing since the Euromaidan protests and the onset of the war in the Donbas. In his post-Euromaidan article, "National Heroes for a New Ukraine," Yekelchyk details recent initiatives on the governmental level, as well as in the arts, to transform "national memory" in Ukraine (121). He gives the most curious example of the recent efforts of Ukraine's Ministry of Defence to marry the "Soviet" and the "nationalist" visions of Ukraine in a TV commercial: "Two elderly actors, familiar from Soviet-era war films, portray decorated World War II veterans who receive phone calls from their grandchildren currently serving in the Ukrainian army. At the end of their brief conversations in Russian, the present-day soldiers congratulate their grandparents on Victory Day, to which they

reply, also in Russian, 'Glory to Ukraine!'" (121). On the significance of this greeting and the changes in its connotations during the Euromaidan, see chapter 6, note 3.

13 Hutsuls are an ethnographic group of highlanders who live in the Carpathian Mountains in Western Ukraine; they speak a distinctive Hutsul dialect of Ukrainian and have preserved a rich array of folk traditions.

14 As Matios stressed in one of her interviews about *The Nation*, her account of "the nation" is personal and subjective: "I attempted to create *my own* – living – picture of Ukrainian life and its recent – post-war – history" (*Vyrvani storinky* 293; my emphasis).

15 Brown notes that one of the first initiatives of the occupying Nazi administration was to single out ethnic Germans and Jews, for which they used "Soviet records and read the demographic maps drawn up by Soviet cartographers in the mid-twenties" (198).

16 In this story, Matios does not portray the period of the Romanian occupation in detail, although she writes about the persecution of the Jews during the Second World War, including the Nazi-allied Romanian administration in Bukovyna, in her novel *Sweet Darusia*; in her 2011 collection of essays and autobiographical fragments, *Pages Torn Out of My Autobiography*; in newspaper articles (see, for example, "Omelian Kovch and Emil' Klugman"); and, most fully and poignantly, describing local collaboration, in her 2013 novel, *Cherevychky Bozhoi materi (Shoes of the Mother of God).*

17 For a Derridean reading of this short story, in which the concept of undecidability is central, see Szymczyszyn.

18 *Kulak*, or *kurkul* in Ukrainian, was a term for a well-to-do peasant in the Russian Empire and later in the Soviet Union. The criteria for defining a *kulak* became very arbitrary in the Soviet period, and especially during Stalin's collectivization campaign, when kulaks were declared class enemies marked for "liquidation." Their property was confiscated and the peasants themselves, together with their families, were deported to remote areas of the Soviet Empire.

19 An interpretation suggested by Irina Zherebkina in *Gendernye 90-e* (160).

20 "Prosyly tato-mama ..." (My father is asking, my mother is asking ...) is a traditional beginning of the ritual Ukrainian oral invitation to a wedding, still used in rural Ukraine today.

21 Nowhere in her texts does Matios call the guerrillas "UPA" but rather "those from the forest" or simply "the forest," a euphemism used by the locals at the time of the movement's activity and until Ukraine's independence.

22 *Skaz* is a form of narration that imitates oral, often folksy, speech, including dialectal features and slang, in order to characterize the literary heroes and their milieu.

23 Sociologist James W. Messerschmidt, among others, writes of the widespread use of mass rape in the Second World War, both by Nazi and Soviet troops. In particular, he analyses motivations behind the mass rapes of German women in Berlin by the Red Army soldiers in 1945, concluding that they "functioned ... to establish masculine domination over Other women, Other men, and the Other nation" and "to frighten and intimidate the Berlin civilian population" (710).

24 In *Pages Torn Out of My Autobiography*, Matios mentions her aunt Hafia, the mother of a one-year-old at the time when she was interrogated and tortured by the MGB – in ways similar to those used with Matronka (126).

25 In *Pages Torn Out of My Autobiography*, Matios writes that she grew up almost ignorant of the real Second World War events that occurred in her village and in Bukovyna in general. Her grandparents, and especially her grandmother, were afraid to tell the truth to their children and grandchildren. She began to learn these historical facts and collect oral histories in rural Bukovyna only in the late 1980s.

26 Solovey 58; Strikha, "Dzerkalo doby imitatsii."

27 *Homo Sovieticus* is a derogatory term for a stereotypical Soviet citizen, characterized by lack of initiative, conformism, tolerance for corruption, and other negative features that became common in Soviet society. The term was made popular thanks to the book *Homo Sovieticus* (1982), by Soviet Russian writer Aleksandr Zinovyev.

28 *Zrivnialivka* was the Soviet practice of economic levelling, grounded in the belief that no individual should be much wealthier than another.

29 *Surzhyk* is a mix of Russian and Ukrainian languages often used in Central and Eastern Ukraine.

30 I do not mean to say that the differences between Kyiv and Eastern Ukrainian regions do not exist – only that the dynamics of othering tends to construct on their basis a divisive internal boundary. In the post-Soviet era, historians and political scientists have written much about different regional identities in Ukraine. In 2000, political scientist Kataryna Wolczuk, for example, analysed the strong "regional identity" of Donbas, formed in the Soviet era, when this part of Ukraine "played the role of a shop window of Soviet communism" (673). Since the war in the Donbas, academic writing about this region has exploded. See, for example, a comprehensive work by historians Stanislav Kul'chyts'kyi and Larysa Iakubova, *Trysta rokiv samotnosti*.

5 Excavating the (Gendered) Nation

1 In her interview with Khruslinska, Zabuzhko stated that her conception of *The Museum of Abandoned Secrets* included a deliberate focus on women's deaths and the reasons behind them (Khruslins'ka 222).

2 Zabuzhko has mentioned in interviews that the story of the concert hall was based on real events. Palace "Ukraine" was first built in the 1970s upon the approval of the project in Moscow; however, when the local authorities realized that their palace turned out to be more opulent than the Kremlin Palace of Congresses in Moscow, they shut it down "for repairs," stripped it of its elegant furnishings, reopened it soon after, and placed the blame for this "oversight" on the project's architects.

3 All quotations from this novel come from Nina Shevchuk-Murray's 2012 translation (Zabuzhko, *The Museum of Abandoned Secrets*).

4 For a detailed reading of these conversations, and of the entire novel as Michel de Certeau's "zoo of everyday practices" (78), see my article in *The Everyday of Memory*, edited by Marta Rabikowska (Shchur, "Ukrainian Women between Communism and Post-Communism").

5 In this seemingly overdramatic episode, Zabuzhko actually addresses a widespread gender issue of post-Soviet transition in Ukraine. As recently as 2009, Ukraine still had "the worst human trafficking problem in the world" (Hankivsky and Salnykova 7), with about half of the victims being women and girls who were trafficked for the purposes of "sexual exploitation" ("Human Trafficking and Modern-Day Slavery"). This is despite large-scale awareness-raising and prevention campaigns operating in Ukraine since the late 1990s and sponsored by Western donors, such as USAID, and various European Union agencies, as well as legislation adopted by the Ukrainian government to eliminate trafficking (Hrycak, "Women as Migrants").

6 For an exploration of the literary connections between the secret police and the devil in Soviet literature, see Vatulescu.

7 This is in contrast to Matios, who was elected to the Ukrainian parliament in 2012.

8 See Zhurzhenko, *Gendernye rynki Ukrainy* and "Feminist (De)Constructions of Nationalism."

9 For this argument made in detail, see Hrycak and Rewakowicz, "Feminism, Intellectuals and the Formation of Micro-Publics in Postcommunist Ukraine."

10 See Zabuzhko, "Zhinka-avtor u kolonial'nii kul'turi."

11 It is in part for this reason that Maria Rewakowicz considers "Zabuzhko's bulky novel ... her least feminist work to date" (*Ukraine's Quest for Identity* 107).

12 As mentioned in the previous chapter, Matios's *Sweet Darusia* received the 2005 Taras Shevchenko National Prize and the title of "The Most Widely Read Book in 2007" in Ukraine. Kononenko's *Imitation* was the winner of the 2001 Ukrainian national rating "Book of the Year" and received the prize of the literary journal *Suchasnist'*. Finally, Zabuzhko's *The Museum of Abandoned Secrets* earned the author a number of accolades: it was the winner of the 2010 Ukrainian national rating "Book of the Year" and was named "The Best Ukrainian Book of 2010" by the *Korrespondent* magazine; it was nominated for 2010 BBC Book of the Year award; and it received the prestigious Angelus Central European Literature Award in 2013.

13 Pavlyshyn notes this particular contribution of Matios in contemporary Ukrainian literature, considering her to be one of very few authors whose writing is truly postcolonial rather than displaying an anticolonial animus. See Pavlyshyn, "The Tranquil Lakes of the Transmontane Commune," p. 75.

6 New National Chronicles

1 In a 2012 theorization of *communitas*, Edith Turner defined this phenomenon as "the sense felt by a group of people when their life together takes on full meaning" (1).

2 See Pavlyshyn, "Literary History," p. 77, and Shore, p. 80. For a theorization of how Euromaidan enabled the emergence of a new civic Ukrainian identity through performance, see Hundorova, "Ukrainian Euromaidan as Social and Cultural Performance."

3 The greeting "Slava Ukraini!" (Glory to Ukraine!) and its customary response "Heroiam slava!" (Glory to the Heroes!) was commonly used in the 1930s by the members of the OUN and the UPA. It became one of the Maidan's most common slogans, but many protesters have argued that it lost its radical nationalist connotations in the process. For different reactions to the slogan, see Shore, pp. 52–3, 55.

4 Non-fiction genres are by no means new literary territory for Zabuzhko or for Matios. As mentioned in chapter 2 and elsewhere in this book, both writers had earlier in their careers published highly successful non-fiction volumes, many of which provided insightful commentary on Ukrainian history, culture, and politics. That such works can attract a lot of attention in Ukraine was demonstrated, for example, by Matios's 2011 collection of essays and autobiographical fragments, *Pages Torn Out of My Autobiography*. This volume "generated a scandal of national proportions" over some comments it made and led to the author's harassment by the Yanukovych government (Tytarenko, "Female Narrative Journalism" 46). For more on this incident, see also Tytarenko, "Women's Voices," pp. 172–75. Finally, Zabuzhko's most recent volume of non-fiction writing, *I znov ia vlizaiu v tank …* (*And Once Again I Am Climbing into a Tank …*), earned her the Taras Shevchenko Prize in 2019.

5 For an excellent recent elaboration of Aristotle's classic definition of a plot, see Belknap, *Plots*, esp. pp. 34–7.

6 *Nebesna Sotnia* (the Heavenly Hundred) was a collective name given to about a hundred protesters who were killed during the Euromaidan. The term "sotnia" referred to a Cossack military formation of about a hundred men in the sixteenth to eighteenth centuries. The term was first adopted on the Maidan to designate self-defence units and was later expanded to various groupings of protesters united by a common initiative or activity, such as *Mystetska Sotnia* (the Arts Hundred).

7 The hero's mother stays home and worries about her son's well-being; the hero's girlfriend leaves Kyiv before the most dangerous phase of the protests begins, inspiring and reassuring him during their phone conversations; and the hero's death acquires an especially heroic colouring because he is shot while trying to protect an elderly woman on the Maidan.

8 *Titushky* was a term coined to designate the thugs hired by the Yanukovych regime to intimidate and commit violence against the protesters during the Euromaidan.

9 "Deputy" or "people's deputy" is the term that designates a member of the Ukrainian parliament, a legislative body that consists of 450 members.

10 See Martsenyuk, "Women's Top-Level Political Participation," p. 33.

11 A relic of the Soviet era, internal troops were a gendarme-like force subordinate to the Ministry of Internal Affairs of Ukraine. They existed in Ukraine until 2014 and were used along with the riot police against the Euromaidan protesters.

12 For a detailed discussion of the mother's authority in the traditional Ukrainian family, see Kis', *Zhinka v tradytsiinii ukrains'kii kul'turi*, especially pp. 178–80.

13 Matios's gendered strategies of protest action during the Euromaidan were not a unique phenomenon. In her excellent study of the Euromaidan "as pure subjective experience" (xiv), based on numerous interviews with both male and female protest participants, Marci Shore gives an example of similar strategic deployment of gender identity by women in the march of the "Sisters' *Sotnia*," an all-woman demonstration in Dnipropetrovsk (193). Because they knew that "men would not want to attack women, ... Victoria and her fellow organizers asked the men to stay to the side while a hundred or so women of all ages carrying pots, pans, buckets, and drums marched to the administration building – that is, precisely where everyone was now afraid to go" (193).

14 The activities of this group fully accord with the analysis of the maternalist discourse by Phillips as well as Khromeychuk's argument about women speaking out as mothers on behalf of their children. This group is prominently featured in the documentary film *Women of Maidan*, by Olha Onyshko, which mostly gives a traditionalist representation of women's participation in the protests. For more on the film, see Roßmann, "To Serve Like a Man," p. 205.

15 For the analysis of these roles' incompatibility in Ukrainian culture, see Kis, "Choosing without Choice."

16 The anti-democratic laws, popularly known as "dictatorship laws," were passed on 16 January 2014 by the Ukrainian parliament, with numerous violations of the legislative procedure and under pressure from the then president, Yanukovych. They significantly limited freedom of speech and assembly, seeking to criminalize the protesters and put an end to the Euromaidan.

17 For more on women's participation in self-defence on the Euromaidan, see Phillips; Khromeychuk; and Onuch and Martsenyuk, esp. pp. 119–20.

18 For the full argument against women's participation in Euromaidan self-defence, see Mayerchyk and Plakhotnik.

19 See, for example, Karpov, "Politika iskazheniia roli zhenshchin."

20 See, for example, the evidence from the interviews which Khromeychuk conducted with the female leaders of the all-female *sotnias*, in "Gender and Nationalism on the Maidan."

21 Finnin, "Nationalism and the Lyric," pp. 51–2.

22 This general sense is also present in the representation of the protests in the critically acclaimed cinematic chronicle of the Euromaidan, Sergey Loznitsa's documentary *Maidan* (2014). It is partly so because *The Chronicle* and the film share the chronicle genre and include a variety of protesters' voices. Dispensing with the overarching narrative voiceover and simply capturing whatever sound is emanating from the protest square and the nearby streets, the film shows, for instance, both male and female poets reciting their amateur poetry from the stage and both men and women running the Maidan kitchen. Like *The Chronicle*,

the documentary also includes some evidence of traditionalist views of women's protest roles – for example, appeals from the Maidan stage for women to leave the barricades during the storming of the square by the riot police. *The Chronicle*, however, ends up being much more effective than the film in representing women's varied participation in the Euromaidan because it features many women protesters' own reflections on the events and on their motivation to participate in them.

23 On Ukrainian women's greater participation in the political and security processes in Ukraine since the Euromaidan, as well as on the challenges that persist, see Benigni.

24 See, for instance, Onuch and Martsenyuk's polemics with Phillips in "Mothers and Daughters of the Maidan," as well as Mayerchyk and Plakhotnik's arguments against Martsenyuk's position in "Ukrainian Feminism."

Conclusion

1 See, for example, Hobsbawm, *Nations and Nationalism since 1780*, pp. 190–2.

2 See, for instance, *Z nepokrytoiu holovoiu: Ukrains'ka zhinocha proza* (2014), edited by Aheieva and published by KOMORA, a Kyiv-based publishing house started by Zabuzhko and her colleagues.

3 The call is issued explicitly by Sorensen in *Postcolonial Studies and the Literary*, but it is also strongly present, for example, in Nicholas Harrison's *Postcolonial Criticism* and Derek Attridge's companion volumes, *The Singularity of Literature* and *J. M. Coetzee: The Ethics of Reading.*

Bibliography

Adel'heim, Ievhen. “Vidchuty sebe spil'nykom usioho sutnioho.” *Kriz' roky: Vybrani pratsi*, Dnipro, 1987, pp. 386–96.

Aheieva, Vira. “Pislia karnavalu, abo restavratsiia pam'iati.” *Dorohy i seredokhrestia: Esei*, Vydavnytstvo Staroho Leva, 2016, pp. 336–47.

– *Poetesa zlamu stolit': Tvorchist' Lesi Ukrainky v postmodernii interpretatsii*. Lybid', 1999.

– *Zhinochyi prostir: Feministychnyi dyskurs ukrains'koho modernizmu*. Fakt, 2003.

– editor. *Z nepokrytoiu holovoiu: Ukrains'ka zhinocha proza*. 2nd ed. Komora, 2014.

“Aktrysa Halyna Stefanova vidklykaie svoie im'ia zi spysku nominantiv na Shevchenkivs'ku premiiu.” *Detektor Media*, 28 Jan. 2008, https://detector.media/withoutsection/article/36169/2008-01-28-aktrisa-galina-stefanova-vidklikae-svoe-imya-zi-spisku-nominantiv-na-shevchenkivsku-premiyu/. Accessed 15 Feb. 2019.

Anderson, Benedict. “Census, Map, Museum.” *Becoming National: A Reader*, edited by Geoff Eley and Ronald Grigor Suny, Oxford UP, 1996, pp. 243–58.

– *Imagined Communities: Reflections on the Origin and Spread of Nationalism*. Rev. ed. Verso, 2016.

Andrukhovych, Yuri. *The Moscoviad*, translated by Vitaly Chernetsky. Spuyten Duyvil, 2008.

Andryczyk, Mark. *The Intellectual as Hero in 1990s Ukrainian Fiction*. U of Toronto P, 2012.

Ashcroft, Bill, et al. *The Empire Writes Back: Theory and Practice in Post-Colonial Literatures*. 2nd ed. Routledge, 2002.

– *Post-Colonial Studies: The Key Concepts*. 2nd ed. Routledge, 2002.

Assmann, Aleida. “Canon and Archive.” *Cultural Memory Studies: An International and Interdisciplinary Handbook*, edited by Astrid Erll and Ansgar Nünning, Walter de Gruyter, 2008, pp. 97–107.

Attridge, Derek. *J.M. Coetzee: The Ethics of Reading: Literature in the Event*. U of Chicago P, 2004.

– *The Singularity of Literature*. Taylor and Francis, 2004.

Bakhtin, Mikhail. *Problems of Dostoevsky's Poetics*, edited and translated by Caryl Emerson. U of Minnesota P, 1984.

Bahri, Deepika. "Feminism in/and Postcolonialism." *The Cambridge Companion to Postcolonial Literary Studies*, edited by Neil Lazarus, Cambridge UP, 2004, pp. 199–220.

Bazhan, Oleh. "Ukrainoznavchi doslidzhennia pid presom ideolohichnykh represii v 1970–1980-kh rokakh." *Kraieznavstvo*, vols. 1–4, 2008, pp. 45–55.

Belknap, Robert L. *Plots*, with an introduction by Robin Feuer Miller. Columbia UP, 2016.

Benigni, Eugenia. "Women, Peace and Security in Ukraine: Women's Hardship and Power from the Maidan to the Conflict." *Security and Human Rights*, vol. 27, no. 1–2, 2016, pp. 59–84.

Berlant, Lauren. *The Anatomy of National Fantasy: Hawthorne, Utopia, and Everyday Life*. U of Chicago P, 1991.

Berlin, Isaiah. *Two Concepts of Liberty*. Oxford UP, 1958.

Bhabha, Homi. "Dissemi-Nation: Time, Narrative, and the Margins of the Modern Nation." *Nation and Narration*, edited by Homi Bhabha, Routledge, 1990, pp. 291–322.

– "Of Mimicry and Man: The Ambivalence of Colonial Discourse." *The Location of Culture*, Routledge, 1994, pp. 85–92.

Bichuia, Nina. *Desiat' sliv poeta*: *Povisti*. Kameniar, 1987.

– Personal interview. 12 June 2017.

– "Taka sobi intryha naprykintsi." *Try teatral'ni povisti. Sribne slovo*, 2015, pp. 331–4.

– *Zemli romens'ki*. Piramida, 2003.

Bichuya, Nina. "The Stone Master." *Herstories: An Anthology of New Ukrainian Women Prose Writers*, edited by Michael M. Naydan, translated by Olesia Wallo, Glagoslav Publications, 2014, pp. 32–54.

Blacker, Uilleam. "Nation, Body, Home: Gender and National Identity in the Work of Oksana Zabuzhko." *The Modern Language Review*, vol. 105, no. 2, 2010, pp. 487–501.

Bloom, Harold. *The Anxiety of Influence*. Oxford UP, 1975.

Bodin, Per-Arne. "Kinets' imperii: Roman Iuriia Andrukhovycha 'Moskoviada'." *Slovo i Chas*, no. 5, 2007, pp. 62–6.

Boehmer, Elleke. *Colonial and Postcolonial Literature: Migrant Metaphors*. 2nd ed. Oxford UP, 2005.

– *Stories of Women: Gender and Narrative in the Postcolonial Nation*. Manchester UP, 2005.

Bohachevsky-Chomiak, Martha. *Feminists Despite Themselves: Women in Ukrainian Community Life, 1884–1939*. The Canadian Institute of Ukrainian Studies, 1988.

Braidotti, Rosi. "Toward a New Nomadism: Feminist Deleuzian Tracks; or, Metaphysics and Metabolism." *Gilles Deleuze and the Theatre of Philosophy*, edited by Constantin Boundas and Dorothea Olkowski, Routledge, 1994, pp. 157–86.

Brennan, Timothy. "The National Longing for Form." *Nation and Narration*, edited by Homi Bhabha, Routledge, 1990, pp. 44–71.

Briukhovets'kyi, Viacheslav. *Lina Kostenko. Narys tvorchosti.* Dnipro, 1990.

Brown, Kate. *Biography of No Place: From Ethnic Borderland to Soviet Heartland.* Harvard UP, 2004.

Buhaichuk, Kateryna. "Zhinochi mifolohichni obrazy u tvorchosti Valeriia Shevchuka." *Volyn'-Zhytomyrshchyna. Istoryko-filolohichnyi zbirnyk z rehional'nykh problem*, vol. 20, 2010, pp. 47–54.

Carey-Webb, Allen. *Making Subject(s): Literature and the Emergence of National Identity.* Garland, 1998.

Carter, Ian. "Positive and Negative Liberty." *The Stanford Encyclopedia of Philosophy*, edited by Edward N. Zalta, Spring 2012, http://plato.stanford.edu/archives/spr2012/entries/liberty-positive-negative/. Accessed 12 Feb. 2019.

Cavanagh, Clare. "Postcolonial Poland." *Common Knowledge*, vol. 10, no. 1, 2004, pp. 82–92.

Certeau, Michel de. *The Practice of Everyday Life*, translated by Steven Rendall. U of California P, 1984.

Chari, Sharad, and Katherine Verdery. "Thinking between the Posts: Postcolonialism, Postsocialism, and Ethnography after the Cold War." *Comparative Studies in Society and History*, vol. 51, no. 1, 2009, pp. 6–34.

Chatterjee, Partha. *The Nation and Its Fragments: Colonial and Postcolonial Histories.* Princeton UP, 1993.

Chebotnikova, Iryna. "Tvir pro tvir: Mariia Matios 'Natsiia'." *HASLO: Holovnyi analitychnii sait livoi opozytsii*, 20 Aug. 2012, http://gaslo.info/?p=1726. Accessed 2 Jan. 2019.

Chernetsky, Vitaly. "Identity Quests: Postcolonial Journeys in Contemporary Ukrainian Writing." *Postcolonial Slavic Literatures after Communism*, edited by Klavdia Smola and Dirk Uffelmann, Peter Lang, 2016, pp. 327–46.

– *Mapping Postcommunist Cultures: Russia and Ukraine in the Context of Globalization.* McGill-Queen's UP, 2007.

– "The Trope of Displacement and Identity Construction in Post-Colonial Ukrainian Fiction." *Journal of Ukrainian Studies*, vol. 27, no. 1–2, 2002, pp. 215–32.

Clark, Katerina. *The Soviet Novel: History as Ritual.* 3rd ed. Indiana UP, 2000.

Connor, Walker. *Ethnonationalism: The Quest for Understanding.* Princeton UP, 1994.

Craig, Cairns. *The Modern Scottish Novel: Narrative and the National Imagination.* Edinburgh UP, 2002.

Cutter, Martha J. *Unruly Tongue: Identity and Voice in American Women's Writing, 1850–1930.* UP of Mississippi, Jackson, 1999.

Dakh, Marta. *Literaturne zhyttia narodnoi ballady 'Oi ne khody, Hrytsiu …': Problema oliteraturennia siuzhetu i zhanru.* L'vivs'kyi natsional'nyi universytet imeni Ivana Franka, Avtoreferat dysertatsii, 2001.

Diachenko, Oleksandr. "Pro nashykh suchasnykiv." *Vitchyzna*, no. 10, 1976, pp. 205–7.

Dmitriieva, Mariia. "Zhinky na Maidani – stari mikhy, nove vyno?" *Krona: Gendernyi informatsiyno-analitychnyi tsentr*, 16 May 2014, http://krona.org.ua/zhinki-na-majdani-stari-mixi-nove-vino.html. Accessed 30 Jan. 2019.

Dobrenko, Evgeny. *Stalinist Cinema and the Production of History: Museum of the Revolution*, translated by Sarah Young. Edinburgh UP, 2008.

Donchik, Vitalii. "Zaglianut' v budushchee." *Literaturnaia gazeta*, no. 22, 31 May 1978, p. 4.

Donchyk, Vitalii. "Dokument i poetyzatsiia: Povist'. Rik 1976." *Dnipro*, no. 12, Dec. 1977, pp. 138–47.

Dukhnich, Olga. "Pochemu ia poidu na Maidan." *Litopys samovydtsiv: Dev'iat' misiatsiv ukrains'koho sprotyvu*, conceived by Oksana Zabuzhko, edited by Tetiana Teren, with a foreword by Svetlana Alexievich, Komora, 2014, pp. 8–10.

Dziuba, Ivan. "Palitra 'mis'koi povisti' (notatky pro tvorchist' Niny Bichui)." *Z krynytsi lit*, vol. 2, Vydavnychyi dim 'Kyievo-mohylians'ka akademiia', 2006, pp. 561–74.

Eakin, Paul John. *How Our Lives Become Stories: Making Selves*. Cornell UP, 1999.

"Empire, Union, Center, Satellite: The Place of Post-Colonial Theory in Slavic/Central and Eastern European/(Post-)Soviet Studies." Special issue of *Ulbandus*, edited by Jonathan Brooks Platt, vol. 7, 2003.

Erofeev, Venedikt. *Moskva-Petushki*. Prometei, 1989.

"Fanfaron." *Etymolohichnyi slovnyk ukrains'koi movy*, vol. 6, Naukova dumka, 2012, p. 73.

"Fanfaron." *Slovnyk ukrains'koi movy*, vol. 10, Naukova dumka, 1979, p. 562.

Filonenko, Sofia. "Typ mysliachoi zhinky v ukrains'kii zhinochii prozi 90-kh rokiv XX stolittia." *Visnyk Luhans'koho natsional'noho pedahohichnoho universytetu im. Tarasa Shevchenka*, edited by O. Halych, LDPU, 2006, pp. 123–36.

Finnin, Rory. "Nationalism and the Lyric, or How Taras Shevchenko Speaks to Compatriots Dead, Living, and Unborn." *The Slavonic and East European Review*, vol. 89, no. 1, 2011, pp. 29–55.

First, Joshua. *Ukrainian Cinema: Belonging and Identity during the Soviet Thaw*. I.B. Tauris, 2015.

Forostyna, Oksana. "Iza Khruslins'ka. Ukrainskyi palimpsest: Oksana Zabuzhko u rozmovi z Izoiu Khruslins'koiu." *Krytyka*, Dec. 2014, https://krytyka.com/ua/reviews/ukrayinskyy-palimpsest-oksana-zabuzhko-u-rozmovi-z-izoyu-khruslinskoyu. Accessed 12 Nov. 2018.

Franko, Roma, translator, and Sonia Morris, editor. *For a Crust of Bread: Selected Prose Fiction by Olena Pchilka, Nataliya Kobrynska, Lyubov Yanovska, Olha Kobylianska, Yevheniya Yaroshynska, Hrytsko Hryhorenko, and Lesya Ukrainka*. Language Lanterns Publications, 1998.

Gabor, Vasyl'. *Neznaioma: Antolohiia ukrains'koi "zhinochoi" prozy ta eseistyky druhoi polovyny XX-pochatku XXI stolit'*. Piramida, 2005.

– "'Vyvorozhy mene cherez p'iatsot lit' (Eskiz do portreta Niny Bichui)." *Vid Dzhoisa do Chubaia: Esei, literaturni rozvidky ta interv'iu*. Piramida, 2010, pp. 26–33.

George, Rosemary Marangoly. "Feminists Theorize the Colonial/Postcolonial." *The Cambridge Companion to Feminist Literary Theory*, edited by Ellen Roney, Cambridge UP, 2006, pp. 211–31.

Gerasimov, Ilya. "Ukraine 2014: The First Postcolonial Revolution. Introduction to the Forum." *Ab Imperio*, vol. 3, 2014, pp. 22–44.

Gilbert, Paul. *The Philosophy of Nationalism*. Westview Press, 1998.

Gilbert, Sandra, and Susan Gubar. *The Madwoman in the Attic: The Woman Writer and the Nineteenth-Century Literary Imagination*. Yale UP, 1979.

Gillis, John R. "Introduction. Memory and Identity: The History of a Relationship." *Commemorations: The Politics of National Identity*, edited by John R. Gillis. Princeton UP, 1996, pp. 3–24.

Goscilo, Helena. *Dehexing Sex: Russian Womanhood during and after Glasnost*. U of Michigan P, 1996.

Gourgouris, Stathis. *Dream Nation: Enlightenment, Colonization and Institution of Modern Greece*. Stanford UP, 1996.

Grabowicz, George G. *The Poet as Mythmaker: A Study of Symbolic Meaning in Taras Ševčenko*. Harvard UP, 1982.

Grothe, Anja. *Medusa, Cassandra, Medea: Re-Inscribing Myth in Contemporary German and Russian Women's Writing*. CUNY, PhD diss., 2000.

Hall, Stuart. "Ethnicity: Identity and Difference." *Becoming National: A Reader*, edited by Geoff Eley and Ronald Grigor Suny, Oxford UP, 1996, pp. 339–49.

Hankivsky, Olena, and Anastasiya Salnykova. "Gender in Transition: Legacies, Opportunities, and Milestones in Post-Soviet Ukraine." *Gender, Politics, and Society in Ukraine*, edited by Olena Hankivsky and Anastasiya Salnykova, U of Toronto P, 2012, pp. 3–25.

Harrison, Nicholas. *Postcolonial Criticism: History, Theory, and the Work of Fiction*. Polity Press, 2003.

Himka, John-Paul. "The Basic Historical Identity Formations in Ukraine: A Typology." *Harvard Ukrainian Studies*, vol. 28, nos. 1–4, 2006, pp. 483–500.

Hirsch, Francine. "The Soviet Union as a Work-in-Progress: Ethnographers and the Category Nationality in the 1926, 1937, and 1939 Censuses." *Slavic Review*, vol. 56, no. 2, Summer 1997, pp. 251–78.

– "Toward an Empire of Nations: Border-Making and the Formation of Soviet National Identities." *The Russian Review*, vol. 59, Apr. 2000, pp. 201–26.

Hirsch, Marianne. "The Generation of Postmemory." *Poetics Today*, vol. 29, no. 1, Spring 2008, pp. 103–28.

Hnatiuk, Olia. *Proshchannia z imperiieiu. Ukrains'ki dyskusii pro identychnist'*. Kyiv: Krytyka, 2005.

– "Zhinoche oblychchia ukrains'koho modernizmu." *Krytyka*, nos. 1–2, Jan.–Feb. 2017, pp. 20–7.

Hobsbawm, E.J. *Nations and Nationalism since 1780. Programme, Myth, Reality.* Cambridge UP, 1990.

Hogan, Patrick Colm. *Understanding Nationalism: On Narrative, Cognitive Science, and Identity.* Ohio State UP, 2009.

Holmgren, Beth. "Writing the Female Body Politic (1945–1985)." *A History of Women's Writing in Russia*, edited by Adele Marie Barker and Jehanne M. Gheith, Cambridge UP, 2003, pp. 225–42.

Horak, Roman. *Kynuty kamenem: Esei pro Irynu Vil'de.* Apriori, 2016.

Hordasevych, Halyna. "Taiemnytsi zhinochoho svitu." *Kyiv*, no. 4, Apr. 1984, pp. 116–20.

Hrabovych, Hryhorii. "Kokhannia z vid'mamy." *Teksty i masky.* Krytyka, 2005, pp. 283–98.

Hrycak, Alexandra. "Orange Harvest? Women's Activism and Civil Society in Ukraine, Belarus and Russia since 2004." *Canadian-American Slavic Studies*, vol. 44, 2010, pp. 151–77.

– "Women as Migrants on the Margins of the European Union." *Mapping Difference: The Many Faces of Women in Contemporary Ukraine*, edited by Marian J. Rubchak, Berghahn Books, 2011, pp. 47–64.

Hrycak, Alexandra, and Maria G. Rewakowicz. "Feminism, Intellectuals and the Formation of Micro-Publics in Postcommunist Ukraine." *Studies in East European Thought.* Special issue, "Wither the Intelligentsia: The End of the Moral Elite in Eastern Europe," edited by Serguei Alex. Oushakine, vol. 61, 2009, pp. 311–33.

Hryn, Halyna, and Oksana Zabuzhko. "A Conversation with Oksana Zabuzhko." *Agni*, vol. 53, 2001, pp. 17–22.

Hrytsak, Yaroslav. "Postcolonial Is Not Enough." *Slavic Review*, vol. 74, no. 4, Winter 2015, pp. 732–7.

– "Tezy do dyskusii pro UPA." *Strasti za natsionalizmom. Istorychni esei.* Krytyka, 2004, pp. 90–113.

"Human Trafficking and Modern-Day Slavery in the Early Years of the 21st Century," 2009, http://gvnet.com/humantrafficking/Ukraine.htm. Accessed 1 Dec. 2018.

Hundorova, Tamara. "'Bu-Ba-Bu,' karnaval i kich." *Krytyka*, vols. 7–8, 2000, pp. 13–18.

– *Femina Melancholica: Stat' i kul'tura v gendernii utopii Ol'hy Kobylians'koi.* Krytyka, 2002.

– *Pisliachornobyl's'ka biblioteka. Ukrains'kyi literaturnyi postmodern.* Krytyka, 2005.

– "Posttotalitarnyi kemp: Ledi Iu i Ledi Kich." *Tranzytna kul'tura. Symptomy postkolonial'noi travmy: statti ta esei.* Hrani-T, 2013, pp. 490–546.

– "Uiava i pam'iat' v postkolonial'nomu romani." *Tranzytna kul'tura. Symptomy postkolonial'noi travmy: statti ta esei*, Hrani-T, 2013, pp. 110–49.

– "Ukrainian Euromaidan as Social and Cultural Performance." *Revolution and War in Contemporary Ukraine: The Challenge of Change*, edited by Olga Bertelsen, ibidem-Verlag, 2017, pp. 161–79.

Iankovs'ka, Olena. "Zhinky na Maidani: Ne kanapkamy iedynymy." *Vholos*, 16 Sept. 2014, https://vgolos.com.ua/news/zhinky-na-majdani-ne-kanapkamy-yedynymy_157316.html. Accessed 2 Feb. 2019.

Il'nyts'kyi, Mykola. *Drama bez katarsysu: Storinky literaturnoho zhyttia L'vova druhoi polovyny XX stolittia*. Instytut ukrainoznavstva im. Kryp'iakevycha NAN Ukrainy, 2003.

– "Vyvorozhy mene, zvizdariu ..." *Vitchyzna*, no. 9, Sept. 1970, pp. 195–7

Ivanchenko, Raisa. *Liubyty ne prosto*. Radians'kyi pys'mennyk, 1976.

– *Ne rozmynys' iz soboiu*. Molod', 1980.

Ivanychuk, Roman. *Blahoslovy, dushe moia, Hospoda ... Shchodennykovi zapysy, spohady i rozdumy*. Prosvita, 1993.

– "Tema liuds'koi tvorchosti: Sproby peretvorennia (Shtrykhy do portreta Niny Bichui)." *Ukrains'ka mova i literatura v shkoli*, no. 8, Aug. 1987, pp. 9–14.

– "U poshukakh liuds'koi chystoty." *Zhovten'*, no. 8, Aug. 1975, pp. 141–5.

Jameson, Fredric. *The Political Unconscious: Narrative as a Socially Symbolic Act*. Cornell UP, 1981.

Jayawardena, Kumari. *Feminism and Nationalism in the Third World*. Zed Press, 1986.

Johnson, Janet Elise, and Jean C. Robinson, editors. *Living Gender after Communism*. Indiana UP, 2006.

Kaganovsky, Lilya. *How the Soviet Man Was Unmade: Cultural Fantasy and Male Subjectivity under Stalin*. Pittsburgh UP, 2008.

Kaplan, Caren, et al., editors. *Between Woman and Nation: Nationalisms, Transnational Feminisms, and the State*. Duke UP, 1999.

Karpov, Vladimir. "Politika iskazheniia roli zhenshchin v voenno-politicheskikh sobytiiakh (Na primere izobrazheniia v SMI Evromaidana i voiny na vostoke Ukrainy)." *Ia*, vol. 37, no. 1, 2015, pp. 10–14.

Kasianov, Georgiy. "'Nationalized' History: Past Continuous, Present Perfect, Future ..." *Laboratory of Transnational History: Ukraine and Recent Ukrainian Historiography*, edited by Georgiy Kasianov and Philipp Ther, Central European UP, 2008, pp. 7–23.

Kas'ianov, Heorhii. *Nezhodni: Ukrains'ka intelihentsiia v rusi oporu 1960–80-kh rokiv*. Lybid', 1999.

Kelertas, Violeta, editor. *Baltic Postcolonialism*. Rodopi, 2006.

Kharchuk, Roksana. *Suchasna ukrains'ka proza. Postmodernyi period*. Akademiia, 2008.

Khromeychuk, Olesya. "Gender and Nationalism on the Maidan." *Ukraine's Euromaidan: Analyses of a Civil Revolution*, edited by David R. Marples and Frederick V. Mills, ibidem-Verlag, 2015, pp. 123–45.

Khruslins'ka, Iza. *Ukrainskyi palimpsest: Oksana Zabuzhko u rozmovi z Izoiu Khruslins'koiu*, translated by Dzvenyslava Matiiash, edited by Ivan Andrusiak and Oksana Zabuzhko, Komora, 2014.

Khudyts'kyi, Vasyl'. "Nina Bichuia: 'Z shesty rokiv ia znala, khto takyi Stalin i pravdu pro Holodomor'." *Dzerkalo tyzhnia. Ukraina*, 11 June 2016. *ZN,UA*, https://dt.ua/CULTURE/nina-bichuya-z-shesti-rokiv-ya-znala-hto-takiy-stalin-i-pravdu-pro-golodomor-_.html. Accessed 6 Dec. 2017.

Kis, Oksana. "Biography as Political Geography: Patriotism in Ukrainian Women's Life Stories." *Mapping Difference: The Many Faces of Women in Ukraine*, edited by Marian J. Rubchak, Berghahn Books, 2011, pp. 89–108.

– "Choosing without Choice: Dominant Models of Femininity in Contemporary Ukraine." *Gender Transitions in Russia and Eastern Europe*, edited by Ildiko Asztalos Morell et al., Forlags ab Gondolin, 2005, pp. 105–29.

– "(Re)Constructing Ukrainian Women's History: Actors, Agents, and Narratives." *Gender, Politics, and Society in Ukraine*, edited by Olena Hankivsky and Anastasiya Salnykova, U of Toronto P, 2012, pp. 152–79.

Kis', Oksana. *Zhinka v tradytsiinii ukrains'kii kul'turi (druha polovyna XIX-pochatok XX st.).* Instytut narodoznavstva NAN Ukrainy, 2008.

Klymenko, Valentyna. "Poliovi doslidzhennia Shevchenkivs'koi premii: Aktrysa Halyna Stefanova vidklykaie svoie im'ia zi spysku shevchenkivs'kykh nominantiv." *Ukraina Moloda*, 30 Jan. 2008, http://www.umoloda.kiev.ua/number/1093/116/39129/. Accessed 2 Feb. 2019.

Knight, Stephen. *Form and Ideology in Crime Fiction*. Indiana UP, 1980.

Kobets, Svitlana. "Rev. of *Poliovi doslidzhennia z ukrains'koho seksu*, by Oksana Zabuzhko." *The Slavic and East European Journal*, vol. 41, no. 1, Spring 1997, pp. 183–5.

Kobylians'ka, Ol'ha. *V nediliu rano zillia kopala*. *Ukrains'kyi Tsentr*, http://www.ukrcenter.com/Література/Ольга-Кобилянська/20662-1/В-неділю-рано-зілля-копала. Accessed 11 Dec. 2017.

Komitet z Natsional'noi premii Ukrainy imeni Tarasa Shevchenka, http://www.knpu.gov.ua/. Accessed 12 Dec. 2017.

Koniaieva, Tetiana. "Ievheniia Kononenko: 'Chasy Maidanu povernuly zhinku do arkhaiichnoho spryiniattia – u tsentri svitobudovy cholovik'." *Vysokyi zamok*, 13 Oct. 2014, https://wz.lviv.ua/interview/128906-yevheniia-kononenko-chasy-maidanu-povernuly-zhinku-do-arkhaichnoho-spryiniattia-u-tsentri-svitobudovy-cholovik. Accessed 2 Feb. 2019.

Kononenko, Ievheniia. *Bez muzhyka. Zbirka korotkoi prozy.* Kal'variia, 2005.

– *Heroini ta heroi. Zbirka ese.* Hrani-T, 2010.

– "Ievanheliie vid poetiv." *Krytyka*, vols. 3–4, 2015, pp. 20–7.

– *Imitatsiia*. Kal'variia, 2001.

– *Nostal'hiia*. Kal'variia, 2013.

– "On Sunday Morning." Translated by Svitlana Kobets. *Ukrainian Literature: A Journal of Translations*, vol. 1, 2004, pp. 151–5, http://sites.utoronto.ca/elul/Ukr_Lit/Vol01/. Accessed 10 Nov. 2018.

– *Ostannie bazhannia*. Vydavnytstvo Anetty Antonenko, 2015.

- *Rosiis'kyi siuzhet*. Kal'variia, 2012.
- "Spivocha dusha Ukrainy (Marusia Churai, Lesia Ukrainka, Lina Kostenko)." *Heroi ta znamenytosti v ukrains'kii kul'turi*, edited by Oleksandr Hrytsenko, Ukrains'kyi tsentr kul'turnykh doslidzhen', 1999, pp. 234–48.
- "U nediliu rano." *Kolosal'nyi siuzhet*, Zadruha, 1998, pp. 3–8.
- *Zrada. ZRADA made in Ukraine*. Kal'variia, 2002.

Korek, Janusz, editor. *From Sovietology to Postcoloniality: Poland and Ukraine from a Postcolonial Perspective*. Södertörns högskola, 2007.

Kostenko, Lina. *Marusia Churai. Istorychnyi roman u virshakh*. Radians'kyi pys'mennyk, 1979.

Kostenko, Lina, and Oksana Pakhliovs'ka. "Tse nazyvalos' – tvorchi seminary." *Harmoniia kriz' tuhu dysonansiv ...*, edited by Ivan Dziuba et al., Lybid', 2016, pp. 156–68.

Kozulia, Oles'. *Zhinky v istorii Ukrainy*. Ukrains'kyi tsentr dukhovnoi kul'tury, 1993.

Krys, Svitlana. "A Comparative Feminist Reading of Lesia Ukrainka's and Henrik Ibsen's Dramas." *Canadian Review of Comparative Literature*, vol. 34, no. 4, Dec. 2007, pp. 389–409.

Kuehnast, Kathleen, and Carol Nechemias, editors. *Post-Soviet Women Encountering Transition: Nation Building, Economic Survival, and Civic Activism*. Woodrow Wilson Center Press, 2004.

Kulish, Mykola. *Patetychna sonata. Tvory v dvokh tomakh*, vol. 2. Dnipro, 1990, pp. 173–260.

Kul'chyts'kyi, Stanislav, and Larysa Iakubova. *Trysta rokiv samotnosti: Ukrains'kyi Donbas u poshukakh smysliv i Bat'kivshchyny*. Klio, 2016.

Kuzio, Taras. "History, Memory and Nation Building in the Post-Soviet Colonial Space." *Nationalities Papers*, vol. 30, no. 2, 2002, pp. 241–64.

Lanser, Susan Sniader. *Fictions of Authority: Women Writers and Narrative Voice*. Cornell UP, 1992.

Lazurkevych, Sofiia. "Oksana Kis': Zhinky chasto maiut' alerhiiu na feminism." *Interv'iu z Ukrainy*, 29 Oct. 2015, https://rozmova.wordpress.com/2015/11/02/oksana-kis-2/. Accessed 2 Feb. 2017.

Lemko, Il'ko. *L'viv ponad use: Spohady l'viv'ianyna druhoi polovyny 20-ho stolittia*. Piramida, 2003.

Leshchenko, M.P. *Vanda Vasylevs'ka: Narys zhyttia i tvorchosti*. Dnipro, 1986.

Levkova, Anastasiia. "Nina Bichuia: 'U misti ia isnuiu i ne znaiu, chy mohla by isnuvaty poza nym'." *LitAktsent*, 28 Jan. 2013, http://litakcent.com/2013/01/28/nina-bichuja-u-misti-ja-isnuju-j-ne-znaju-chy-mohla-by-isnuvaty-poza-nym/. Accessed 3 May 2017.

Litopys samovydtsiv. Dev'iat' misiatsiv ukrains'koho sprotyvu, conceived by Oksana Zabuzhko, edited by Tetiana Teren, with a foreword by Svetlana Alexievich, Komora, 2014.

Lomazova, Kira. "Pidemo zustrichaty vesnu." *Literaturna Ukraina*, no. 55, 10 July 1979, p. 2.

Loznitsa, Sergei, director. *Maidan*. Atom and Void, 2014.

Lynch, Deidre, and William B. Warner. "Introduction: The Transport of the Novel." *Cultural Institutions of the Novel*, edited by Deidre Lynch and William B. Warner, Duke UP, 1996, pp. 1–10.

Malmgren, Carl D. "Anatomy of Murder: Mystery, Detective, and Crime Fiction." *Journal of Popular Culture*, vol. 30, no. 4, 1997, pp. 115–35.

Marples, David. *Heroes and Villains: Creating National History in Contemporary Ukraine*. CEU Press, 2007.

Martsenyuk, Tamara. "Women's Top-Level Political Participation: Failures and Hopes of Ukrainian Gender Politics." *New Imaginaries: Youthful Reinvention of Ukraine's Cultural Paradigm*, edited by Marian J. Rubchak, Berghahn, 2015, pp. 33–52.

Matios, Mariia. *Armahedon uzhe vidbuvsia*. Piramida, 2011.

– *Cherevychky Bozhoi materi*. Piramida, 2013.

– *Natsiia. Odkrovennia*. Kal'variia, 2006.

– "Omelian Kovch i Emil' Klugman u chas liudynoneliubstva." *Ukrains'ka Pravda*, 8 Dec. 2011, http://www.istpravda.com.ua/articles/2011/12/8/64486/. Accessed 13 Dec. 2017.

– *Pryvatnyi shchodennyk. Maidan. Viina* ... Piramida, 2015.

– *Solodka Darusia*. 4th ed. Piramida, 2007.

– *Vyrvani storinky z avtobiohrafii*. Piramida, 2011.

Mayer, Tamar. "Gender Ironies of Nationalism: Setting the Stage." *Gender Ironies of Nationalism: Sexing the Nation*, edited by Tamar Mayer, Routledge, 2000, pp. 1–23.

Mayerchyk, Mariya. "Seizing the Logic/A World without Women." *Krytyka*, 25 Jan. 2014, https://krytyka.com/en/community/blogs/seizing-logic-world-without-women. Accessed 2 Feb. 2019.

Mayerchyk, Mariya, and Olga Plakhotnik. "Ukrainian Feminism at the Crossroad of National, Postcolonial, and (Post)Soviet: Theorizing the Maidan Events 2013–2014." *Krytyka*, 24 Nov. 2015, https://krytyka.com/en/community/blogs/ukrainian-feminism-crossroad-national-postcolonial-and-postsoviet-theorizing-maidan. Accessed 2 Feb. 2019.

McClintock, Anne. "Family Feuds: Gender, Nation, and the Family." *Feminist Review*, vol. 44, 1993, pp. 61–80.

– "No Longer in a Future Heaven: Nationalism, Gender and Race." *Becoming National: A Reader*, edited by Geoff Eley and Ronald Grigor Suny, Oxford UP, 1996, pp. 260–84.

McClintock, Anne, Aamir R. Mufti, and Ella Shohat, editors. *Dangerous Liaisons: Gender, Nations, and Postcolonial Perspectives*. U of Minnesota P, 1997.

Messerschmidt, James W. "The Forgotten Victims of World War II: Masculinities and Rape in Berlin, 1945." *Violence against Women*, vol. 12, no. 7, July 2006, pp. 706–12.

Monakhova, Natalia. "National Identity in the Postcolonial Situation: A Comparative Study of the Caribbean and Ukrainian Cases – Jamaica Kincaid and Oksana Zabuzhko." *Atlantic Literary Review Quarterly* (Special Issue on Postcolonial Feminist Writing), vol. 4, no. 4, 2003, pp. 173–98.

– "'Pidporiadkovane' v ukrains'komu konteksti." *Suchasnist'*, vol. 4, 2003, pp. 124–42.

Moore, Amy Elisabeth. *Feminism and Nationalism in the Works of Nicole Brossard and Oksana Zabuzhko*. U of California, PhD diss., 2009.

Moore, David Chioni. "Is the Post- in Postcolonial the Post- in Post-Soviet? Toward a Global Postcolonial Critique." *PMLA*, vol. 116, no. 1, 2001, pp. 111–28.

Mullaney, Julie. *Postcolonial Literatures in Context*. Continuum, 2010.

Murav, Harriet. "Engendering the Russian Body Politic." *Postcommunism and the Body Politic*, edited by Ellen E. Berry, New York UP, 1995, pp. 32–56.

– *Holy Foolishness: Dostoevsky's Novels and the Poetics of Cultural Critique*. Stanford UP, 1992.

Murphy, Peter F. "Living by His Wits: The Buffoon and Male Survival." *Signs*, vol. 31, no. 4, 2006, pp. 1125–42.

Musiienko, Iryna. "Politychni represii na pivnichnii Bukovyni ta Khotynshchyni u 1940–1941 rr." *Z arkhiviv VUCHK-GPU-NKVD-KGB*, vols. 2–4, 2000, pp. 472–85.

Nash, Catherine. "Remapping and Renaming: New Cartographies of Identity, Gender and Landscape in Ireland." *Feminist Review*, vol. 44, Summer 1993, pp. 39–57.

Naydan, Michael M. "'A Conspicuous Blossoming': The Emergence of Prose Writing by Ukrainian Women." *Belletrista*, http://belletrista.com/2011/Issue11%20/features_2.php. Accessed 20 Dec. 2017.

– "Emerging Ukrainian Women Prose Writers: At Twenty Years of Independence." *Herstories: An Anthology of New Ukrainian Women Prose Writers*, edited by Michael M. Naydan, Glagoslav Publications, 2014, pp. 14–23.

"On Colonialism, Communism and East-Central Europe – Some Reflections." Special Issue of *The Journal of Postcolonial Writing*, edited by Dorota Kołodziejczyk and Cristina Şandru, vol. 48, no. 2, 2012.

Onuch, Olga, and Tamara Martsenyuk. "Mothers and Daughters of the Maidan: Gender, Repertoires of Violence, and the Divison of Labour in Ukrainian Protests." *Social, Health, and Communication Studies Journal*, vol. 1, no. 1, Nov. 2014, pp. 105–26.

Onyshko, Olha, director. *Women of Maidan*, produced by Olha Onyshko and Petro Didula, 2016.

Oushakine, Serguei Alex. "Introduction: Wither the Intelligentsia: The End of the Moral Elite in Eastern Europe." *Studies in East European Thought*, vol. 61, 2009, pp. 243–8.

– "The Terrifying Mimicry of Samizdat." *Public Culture*, vol. 13, no. 2, 2001, pp. 191–214.

Pakhliovs'ka, Oksana. *Ave, Europa!* Pul'sary, 2008.

Panchenko, Volodymyr. "Lohika kharakteriv? Ni, lohika dumok." *Vitchyzna*, no. 4, Apr. 1979, pp. 200–3.

Parts, Lyudmila. *The Chekhovian Intertext: Dialogue with a Classic*. Ohio State UP, 2008.

Pavlychko, Solomia. *Dyskurs modernizmu v ukrains'kii literaturi*. Lybid', 1997.

– "Kanon klasykiv iak pole gendernoi borot'by." *Feminizm*, edited by Vira Aheieva, Osnovy, 2002, pp. 213–18.

– "Vyklyk stereotypam: novi zhinochi holosy v suchasnii ukrains'kii literaturi." *Feminizm*, edited by Vira Aheieva, Osnovy, 2002, pp. 181–7.

Pavlyshyn, Marko. *Kanon ta ikonostas*. Chas, 1997.

– "Literary Canons and National Identities in Ukraine." *Canadian-American Slavic Studies*, vol. 40, no. 1, 2006, pp. 5–19.

– "Literary History as Provocation of National Identity, National Identity as Provocation of Literary History: The Case of Ukraine." *Thesis Eleven*, vol. 136, no. 1, 2016, pp. 74–89.

– "Literatura i modernist': Dumky pro prozu." *Literatura, natsiia i modernist'*, Tsentr humanitarnykh doslidzhen', 2013, pp. 5–48.

– "'The Tranquil Lakes of the Transmontane Commune': Literature and/against Postcoloniality in Ukraine after 1991." *Postcolonial Slavic Literatures after Communism*, edited by Klavdia Smola and Dirk Uffelmann, Peter Lang, 2016, pp. 59–82.

– "Ukrainian Literature and the Erotics of Postcolonialism: Some Modest Propositions." *Harvard Ukrainian Studies*, vol. 17, nos. 1–2, June 1993, pp. 110–26.

Pavlyshyn, Mark, and J.E.M. Clarke, editors. *Ukraine in the 1990s*. Monash University, Slavic Section, 1992.

Petrenko, Mykola. *Lytsari pera i charky*. Spolom, 2000.

Petrosiuk, Mykola, editor. *Pys'mennyky Radians'koi Ukrainy: Literaturno-krytychni narysy*, vol. 13, Radians'kyi pys'mennyk, 1987.

Petrovsky-Shtern, Yohanan. *The Anti-Imperial Choice: The Making of the Ukrainian Jew*. Yale UP, 2009.

Pettman, Jan Jindy. "Boundary Politics: Women, Nationalism and Danger." *New Frontiers in Women's Studies: Knowledge, Identity and Nationalism*, edited by May Maynard and June Purvis, Taylor and Francis, 1996, pp. 187–202.

Phillips, Sarah D. "The Women's Squad in Ukraine's Protests: Feminism, Nationalism, and Militarism on the Maidan." *American Ethnologist*, vol. 41, no. 3, 2014, pp. 414–26.

Polishchuk, Olena. "Poshuky natsional'noi identychnosti v umovakh postkolonializmu (za prozoiu Iuriia Andrukhovycha)." *Visnyk L'vivs'koho universytetu. Seria filolohii*, vol. 33, no. 2, 2004, pp. 254–9.

Ready, Oliver. "In Praise of Booze: 'Moskva-Petushki' and Erasmian Irony." *The Slavonic and East European Review*, vol. 88, no. 3, 2010, pp. 437–67.

Rewakowicz, Maria G. "Feminism, Nationalism, and Women's Literary Discourse in Post-Soviet Ukraine." *Mapping Difference: The Many Faces of Women in Contemporary Ukraine*, edited by Marian J. Rubchak, Berghahn Books, 2011, pp. 161–72.

– *Ukraine's Quest for Identity: Embracing Cultural Hybridity in Literary Imagination, 1991–2011*. Lexington Books, 2018.

– "Women's Literary Discourse and National Identity in Post-Soviet Ukraine." *Contemporary Ukraine on the Cultural Map of Europe*, edited by Larissa Zaleska Onyshkevych and Maria Rewakowicz, M.E. Sharpe, 2009, pp. 275–94.

Riabchuk, Mykola. *Vid Malorossii do Ukrainy: Paradoksy zapizniloho natsiietvorennia*. Krytyka, 2000.

Ricoeur, Paul. "The Creativity of Language." *Dialogues with Contemporary Continental Thinkers: Paul Ricoeur, Emmanuel Levinas, Herbert Marcuse, Stanislas Breton, Jacques Derrida*, edited by Richard Kearney, Manchester UP, 1984.

Risch, William Ray. *The Ukrainian West: Culture and the Fate of Empire in Soviet Lviv*. Harvard UP, 2011.

Riznyk, Levko. "Pohliad zi storony." *Dzvin*, no. 8, Aug. 2007, pp. 134–9.

Romanets, Maryna. *Anamorphosic Texts and Reconfigured Visions: Improvised Traditions in Contemporary Ukrainian and Irish Literature*. ibidem-Verlag, 2007.

– "Erotic Assemblages: Field Research, Palimpsests, and What Lies Beneath." *Journal of Ukrainian Studies*, vol. 27, nos. 1–2, 2002, pp. 273–85.

Roßmann, Sabine. "'To Serve Like a Man' – Ukraine's Euromaidan and the Questions of Gender, Nationalism and Generational Change." *Eastern European Youth Cultures in a Global Context*, edited by Matthias Schwartz and Heike Winkel, Palgrave Macmillan, 2016, pp. 202–17.

Rubchak, Marian J. "Collective Memory as a Device for Constructing a New Gender Myth." *Contemporary Ukraine on the Cultural Map of Europe*, edited by Larissa M. L. Zaleska Onyshkevych and Maria G. Rewakowicz, M.E. Sharpe, 2009, pp. 139–53.

– "In Search of a Model: Evolution of a Feminist Consciousness in Ukraine and Russia." *European Journal of Women's Studies*, vol. 8, 2001, pp. 149–60.

Rudnevych, Marko. *Ia z Nebesnoii sotni: Povist'*. A-BA-BA-HA-LA-MA-HA, 2014.

Samchuk, Ulas. *Mariia. Khronika odnoho zhyttia*. Mykola Denysiuk Publishing, 1952.

Sandomirskaia, Irina. *Kniga o Rodine: Opyt analiza diskursivnykh praktik*. Wiener Slawistischer Almanach, 2001.

Scott, Joan Wallach. *Gender and the Politics of History*. Columbia UP, 1999.

Shavokshyna, N.V. "Typolohiia smikhovykh personazhiv v ukrains'komu, ches'komu ta rosiis'komu postmodernizmakh (blazen' – pabitel' – iurodyvyi)." *Filolohiia. Literaturoznavstvo. Naukovi pratsi*, vol. 124, no. 11, 2009, pp. 113–19.

Shchur, Oleksandra. "Ukrainian Women between Communism and Post-Communism: Memory and the Everyday of Ideology in Oksana Zabuzhko's *The Museum of Abandoned Secrets*." *The Everyday of Memory: Between Communism and Post-Communism*, edited by Marta Rabikowska, Peter Lang, 2013, pp. 267–89.

Shkandrij, Myroslav. *Jews in Ukrainian Literature: Representation and Identity*. Yale UP, 2009.

– *Russia and Ukraine: Literature and the Discourse of Empire from Napoleon to Postcolonial Times*. McGill-Queen's UP, 2001.

– "The Shifting Object of Desire: The Poetry of Oleksandr Irvanets." *Canadian-American Slavic Studies*, vol. 44, 2010, pp. 67–81.

– *Ukrainian Nationalism: Politics, Ideology, and Literature, 1929–1956*. Yale UP, 2015.

Shore, Marci. *The Ukrainian Night: An Intimate History of Revolution*. Yale UP, 2017.

Shultheis, Alexandra. *Regenerative Fictions: Postcolonialism, Psychoanalysis, and the Nation as Family*. Palgrave Macmillan, 2004.

Slezkine, Yuri. "The USSR as a Communal Apartment, or How a Socialist State Promoted Ethnic Particularism." *Becoming National: A Reader*, edited by Geoff Eley and Ronald Grigor Suny, Oxford UP, 1996, pp. 203–38.

Smith, Anthony D. *Ethno-Symbolism and Nationalism: A Cultural Approach*. Routledge, 2009.

– *National Identity*. U of Nevada P, 1991.

Snyder, Timothy. *Bloodlands: Europe between Hitler and Stalin*. Basic Books, 2010.

Solzhenitsyn, Aleksandr. *Matryona's Home. "We Never Make Mistakes": Two Short Novels*, translated by Paul Blackstock, W.W. Norton & Company, 1996, pp. 89–142.

Solovey, Oleh. "Romany Ievhenii Kononenko: Bestsellery dlia 'elitariiv'?" *Slovo i Chas*, vol. 2, 2003, pp. 58–62.

Sommer, Doris. *Foundational Fictions: The National Romances of Latin America*. U of California P, 1991.

Sorensen, Eli Park. *Postcolonial Studies and the Literary: Theory, Interpretation and the Novel*. Palgrave Macmillan, 2010.

Spivak, Gayatri Chakravorty. "Can the Subaltern Speak?" *Marxism and the Interpretation of Culture*, edited by Cary Nelson and Lawrence Grossberg, U of Illinois P, 1988, pp. 271–313.

Stadnik, Aliona. "40 dnei po Ustymu, ili 400 km tuda i obratno." *Litopys samovydtsiv: Dev'iat' misiatsiv ukrains'koho sprotyvu*, conceived by Oksana Zabuzhko, edited by Tetiana Teren, with a foreword by Svetlana Alexievich, Komora, 2014, pp. 199–202.

Stambrook, Fred. "National and Other Identities in Bukovina in Late Austrian Times." *Austrian History Yearbook*, vol. 35, 2004, pp. 185–203.

Staryts'kyi, Mykhailo. *Oi ne khody, Hrytsiu, ta i na vechornytsi. Tvory u dvokh tomakh*, vol. 2. Dnipro, 1984, pp. 158–222.

Stiazhkina, Olena. *Zhinky v istorii ukrains'koi kul'tury druhoi polovyny XX stolittia*. Skhidnyi vydavnychyi dim, 2002.

Stowe, William S. "Critical Investigations: Convention and Ideology in Detective Fiction." *Texas Studies in Literature and Language*, vol. 31, no. 4, Winter 1989, pp. 570–91.

Strauss, Claudia. "The Imaginary." *Anthropological Theory*, vol. 6, no. 3, 2006, pp. 322–44.

Strikha, Maksym. "Dzerkalo doby imitatsii." *ZN, UA*, 18 Jan. 2002, https://dt.ua/CULTURE/dzerkalo_dobi_imitatsiy.html. Accessed 15 Feb. 2019.

– "Mova." *Narysy ukrains'koi populiarnoi kul'tury*, edited by Oleksandr Hrytsenko. Ukrains'kyi tsentr kul'turnykh doslidzhen', 1998, pp. 397–426.

Suchland, Jennifer. "Is Postsocialism Transnational?" *Signs*, vol. 36, no. 4, 2011, pp. 837–62.

Sutcliffe, Benjamin M. *The Prose of Life: Russian Women Writers from Khurshchev to Putin*. U of Wisconsin P, 2009.

Sverstiuk, Ievhen. "Na sviato zhinky." *Na sviati nadii: esei, literaturno-krytychni statti. Ukrains'ke zhyttia v Sevastopoli*, http://ukrlife.org/main/sverstuk/to_women.htm. Accessed 2 Nov. 2017.

Szymczyszyn, Mariia. "Diialoh identychnostei v opovidanni Marii Matios *Apokalipsys*." Teka Kom. Pol.-Ukr. Związ. Kult, OL PAN, 2009, pp. 192–9.

Taran, Liudmyla. "Lantsiuhova reaktsiia. Retseptsiia retseptsii 'Poliovykh doslidzhen' z ukrains'koho seksu' Oksany Zabuzhko." *Zhinocha rol': Zhinka-avtor u suchasnii ukrains'kii prozi. Emansypatsiinyi dyskurs*, Osnovy, 2007, pp. 110–22.

– *Zhinocha rol': Zhinka-avtor u suchasnii ukrains'kii prozi. Emansypatsiinyi dyskurs*, Osnovy, 2007.

Taylor, Diana. "Performing Gender: Las Madres de la Plaza de Mayo." *Negotiating Performance: Gender, Sexuality, and Theatricality in Latin/o America*, edited by Diana Taylor and Juan Villegas, Duke UP, 1994, pp. 275–305.

Tebeshevs'ka-Kachak, Tetiana. "Avtobiohrafizm iak pryntsyp naratsii ta kharakterotvorennia u prozi Oksany Zabuzhko." *Slovo i Chas*, vol. 2, 2004, pp. 39–47.

Teren, Tetiana. "Oksana Zabuzhko: 'Ia napysala roman narodu, pozbavlenoho napysanoi istorii'." *LB.ua*, 12 Jan. 2010, https://lb.ua/culture/2010/01/12/19304_oksana_zabuzhko_ya_napisala_roma.html. Accessed 15 Feb. 2019.

Tlostanova, Madina. *Postsovetskaia literatura i estetika transkul'turatsii. Zhyt' nikogda, pisat' niotkuda*. Editorial URSS, 2004.

Tsvetaeva, Marina. "Moi pis'mennyi vernyi stol!.." *Sobranie stikhotvorenii, poem i dramaticheskikh proizvedenii v 3-kh tomakh*, vol. 3. PTO "Tsentr," 1993, pp. 37–9.

Turner, Edith. *Communitas: The Anthropology of Collective Joy*. Palgrave Macmillan, 2012.

Tytarenko, Mariya. "Female Narrative Journalism in Contemporary Ukraine." *World Literature Today*, vol. 86, no. 2, 2012, pp. 45–9.

– "Women's Voices in Contemporary Ukrainian Literary Journalism." *New Imaginaries: Youthful Reinvention of Ukraine's Cultural Paradigm*, edited by Marian J. Rubchak, Berghahn Books, 2015, pp. 170–88.

Ukrainka, Lesia. *Kaminnyi hospodar. Orhiia: Dramatychni poemy*. Osnovy, 2001, pp. 545–642.

– *Kassandra. Tvory v 4 tomakh*, vol. 2. Dnipro, 1981.

Vasyliv, Marta. "Komisar Vanda – zhinka u shtaniakh." *Druh chytacha*, 21 June 2010, https://vsiknygy.net.ua/person/5897/. Accessed 25 May 2019.

Vatulescu, Cristina. *Police Aesthetics: Literature, Film, and the Secret Police in Soviet Times*. Stanford UP, 2010.

Vickers, Jill. "Bringing Nations In: Some Methodological and Conceptual Issues in Connecting Feminisms with Nationhood and Nationalisms." *International Feminist Journal of Politics*, vol. 8, no. 1, Mar. 2006, pp. 84–109.

Vil'de, Iryna. *Sestry Richyns'ki*. Zelenyi pes, 2010.

Wachtel, Andrew Baruch. *Remaining Relevant after Communism: The Role of the Writer in Eastern Europe*. U of Chicago P, 2006.

Walsh, Kevin. *The Representation of the Past: Museums and Heritage in the Post-Modern World*. Routledge, 1992.

Walsh, Michael. "National Cinema, National Imaginary." *Film History*, vol. 8, no. 1, 1996, pp. 5–17.

Watkins, Susan. *Doris Lessing: Contemporary World Writers*. Oxford UP, 2010.

Wertsch, James V. "National Narratives and the Conservative Nature of Collective Memory." *Neohelicon*, vol. 34, no. 2, 2007, pp. 23–33.

– *Voices of Collective Remembering*. Cambridge UP, 2002.

White, Hayden V. *The Content of the Form: Narrative Discourse and Historical Representation*. Johns Hopkins UP, 1987.

– "The Value of Narrativity in the Representation of Reality." *The Content of Form: Narrative Discourse and Historical Representation*. Johns Hopkins UP, 1987, pp. 1–25.

Wilson, Andrew. *The Ukrainians: Unexpected Nation*. 3rd ed. Yale UP, 2009.

Wolczuk, Kataryna. "History, Europe and the 'National Idea': The 'Official' Narrative of National Identity in Ukraine." *Nationalities Papers*, vol. 28, no. 4, 2000, pp. 671–94.

Yekelchyk, Serhy. "National Heroes for a New Ukraine: Merging the Vocabularies of the Diaspora, Revolution, and Mass Culture." *Ab Imperio*, vol. 3, 2015, pp. 97–123.

– *Stalin's Empire of Memory: Russian-Ukrainian Relations in the Soviet Historical Imagination*. U of Toronto P, 2004.

Yurchak, Alexei. *Everything Was Forever, Until It Was No More: The Last Soviet Generation*. Princeton UP, 2006.

Yuval-Davis, Nira. *Gender and Nation*. Sage Publications, 1997.

Zabuzhko, Oksana. *Fieldwork in Ukrainian Sex*. Translated by Halyna Hryn. AmazonCrossing, 2011.

– *Inoplanetianka. Sestro, Sestro. Povisti ta opovidannia*, Fakt, 2003, pp. 169–226.

– *I znov ia vlizaiu v tank*... Komora, 2016.

– *Let My People Go: 15 tekstiv pro ukrains'ku revoliutsiiu*. Fakt, 2005.

– "Mova i vlada." *Khroniky vid Fortinbrasa: Vybrana eseistyka 90-kh*, Fakt, 1999, pp. 99–124.

– *The Museum of Abandoned Secrets*. Translated by Nina Shevchuk-Murray. AmazonCrossing, 2012.
– *Muzei pokynutykh sekretiv*. 2nd ed. Fakt, 2010.
– *Notre Dame d'Ukraine: Ukrainka v konflikti mifolohii*. Fakt, 2007.
– *Poliovi doslidzhennia z ukrains'koho seksu*. Zhoda, 1996.
– *Sestro, Sestro. Povisti ta opovidannia*. Kyiv: Fakt, 2003.
– "Zamist' epihrafa." *Litopys samovydtsiv. Dev'iat' misiatsiv ukrains'koho sprotyvu*, conceived by Oksana Zabuzhko, edited by Tetiana Teren, with a foreword by Svetlana Alexievich, Komora, 2014, p. 7.
– "Zhinka-avtor u kolonial'nii kul'turi, abo znadoby do ukrains'koi gendernoi mifolohii." *Khroniky vid Fortinbrasa: Vybrana eseistyka 90-kh*, Fakt, 1999, pp. 152–93.

Zakharchuk, Iryna. "Genderna asymetriia kanonu sotsialistychnoho realizmu: Versiia Iryny Vil'de." *Dyvoslovo*, no. 6, June 2006, pp. 48–53.

Zborovs'ka, Nila. *Feministychni rozdumy: Na karnavali mertvykh potsilunkiv*. Litopys, 1999.

Zherebkina, Irina. *Gendernye 90-e, ili fallosa ne sushchestvuiet*. Aleteya, 2003.

Zhurzhenko, Tatiana. "Feminist (De)Constructions of Nationalism in the Post-Soviet Space." *Mapping Difference: The Many Faces of Women in Contemporary Ukraine*, edited by Marian J. Rubchak, Berghahn Books, 2011, pp. 173–91.
– *Gendernye rynki Ukrainy: Politicheskaia ekonomiia natsional'nogo stroitel'stva*. European Humanities University, 2008.

Ziolkowski, Margaret. *Literary Exorcisms of Stalinism: Russian Writers and the Soviet Past*. Camden House, 1998.

Zubovskaia, Ol'ga. "Primenima li i kak zapadnaia postkolonial'naia teoriia dlia analisa postsovetskogo feminizma (na primere kategorii sovetskogo i postsovetskogo 'vostoka')?" *Gendernye issledovaniia*, vol. 18, 2008, pp. 177–99, http://www.intelros.ru/pdf/gender_issledovaniya/2008_18/09.pdf. Accessed 20 Feb. 2019.

Index

www.ingramcontent.com/pod-product-compliance
Lightning Source LLC
LaVergne TN
LVHW090159080826
844660LV00013B/869/J

* 9 7 8 1 4 8 7 5 0 6 0 0 1 *